THE NEEDLEWORK LIBRARY

BY ELIZABETH LAIRD MATHIESON

A MODERN MANUAL OFFERING
FULL INSTRUCTIONS IN EMBROIDERY,
KNITTING, TATTING, AFGHANS, QUILTS,
CROCHET, RUGS, AND PINEAPPLES

THE WORLD PUBLISHING COMPANY

CLEVELAND AND NEW YORK

PUBLISHED BY *The World Publishing Company*

2231 West 110th Street · Cleveland 2 · Ohio

First Published April 1949

ACKNOWLEDGMENTS

I wish to extend my sincere thanks to Mrs. George Frasher, Mrs. Anna Darragh and Miss Edna A. Walker for their valuable assistance in the preparation of this book. An expression of appreciation is also due for the efforts of Mrs. George Lynch, Mrs. Antonio Di Marco, and Mrs. Wallace E. Ryan.

Elizabeth Laird Mathieson

CONTENTS

PREFACE

WE SHOULD LIKE to take you into our confidence and tell you our purpose in compiling this book. To some people, adventure can only be found in a trip to romantic, faraway places. To others — and it is to these people we dedicate our book — it lies within the four walls of home, in the familiar tasks of daily living, in the odd moments of leisure in which to create with needle and thread, the unparalleled beauty of handwork.

In compiling "THE NEEDLEWORK LIBRARY" we were thinking of the thousands of women who appreciate and admire beautiful handwork and who are forever wistfully longing to "learn how." In this book, we embrace several branches of needlework, cramming it full of lovely and useful things to make and to own. We hope it will prove an irresistible temptation to the novice to learn a handcraft that will surely repay her with a lifetime of pleasure. We hope, too, that many women who are skilled at knitting or crochet will be induced to try their hands at quilting, embroidery, tatting or rug making. In other words, we have tried to make our own modest contribution to the renaissance of needlework arts. Explanatory steps have been included in the chapters on Crochet, Knitting and Tatting, so that the timid steps of the beginner will soon become the masterful strides of the expert.

We hope that "THE NEEDLEWORK LIBRARY" will provide the necessary incentive and instruction for the novice and fresh inspiration for the accomplished needlewoman . . . we shall feel it our greatest reward if we have been able to give our readers a key to treasure—and many future hours of pleasure!

Elizabeth Laird Mathieson

CHAPTER I

EMBROIDERY . . . *exquisite handmaiden of the arts*

*F*OR CENTURIES a pretty woman at her embroidery has been a favorite subject for artists. There is something graceful, charming and infinitely feminine about the flashing thrust of the needle, the play of light on colored floss, the toy-like scissors . . . the gradual blossoming of petal or leaf.

Every country, every civilization has made its contribution to the development of embroidery. We have gathered together a group of attractive, varied embroidery designs from many sources . . . designs that lend themselves to modern taste and usage.

You will find that embroidery works a special magic, transforms the commonplace into the unusual . . . You will discover that in the techniques of embroidery you have a new magic wand for surrounding yourself with lovely things.

EMBROIDERY

EMBROIDERY THREADS . . . Your choice of threads will depend upon the type of embroidery on which you intend to work. Mercerized threads may be used on most lightweight fabrics. Heavier cotton thread produces a rich and unusual effect in certain designs. Wool is suitable for use on heavier fabrics.

All embroidery threads should be boilfast. To work with inferior materials and threads is a foolish waste of time. When the working thread begins to acquire a fuzz or becomes untwisted, take a new one.

EMBROIDERY NEEDLES . . . The needle with which you embroider opens the weave of the material to enable the embroidery thread to slide through easily. Therefore, when you choose an embroidery needle, the eye should be slightly larger than the thickness of the embroidery thread. Almost all embroidery needles have a much longer eye than sewing needles. The needle ordinarily used is called a crewel needle. The length of the average embroidery needle is about 1¾ inches. A longer needle hinders the worker in gaining speed.

SCISSORS . . . Embroidery scissors should be about 4 to 5 inches long and should have very sharp points.

BEGINNINGS AND FINISHINGS . . . The wrong side of the work should look equally as well as the right side. To begin a piece of embroidery *do not use a knot,* but make a close running stitch toward the starting point, then make a small back stitch and begin to embroider in the direction specified.

To end your thread, weave the needle in and out of the material under the piece which has just been completed, but do not allow your needle to pick up any of the embroidery stitches. When you feel that the end of the thread is perfectly secure, cut the thread close to the embroidery. *Do not carry your thread from one design to the other,* as this produces very untidy work.

PRESSING . . . All embroidery should be pressed on a thickly padded surface. The raised face of the embroidery sinks into the softness of the padding and is not flattened by the iron. Place the embroidery piece wrong side up. Cover with a damp cloth. With a moderately hot iron press heavily. Remove the damp cloth and iron until dry. Turn work and, on right side, iron only the hems.

HOW TO TRANSFER DESIGNS . . . Trace the outline of the full-sized design onto white tracing paper. Determine the position of your design on the fabric. Place a sheet of carbon paper face down on it. Use orange or white carbon paper to transfer designs onto dark fabric. Place the tracing paper over the carbon paper and go over the entire design very carefully with a sharp pencil. To avoid smudging fabric, do not let the weight of your hand rest on the paper.

FRAMES . . . There are several types of embroidery frames. The hand frames are most commonly used. They can be bought at a very low cost and are made in two shapes, round and oval. When frames are adjusted over a small area of the work, the material is held taut and the work cannot pucker. Larger frames for larger pieces are also available and may be adjusted for almost any size or type of embroidery.

ALL DESIGNS ARE ACTUAL SIZE

EMBROIDERY STITCHES

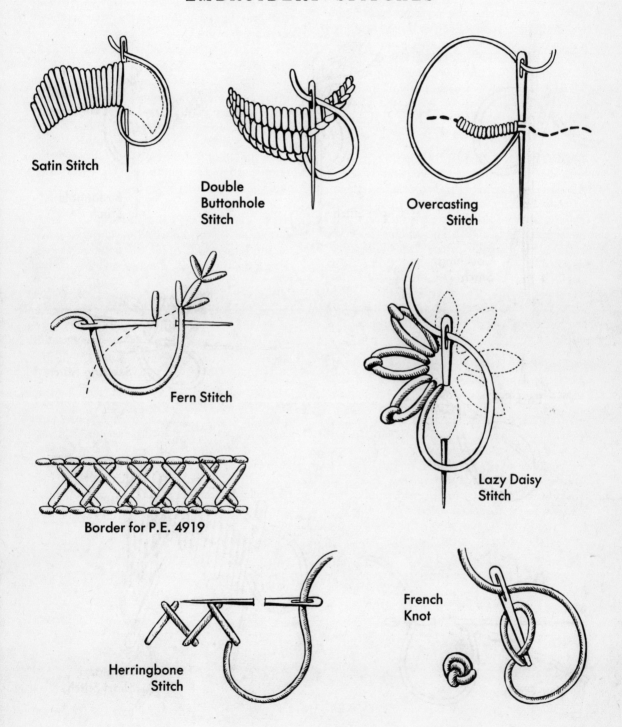

Satin Stitch

Double Buttonhole Stitch

Overcasting Stitch

Fern Stitch

Lazy Daisy Stitch

Border for P.E. 4919

Herringbone Stitch

French Knot

EMBROIDERY STITCHES

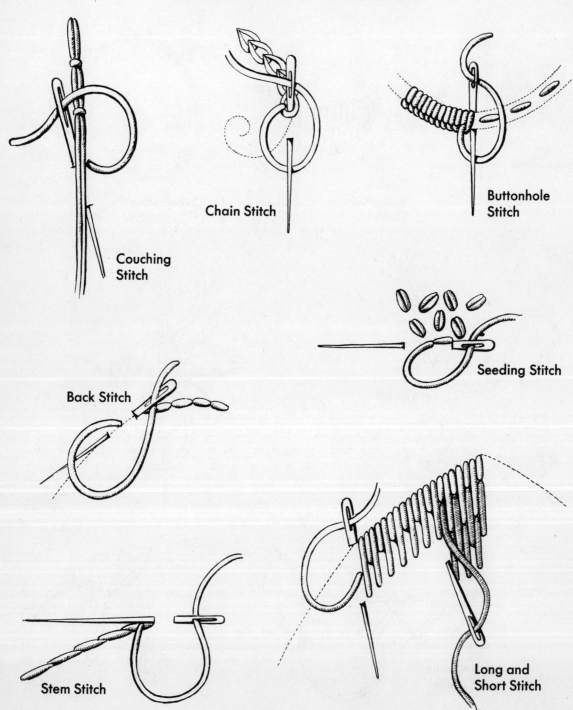

Couching Stitch

Chain Stitch

Buttonhole Stitch

Seeding Stitch

Back Stitch

Stem Stitch

Long and Short Stitch

EMBROIDERY STITCHES

Fly Stitch

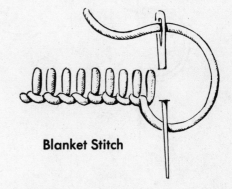

Blanket Stitch

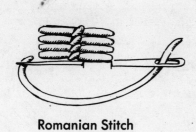

Romanian Stitch

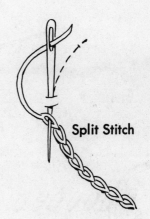

Split Stitch

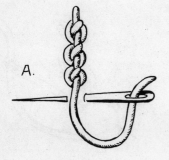

A.

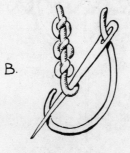

B.

C.

Double Knot Stitch

EMBROIDERY STITCHES

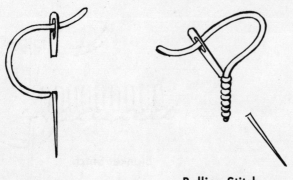

Bullion Stitch

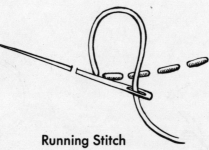

Running Stitch

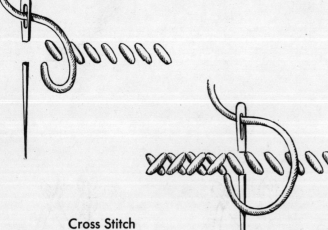

Cross Stitch

Detached Chain Stitch

Zigzag Chain Stitch

No. P. E. 4910 . Linen Beach Coat

Materials: Six Strand Floss, *4 skeins each of Light Cardinal and Orange; 3 skeins each of China Blue and Fern Green . . . Cream linen beach coat . . . Crewel Needle No. 5.*

Use 6 Strands Throughout

Trace complete design onto right front of coat, 3½ inches from shoulder seam, and trace in reverse for other front. Trace large section of design only on right pocket and trace in reverse for left pocket.

Follow diagram and number key for placing of colors and stitches. The stitches used are as follows: Stem stitch (page 16), Satin stitch (page 15), Herringbone stitch (page 15), Running stitch (page 18). With Light Cardinal, work a row of running stitch ½ inch from edge around front edges, pockets and cuffs.

Stitch and Color Key

STEM STITCH
1. Fern Green
2. Orange

SATIN STITCH
3. Light Cardinal

HERRINGBONE STITCH
4. China Blue
5. Light Cardinal
6. Orange

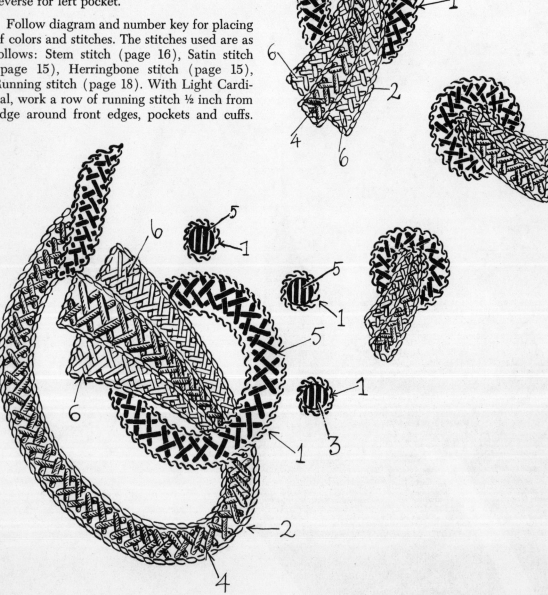

P.E. 4911

No. P. E. 4911 . . . . . Felt Belt

Materials: SIX STRAND FLOSS, *2 skeins each of Yellow and Dark Lavender; 1 skein each of Purple, Dark Orange, Steel Blue, Fern Green, Deep Rose, Sea Green, Blue, Beauty Pink . . . 1 strip of black felt, 5½ x 33½ inches . . . 1 strip of yellow felt, 6 x 34 inches . . . Crewel Needle No. 6.*

Use 3 Strands Throughout

Cut a strip of black felt 2 x 33 inches. Shape one end of belt as shown in diagram A and the other as shown in diagram B, marking the dots for snap fasteners. Place this black strip onto the yellow strip and trace slightly larger, so that the yellow felt makes a piping around the black. Cut yellow felt. Trace and cut two flaps and two pocket shapes on the black felt and two larger yellow pockets to make a similar piping.

Follow diagram and key for placing of colors and stitches. The stitches used are as follows: Chain stitch (page 16), Satin stitch (page 15), Fly stitch (page 17), French knots (page 15), Seeding (page 16), Couching (page 16), Running stitch (page 18).

Make up belt, placing pockets at sides of front and working a row of running stitch with Yellow along both edges of belt and around pockets and two rows along center of belt.

21

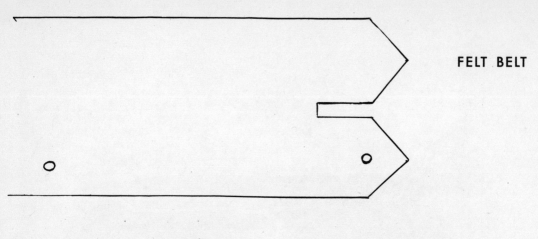

FELT BELT

A

B

Stitch and Color Key

CHAIN STITCH	SATIN STITCH *(cont'd)*	FLY STITCH
1. Yellow	8. Fern Green	17. Yellow
2. Fern Green	9. Dark Orange	
3. Deep Rose	10. Beauty Pink	FRENCH KNOTS
4. Dark Lavender	11. Dark Lavender	18. Yellow
5. Purple	12. Deep Rose	
	13. Dark Lavender	SEEDING
SATIN STITCH	14. Purple	19. Dark Lavender
6. Yellow	15. Blue	
7. Sea Green	16. Steel Blue	COUCHING
		20. Dark Orange

FELT BELT

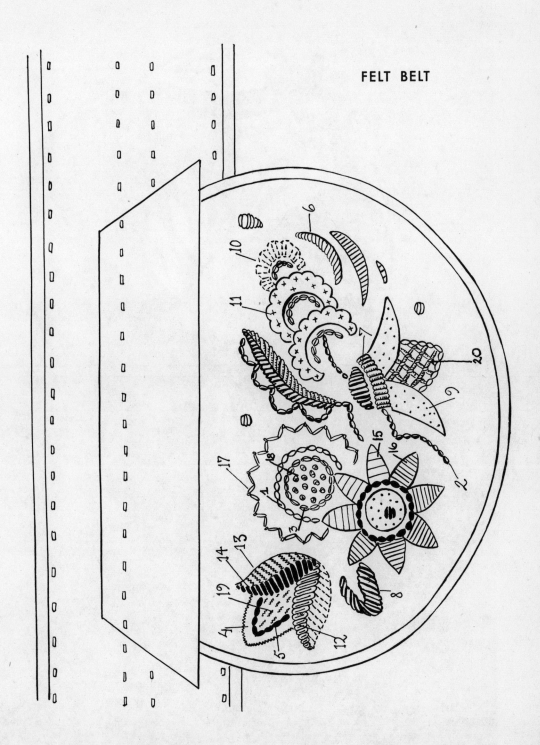

P.E. 4912

No. P. E. 4912 . . Felt Skull Cap

Materials: SIX STRAND FLOSS, *2 skeins each of Beige, Dark Hunter's Green, Black; 1 skein each of Blue, Mid Rose . . . Piece of grey-blue felt 6 x 12 inches . . . Piece of light purple felt 6 x 12 inches . . . Piece of bright yellow felt 3 x 10 inches . . . 1 yard of ½ inch wide velvet ribbon, a shade darker than light purple felt . . . Crewel Needle No. 6.*

Trace section of cap twice onto blue felt and twice onto light purple, then trace small section four times onto yellow felt. Follow diagram and key for placing colors and stitches.

The diagram shown is for the light purple felt sections. For the blue felt sections, substitute 4 for 2 and 6 for 7.

The stitches used are as follows: Chain stitch (page 16), Blanket stitch (page 17). Cut out the four small sections and apply them onto corresponding places on the larger sections. Slip stitch in place with matching thread.

Cut out the four larger sections and work blanket stitch around edges.

Press embroidery on wrong side. Using Black, overcast the sections together, working over the loops of blanket stitch.

Bind bottom of cap with velvet ribbon. Make ribbon loops and attach to top of cap.

Stitch and Color Key

CHAIN STITCH
1. Beige
2. Blue
3. Dark Hunter's Green
4. Mid Rose
5. Black

BLANKET STITCH
6. Dark Hunter's Green
7. Mid Rose

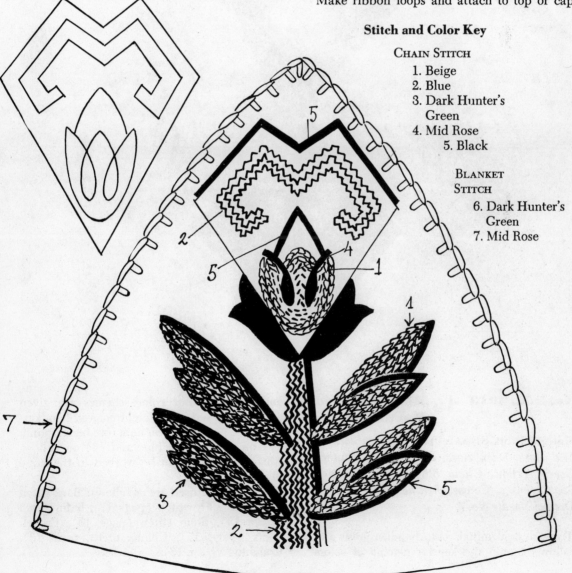

P.E. 4913

No. P. E. 4913 . . Monogrammed Handkerchiefs

Materials: SIX STRAND FLOSS, *1 skein each of Mid Rose, Deep Rose, Nile Green, Hunter's Green, Yellow, China Blue, Light Cardinal, Sea Green . . . Hemstitched handkerchiefs . . . Crewel Needle No. 7.*

Trace desired initials onto handkerchiefs and follow diagram and key for placing of colors and stitches. Four color schemes are given and are worked on different colored handkerchiefs. (1) is worked on light rose background, (2) on red, (3) on blue and (4) on yellow. All other initials can be worked in the same manner.

The stitches used are as follows: Back stitch (page 16), Fly stitch (page 17), Satin stitch (page 15), Stem stitch (page 16), French knots (page 15), Chain stitch (page 16), Couching (page 16).

26

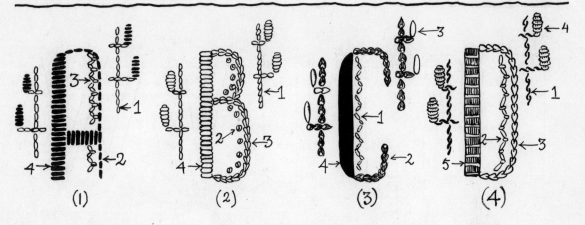

Stitch and Color Key

(1) **BACK STITCH**
   1. Mid Rose
   2. Deep Rose

FLY STITCH
   3. Mid Rose

SATIN STITCH
   4. Deep Rose

(2) **STEM STITCH**
   1. Nile Green

FRENCH KNOTS
   2. Nile Green

CHAIN STITCH
   3. Hunter's Green

SATIN STITCH
   4. Hunter's Green

(3) **BACK STITCH**
   1. Yellow

CHAIN STITCH
   2. China Blue

SATIN STITCH
   3. Yellow
   4. China Blue

(4) **STEM STITCH**
   1. Light Cardinal

COUCHING
   2. Sea Green

CHAIN STITCH
   3. Light Cardinal

SATIN STITCH
   4. Sea Green
   5. Light Cardinal

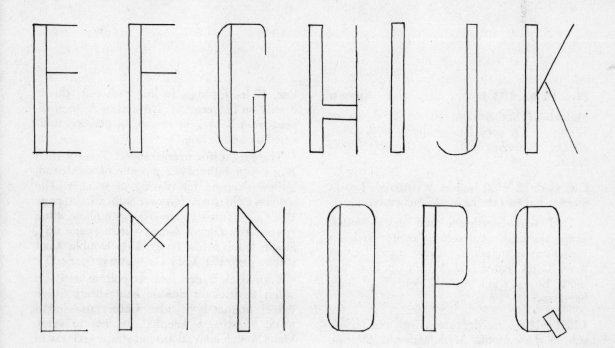

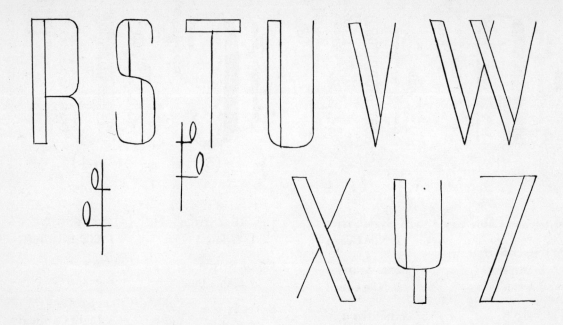

No. P. E. 4914 . . . . . . Apron

Materials: SIX STRAND FLOSS, *6 skeins of White . . . ¾ yard blue material with white checks, 36 inches wide . . . Crewel Needle No. 6.*

Cut skirt 22 x 30 inches, waistband 3 x 18 inches, and two straps 3 x 18 inches.

Fold skirt lengthwise and mark center. Trace section C of design on center fold, 4¼ inches up from edge. * Now trace another motif C on center fold, 1 inch up from last motif. Repeat from * until 6 motifs in all have been traced.

LEFT SIDE . . . Measure ½ inch out on left side of these motifs. Mark with pin. Starting 4¼ inches from lower edge, draw a vertical line, 12 inches long, in line with pin (this is line D on diagram A). Now trace A, then repeat from X to Y in reverse in position indicated alongside line D.

Trace right side to correspond. Trace section B of design 5 times along center of waistband. Follow diagram for placing of stitches. The stitches used are as follows: Satin stitch (page 15), Chain stitch (page 16), Buttonhole stitch (page 16), Zigzag Chain stitch (page 18), Single Satin stitch (page 15), Double Knot stitch (page 17), Lazy Daisy stitch (page 15).

Turn back 2-inch hem at bottom and slip stitch to back of double knot stitch. Stitch ¼-inch hem at both sides. Gather apron skirt to fit waistband, keeping fullness to sides. Make ¼-inch hem all around straps and sew in place at each side of waistband.

P.E. 4914

Stitch and Color Key

Satin Stitch	 1	Lazy Daisy Stitch	4
Chain Stitch	 2	Buttonhole Stitch..	5
Zigzag		Single Satin Stitch.	6
Chain Stitch	 3	Double Knot Stitch	7

(Double Knot Stitch—figure A shows first stitch taken through material; figure B shows second stitch taken through loop made by first stitch with thread below needle as in buttonhole stitch; figure C shows third stitch taken into same loop in same manner).

B.

APRON
P.E. 4914

A

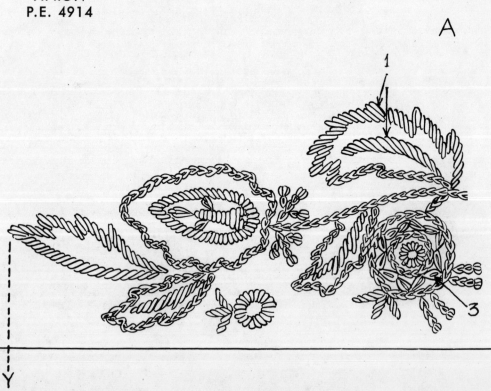

APRON
P.E. 4914

C

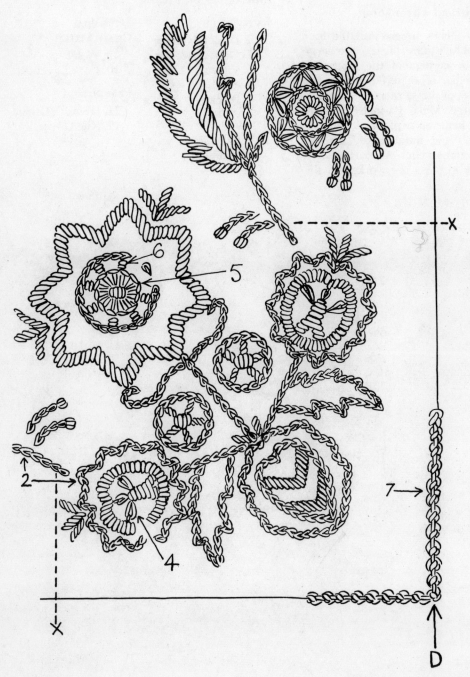

No. P. E. 4919 . . Blue Organdie Tea Cloth and Napkins

Materials: SIX STRAND FLOSS, *3 skeins each of Violet and Dark Lavender; 1 skein each of Yellow, Nile Green, Hunter's Green and Black . . . 2 yards of blue organdie, 45 inches wide . . . Crewel Needle No. 8.*

Use 1 Strand Throughout

Cut the cloth 40 inches square and the four napkins 13½ inches square. Trace the large motif on the four corners of the cloth, 3½ inches in from edge of material. Trace the small motifs on opposite corners of napkins, 2 inches from edge. Make 1¼-inch hems on cloth and ½-inch hems on napkins.

Follow diagram and number key for the placing of colors and stitches. All parts shown similar to numbered parts are worked in the same color and stitch. The stitches used are as follows: Back stitch (page 16), Detached Chain stitch (page 18), Fern stitch (page 15), Herringbone stitch (page 15). All borders are worked in herringbone stitch with a back stitch outline (page 15).

Stitch and Color Key

BACK STITCH
1. Dark Lavender
2. Dark Lavender
3. Violet
4. Yellow
5. Black

HERRINGBONE STITCH
6. Nile Green
7. Yellow
8. Black

DETACHED CHAIN STITCH
9. Violet
10. Dark Lavender

FERN STITCH
11. Hunter's Green
12. Nile Green

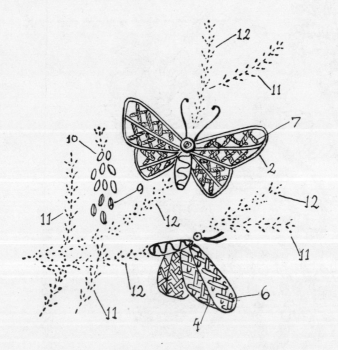

BLUE ORGANDIE TEA CLOTH
and NAPKINS

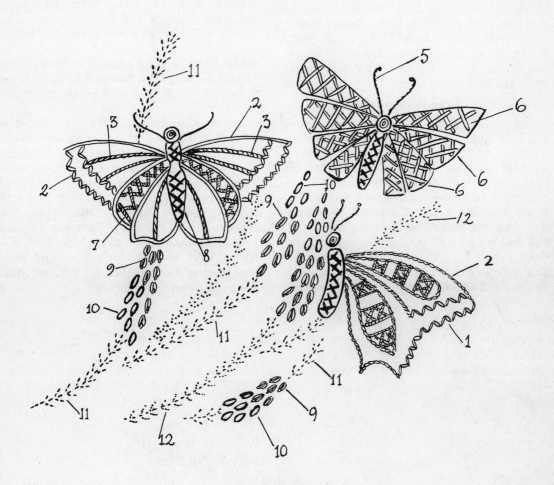

No. P. E. 4920 . . . . . Circular Tablecloth and Napkins

Materials: SIX STRAND FLOSS, *10 skeins of Nile Green; 7 skeins of Dark Hunter's Green; 4 skeins each of Light Rose, Beauty Rose, Deep Rose, Angel Blue, Light Steel Blue, White, Beauty Pink, Orange, Blue . . . Crewel Needle No. 6 . . . 1¾ yards of cream linen, 45 inches wide.*

Use 3 Strands Throughout

Cut a circular cloth, 45 inches in diameter, and four napkins, each 10½ inches square.

CLOTH . . . Trace diagram A in the center of the cloth. Now measure 4½ inches out from center point and draw a circle with this radius. Trace diagrams B and C alternately around this circle, 1½ inches apart, placing the motifs half inside and half outside the circle. Now draw a circle 7½ inches from the center point and trace motifs D and C alternately around this circle, 2¼ inches apart, placing as before.

Draw a third circle, 11 inches from center point, and trace motifs E and C alternately, 4¼ inches apart, placing as before. Now draw a fourth circle, 14½ inches from center point, and trace motifs F and C alternately around the circle 6¼ inches apart, placing as before.

NAPKINS . . . Trace motif C in three corners of each napkin. Then trace motifs B, D, E and F respectively in the fourth corner of the four napkins.

Follow diagrams and key for placing of stitches and colors. The stitches used are as follows: Bullion stitch (page 18), Long and Short stitch (page 16), Lazy Daisy stitch (page 15), Back stitch (page 16), French Knots (page 15), Stem stitch (page 16), Satin stitch (page 15), Romanian stitch (page 17), Blanket stitch (page 17). Turn under ¼-inch hem all around cloth and napkins. With Nile Green, work Blanket stitch all around hems, but making two stitches in the one place (page 36).

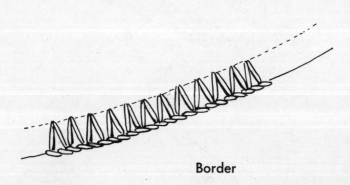

Border

P.E. 4920

Stitch and Color Key

BULLION STITCH
1. Light Rose
2. Beauty Rose
3. Deep Rose

LONG AND SHORT STITCH
4. Angel Blue
5. Light Steel Blue

LAZY DAISY STITCH
6. White

BACK STITCH
7. Beauty Pink
8. Light Steel Blue
9. Orange
10. Angel Blue
11. Blue
12. Nile Green
13. Dark Hunter's Green

FRENCH KNOTS
14. Orange

STEM STITCH
15. Nile Green
16. Dark Hunter's Green

SATIN STITCH
17. Orange
18. Nile Green
19. Dark Hunter's Green

ROMANIAN STITCH
20. Dark Hunter's Green
21. Nile Green

CIRCULAR TABLECLOTH and NAPKINS

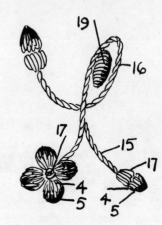

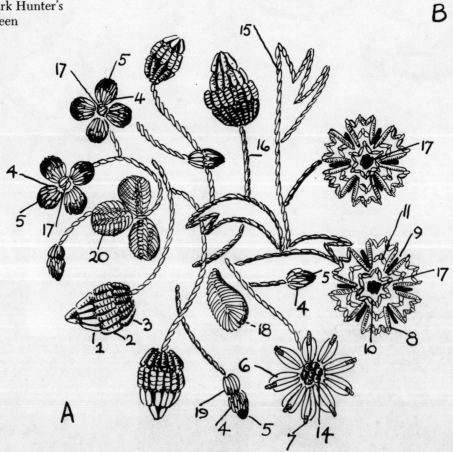

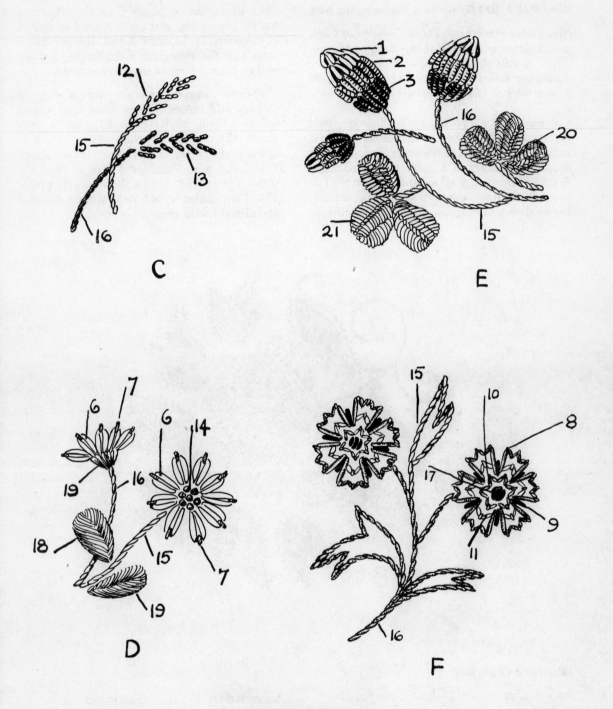

**CIRCULAR TABLECLOTH
and NAPKINS**

No. P. E. 4915 Greek Luncheon Set

Materials: SIX STRAND FLOSS, *7 skeins of Copper, 5 skeins of Black, 3 skeins each of Myrtle, Light Cardinal; 2 skeins of Burnt Orange; 1 skein of Yellow . . . ¾ yard of ecru linen, 36 inches wide . . . Crewel Needle No. 6.*

Cut centerpiece 13½ inches in diameter, two place mats 10¾ inches in diameter, and two glass mats 7¼ inches in diameter. Trace border as shown in diagram A, page 42, on all mats, ¼ inch in from edge all around. Now trace the motif on diagram A onto the centerpiece, placing as shown in diagram. Trace this motif two more times, having points C on the other two motifs joining the first motif traced as shown in diagram. Trace motif B onto the two place mats and the two glass mats, having bottom curl of stem 1 inch in from inner circle.

Follow diagram and key for placing of stitches and colors. The stitches used are as follows: Stem stitch (page 16), Satin stitch (page 15), Romanian stitch (page 17), Buttonhole stitch (page 16), Split stitch (page 17), Long and Short stitch (page 16), Fly stitch (page 17), Herringbone stitch (page 15). Turn under ¼-inch hem around all mats and slip stitch in place.

B

Stitch and Color Key

STEM STITCH	ROMANIAN STITCH	SPLIT STITCH	FLY STITCH
1. Copper	5. Burnt Orange	8. Copper	10. Black
2. Black	6. Light Cardinal		
SATIN STITCH	**BUTTONHOLE STITCH**	**LONG AND SHORT STITCH**	**HERRINGBONE STITCH**
3. Yellow	7. Black	9. Myrtle	11. Copper
4. Copper			

P.E. 4915

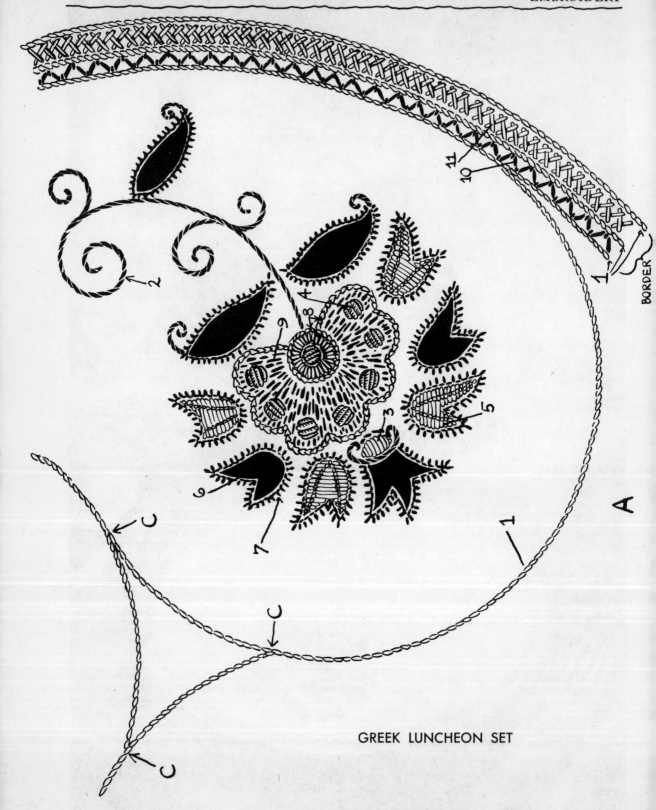

GREEK LUNCHEON SET

P.E. 4917

No. P. E. 4917 . . . . . Tray Mat

Materials: Six Strand Floss, *4 skeins of Sea Green; 3 skeins of White; 2 skeins of Yellow; 1 skein of Deep Rose . . . A piece of green linen 20 x 27 inches . . . Crewel Needle No. 6.*

Use 3 Strands Throughout

Fullsize drawing gives half of motif A (tray mat border) and complete motif B. Trace given half of A at one short end of cloth, then reverse on center line and trace other half to correspond. Continue line C for 9 inches, then trace motif B at center of each side edge. Trace other end of cloth to correspond, continuing line C to meet motifs B.

Follow diagram and key for placing of stitches and colors. The stitches used are as follows: Buttonhole stitch (page 16), Double Buttonhole stitch (page 15), Satin stitch (page 15), Stem stitch (page 16). The sections on diagram marked X are to be cut away.

Stitch and Color Key

Buttonhole Stitch	Satin Stitch
1. White	5. White
2. Yellow	6. Deep Rose
3. Sea Green	
	Stem Stitch
Double	7. Deep Rose
Buttonhole Stitch	
4. Sea Green	

43

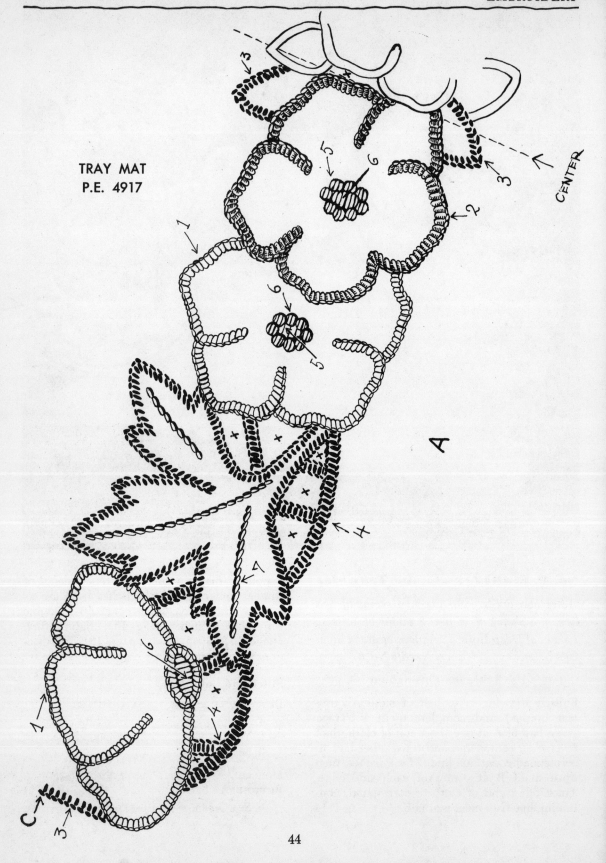

TRAY MAT
P.E. 4917

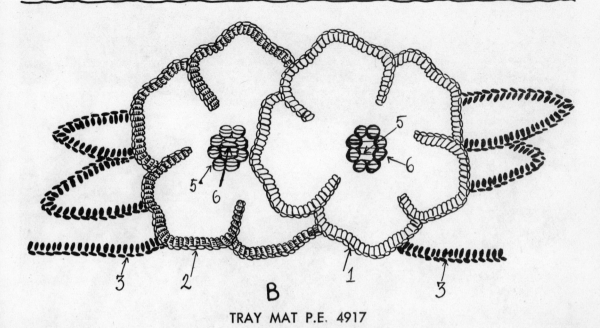

B

TRAY MAT P.E. 4917

CROSS STITCH

Because cross stitch looks easy, people are often careless and mar its beauty by irregular crosses and top threads slanting in opposite directions. Diagram shows how cross stitch is applied to a solid fabric.

When the cross stitch design is not stamped on the background, the best way to work it is over embroidery canvas. The canvas is basted to the fabric to correspond with the weave. The weave of the canvas is a guide for keeping the stitches even. Embroider through both the fabric and the canvas. When embroidery is completed, the canvas is removed by drawing out the threads.

P.E. 4916

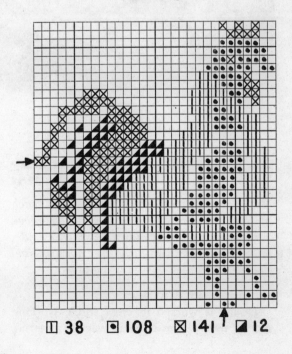

⊞ 38   ⊡ 108   ⊠ 141   ◪ 12

P.E. 4916

No. P. E. 4916 . . Breakfast Tray Mat

Materials: SIX STRAND FLOSS, *1 skein each of Dark Orange, Steel Blue, Devil Red, Black . . . ⅜ yard of cream linen, 36 inches wide, with 36 threads to an inch . . . Tapestry Needle No. 22.*

Cut mat 12½ x 16 inches.

Design is worked in cross stitch, working crosses over 3 threads each way of material.

Follow diagram and key for design and placing of colors. Work one motif in each corner of tray mat, having cockerels facing at each long side. Arrows show points which should be 1¼ inches from edges of material. Draw out one thread of material all around tray mat, 1 inch from edge. Draw out another thread 2½ inches in from edge between each motif. Turn under and sew ⅜-inch hem all around, mitering corners. Hemstitch both lines of drawn thread.

P.E. 4918

No. P. E. 4918 . . . . Place Mats

Algonquin Design

Materials: Six Strand Floss, *12 skeins of Copper; 9 skeins of White; 2 skeins of Colonial Brown . . . ⅜ yard of beige linen, 50 inches wide, with 30 threads to an inch . . . Tapestry Needle No. 22 (for cross stitch) . . . Crewel Needle No. 6 (for stem stitch).*

The design is worked in cross stitch with a row of stem stitch underlining each row of cross stitch. Work the crosses over 3 threads each way of material.

Cut 2 mats, each 12 x 15 inches. Follow diagram and key for placing of colors and stitches. The stitches used are as follows: Cross stitch (page 18), Stem stitch (page 16). The background squares on diagram represent 3 threads of material along and 4 threads down (the latter includes the thread over which the stem stitch is worked). Work the border on other side of mats to correspond. Turn under ½-inch hem around mats and slip stitch in place.

X-132 X-81-A } CROSS STITCH   } -I-STEM STITCH

SWEDISH DARNING

Huck toweling is generally used for Swedish darning. The weave has tiny vertical raised loops which occur at equal intervals, and these are used for darning the designs. A tapestry needle is always used for the darning.

To begin Swedish darning, work from left to right, drawing needle through loops ½ inch away from starting point. Then work from right to left over this woven thread, drawing thread through loops according to the design, taking care that needle does not pass through to back of fabric.

To finish thread, darn back closely over design for ½ inch and cut.

No. P. E. 4849 . . . Guest Towel

Materials: Six Strand Floss, *1 skein each of Dark Hunter's Green, Dark Rose and White*

. . . Crewel Needle No. 6 . . . Light green huck towel.

Use 6 Strands Throughout

Design is worked at one end of towel only. The outside borders are worked with Dark Rose, the small center diamonds with White, and the outer diamonds with Dark Hunter's Green. Follow illustration for design.

No. P. E. 4850 . . . Guest Towel

Materials: Six Strand Floss, *1 skein each of Burnt Orange, Colonial Brown and Nile Green . . . Crewel Needle No. 6 . . . Beige huck towel.*

Use 6 Strands Throughout

Design is worked at one end of towel only. The borders and the inner triangle are worked with Brown, the outer triangle with Green, and the middle triangle in Orange. Follow illustration for design.

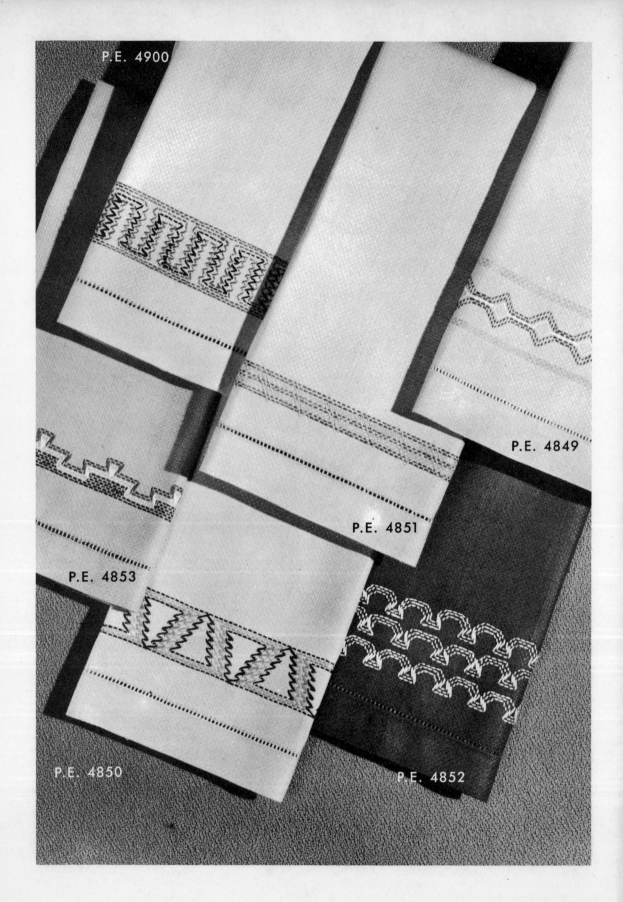

P.E. 4900

P.E. 4849

P.E. 4851

P.E. 4853

P.E. 4850

P.E. 4852

No. P. E. 4851 . . . Guest Towel

Materials: SIX STRAND FLOSS, *1 skein each of Purple and Blue . . . Crewel Needle No. 6 . . . Pink huck towel.*

Use 6 Strands Throughout

Design is worked at one end of towel only. The two horizontal lines at top and bottom, and the two horizontal lines at center are worked with Purple. The remaining two horizontal lines at both sides of center and the zig-zag lines are worked with Blue. Follow illustration for design.

No. P. E. 4852 . . . Guest Towel

Materials: SIX STRAND FLOSS, *2 skeins of White . . . Crewel Needle No. 6 . . . Royal blue huck towel.*

Use 6 Strands Throughout

Design is worked at one end of towel only. The entire design is worked with White. Follow illustration for design.

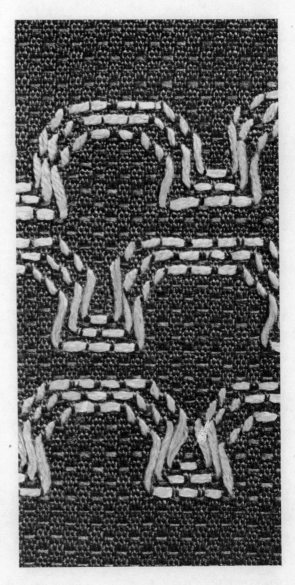

No. P. E. 4853 . . . Guest Towel

Materials: SIX STRAND FLOSS, *1 skein each of China Blue, Devil Red and White . . . Crewel Needle No. 6 . . . Light blue huck towel.*

Use 6 Strands Throughout

Design is worked at one end of towel only. The horizontal lines at base are worked with China Blue, the center of design with White, and the top with Red. Follow illustration for design.

No. P. E. 4900 . . . Guest Towel

Materials: SIX STRAND FLOSS, *1 skein each of Copper and Black . . . Crewel Needle No. 6 . . . Yellow huck towel.*

Use 6 Strands Throughout

Design is worked at one end of towel only. Outer borders and inner zig-zag lines are worked with Copper, outer zig-zag lines with Black. Follow illustration for design.

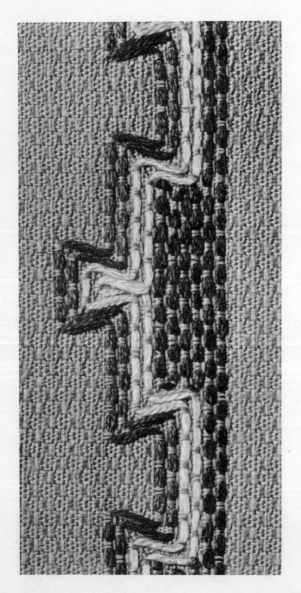

CHAPTER II

QUILTS . . . *rare examples of an early American art*

THE PATCHWORK QUILT is part and parcel of our country's past—and present. While many things on the American scene have changed since Colonial days, the same precise and beautiful quilt patterns that great-great-grandmother made out of scraps of fabric are being followed by women today.

There is a wonderful feeling of continuity, of time flowing and still remaining constant, in seeing re-created, generation after generation, designs that were familiar and alive two hundred years ago. The very names of some of the patterns speak out of the past, evoking in us memories and pride.

Quilts are of two kinds—patchwork and appliqué—and are at home in either rambling ranch house or the most modern of apartments. At one time a bride's trousseau was not complete without a baker's dozen—perhaps you will not want a dozen but surely you won't be satisfied until one of these colorful designs spreads its gayety and warmth across your bed.

PATCHWORK AND QUILTING

PATCHWORK AND QUILTING are two separate arts which were combined by the early settlers of this country to make beautiful quilts.

Patchwork is very simple, requiring only accuracy in making the units. The sewing of Patchwork consists only of a straight seam.

FABRICS . . . Choose only closely woven fabrics with a firm weave and a soft texture such as calico, percale, chintz, muslin or gingham.

COLORS . . . Fast dyes must be chosen or colors will run when quilt is laundered.

MATERIALS . . . All yardages specified are approximate and are figured on 36-inch fabric unless otherwise specified.

SIZES . . . The measurements for the quilts included in this book have been planned for standard size beds. The illustrations show the setting of the quilts.

HOW TO MAKE A PATTERN
(All units illustrated are actual size)

The number of each unit to be cut will be specified with each direction.

1. Trace the design onto a piece of tracing or tissue paper.

2. Cut along tracing line.

3. Place pattern on top of a glazed blotter or sand paper and, holding it firmly in left hand, cut around paper pattern (Fig. 1). Make a number of patterns at one time so that when one pattern is worn a second may be easily picked up.

HOW TO CUT UNITS

1. Even material off by pulling a thread or tearing it.

2. Press material through a damp cloth.

3. The threads that run lengthwise and crosswise are known respectively as the lengthwise and crosswise grain. Place the pattern on the lengthwise grain of the material and with a pencil make a tracing line (Fig. 2).

4. Trace number of units for 1 block, leaving ½ inch space on all sides between each tracing line for seam allowance (Fig. 3).

5. Cut out the units ¼ inch away from tracing line on all sides (Fig. 3).

6. Place pattern directly over the tracing of cut unit and with a moderately hot iron press back the seam allowance over the pattern, thus making a distinct guide line for sewing (Fig. 4).

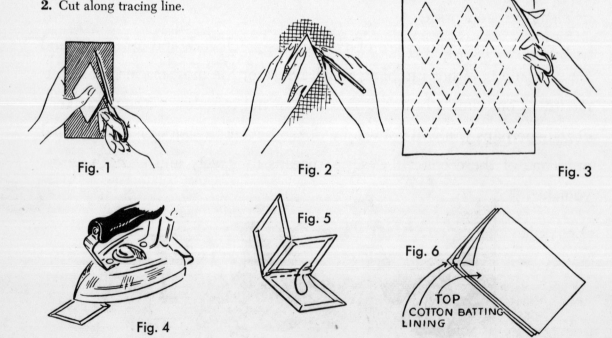

Fig. 1

Fig. 2

Fig. 3

Fig. 5

Fig. 4

Fig. 6

TOP
COTTON BATTING
LINING

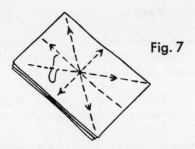

Fig. 7

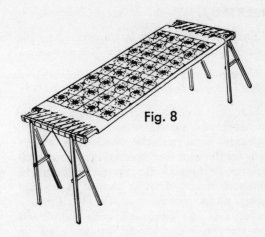

Fig. 8

HOW TO SEW UNITS TOGETHER

The central principle of patchwork is joining the units from the center out. All joinings are made by stitching the units together with a running stitch on wrong side (Fig. 5). A thread approximately 18 inches long is the correct length for sewing.

PRESSING

Pressing the seams frequently improves the appearance of the quilt.

SETTING THE QUILT TOGETHER

This is combining the blocks and the border of the quilt. All borders are described where required. Blocks are joined in strips and then the strips sewed together. The border is sewed on last.

LINING OF QUILT

The backing should be cut the same size as the top unless you wish to bring the edges of the backing over the top for a binding. In the latter case it should be 2½ inches larger all around. The material should be of the same quality as the top. A percale sheet which is soft and free of starch may be used.

INTERLINING OF QUILT

Cotton batting is the most popular and practical interlining. One batt is sufficient for a single size quilt.

PLACING THE THREE LAYERS TOGETHER

Lay the lining flat, smoothing it out. The cotton batting is placed on top of the lining and also smoothed out so that there are no wrinkles. The top is placed over these two layers (Fig. 6), and all three layers are very carefully basted together.

BASTING THE THREE LAYERS TOGETHER

Starting at center of quilt, baste out to each side through all three layers. Then, starting at center again, baste to each corner diagonally. Then baste all outer edges together (Fig. 7).

QUILTING FRAMES

The purpose of a quilting frame is to hold the work taut. All quilting frames have two horizontal bars, 2 inches wide and deep and about 92 inches long. These are held in place by 2 vertical bars, 2 inches wide and about 24 inches long, which have a contrivance for controlling the horizontal bars. To place the quilt on a frame, remove the 2 horizontal bars, then nail a tape, 2 inches wide, to one side of each horizontal bar. Sew the top and bottom edges of the quilt to these tapes. Roll one end up until you reach the width of the vertical bars. Place quilt on frame and roll until it is taut. To hold the sides taut, thread a needle with a strand of PEARL COTTON, Size 5, and make a knot at one end. Insert needle ½ inch in from side edge and draw thread through. Then wind thread over the vertical bar and insert needle in quilt 1 inch away from previous thread. Continue in this manner across the entire length of the vertical bar and fasten end securely. Repeat on the opposite side (Fig. 8).

QUILTING HOOPS

Large hoops, 22 inches in diameter, are also used for quilting.

QUILTING

1. Each quilting design is transferred to the block by pricking the outline with a needle.

2. Thread a needle with an 18-inch length of thread and make a knot at one end.

3. Place the forefinger of left hand over the spot where the needle should come through. With right hand push the needle from underneath up through the three layers of material until needle touches the tip of forefinger of left hand, thus indicating that it is coming through at the correct spot (Fig. 9). Remove forefinger of left hand and with right hand draw the needle and thread through until the knot is concealed in the interlining (Fig. 10).

4. Place the forefinger of left hand under the spot where the needle should come through. With right hand push the needle downward through the three layers, until needle touches the tip of forefinger of left hand (Fig. 11). Remove forefinger and with right hand draw the needle and thread through.

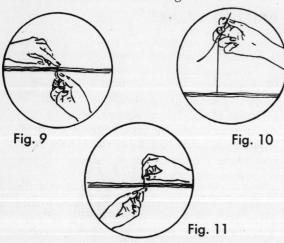

Fig. 9

Fig. 10

Fig. 11

5. Alternate Steps 3 and 4, taking care to fasten the end of each thread securely.

6. The upward and downward movements through the three layers of fabric and the alternating of the position of the hands are the only correct ways of quilting. When you complete the quilting within a comfortable reach, rip out the strands on the sides, roll the quilt toward you and begin again.

7. After the quilting is completed, bind the edges.

Yankee Pride

This pattern is an adaptation of a popular quilt design which originated in New Orleans. It was named the LeMoyne Star in honor of Jacques LeMoyne, Sieur de Bienville, founder of the city. After Louisiana was purchased by the United States in 1803, American women called the design the Lemon Star, and it began to appear in different parts of the country in various forms.

Materials: *For Single Size, 72 x 108 inches—10 yards of white, 6 yards of yellow, 2 yards of red print and 1¼ yards of red. For Double Size, 96 x 108 inches—Make 56 blocks set 7 x 8 before adding border. Use Best Six Cord, or Heavy Duty or Quilting Thread.*

See pages 54, 55 and 56 for general directions.

Each block is made of 4 different kinds of units. Patterns are given for Unit Nos. 1, 2 and 5; Unit Nos. 3 and 4 are respectively a 1⅜ inch and a 3½ inch square.

Number of Each Unit to Cut for 1 Block ...
Unit No. 1: (diamond) 8 print, 24 yellow.
Unit No. 2: (triangle) 12 white. **Unit No. 3:** (1⅜ inch square) 16 white. **Unit No. 4:** (3½ inch square) 4 white.

For Single Size, multiply the above numbers by 40. For Double Size, multiply the above numbers by 56.

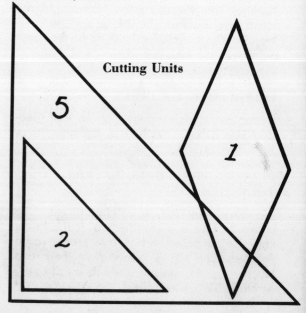

Cutting Units

5

2

1

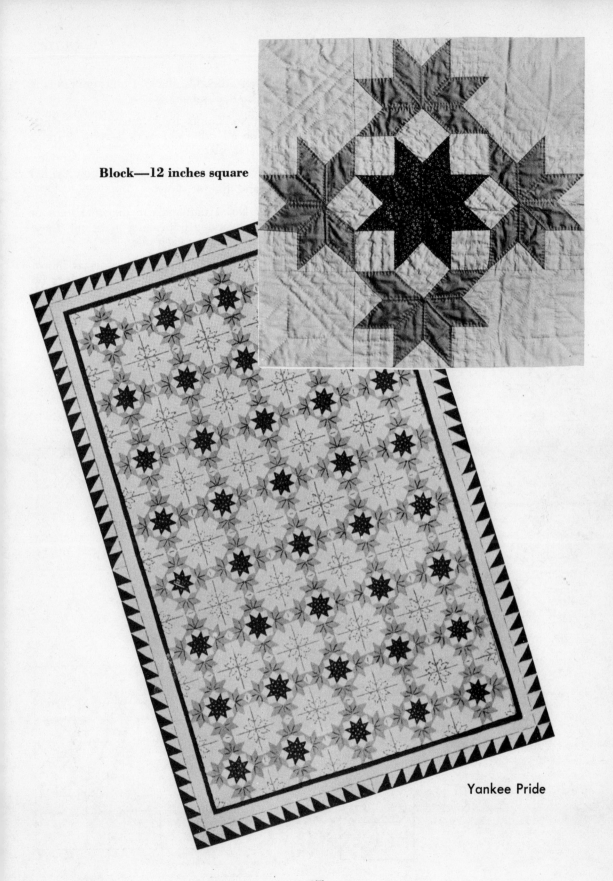

Block—12 inches square

Yankee Pride

How to Combine Units to Form a Block . . .
See Fig. 5, p. 54, for sewing units together.

Step 1—Join 8 print No. 1 units. Step 2—Join 8 No. 3 units to star. Step 3—Join 8 No. 1 units. Step 4—Join 4 No. 1 units. Step 5—Join half star. Step 6—Join No. 2 units. Step 7—Join all other No. 3 units. Step 8—Join No. 4 units.

Setting the Quilt . . . For the border, using red cut 2 strips 1½ x 63 inches and 2 strips 1½ x 99 inches. Using white, cut 2 strips 2½ x 66 inches and 2 strips 2½ x 102 inches. Sew corresponding red strips to each side of quilt, mitering corners. Then sew on the white strips. With red, cut 116 No. 5 units; with white, cut 116 No. 5 units. Make a border by sewing a white and a red triangle together as shown.

Quilting . . . **1.** On all No. 1 units quilt ⅛ inch away from all seams.

2. On No. 3 units divide squares into 3 equal parts on all sides and work 2 vertical and 2 horizontal rows.

3. Divide each side of No. 2 unit into 3 equal parts and quilt as shown.

4. On No. 4 unit make 5 diagonal lines of quilting, working from inner point out—these lines join points on each side.

5. Trace two No. 1 units in corner as shown and quilt. When completed, finish edges by turning in edge of border and lining ½ inch, then slip stitch together.

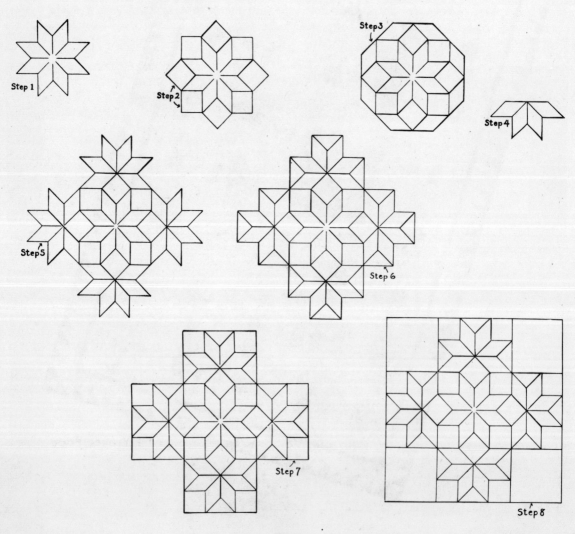

Step 1 · Step 2 · Step 3 · Step 4 · Step 5 · Step 6 · Step 7 · Step 8

Roman Stripe

Early New England women, remembering the thrifty custom which they had observed in Holland, pieced together their scraps of precious material to make comfortable bed coverings. The early patterns were called Crazy Quilts or Hit-and-Miss. The Roman Stripe was an attempt to give a more formal arrangement to this piecing.

Materials *are not given for this quilt, because it is an excellent way to use up scraps. Use Best Six Cord, or Heavy Duty or Quilting Thread.*

Number of Each Unit to Cut . . . See page 54 for making the pattern and cutting the units. For 1 block cut 1 print and 2 solid color units each 1½ x 3½ inches.

How to Combine Units to Form a Block . . . Sew a solid color on each side of a print unit.

Setting the Quilt . . . One block is placed horizontally and the next vertically throughout entire quilt (see illustration).

Quilting . . . Quilt each unit ⅛ inch away from seams on all sides. Then quilt along the center. Bind edges with a solid color.

Block—3 inches square   **Illustration—15 inches square**

Roman Stripe

A Star That Traveled

This star first appeared in New England. The wives and daughters of seafaring men made it in the shape of a Ship's Wheel. The design traveled westward with Cape Cod families. In Pennsylvania, a farm woman saw the doves that gathered at the openings high under the eaves of the great barns. She used the star to put them in a quilt and called it Four Doves In a Window. Farther west in the rich farm lands, the harvest and the autumn colored trees glowing in the sunlight inspired a brilliantly colored star called the Harvest Sun.

HARVEST SUN

Materials: *For Single Size, 72 x 108 inches: 3½ yards blue polka dot, 2½ yards of yellow print, 4 yards red, 3 yards green print, 1½ yards gold, 5 yards of white.*

Fig. I

Harvest Sun

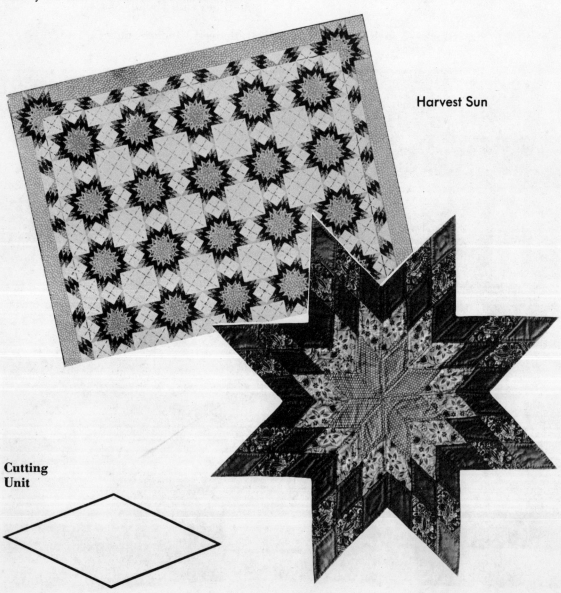

Cutting Unit

SHIP'S WHEEL

Materials: *For Single Size, 72 x 108 inches: 3½ yards red print, 9 yards white, 4 yards of blue print.*

Fig. 2

Ship's Wheel

61

FOUR DOVES IN A WINDOW

Materials: *For Single Size, 72 x 108 inches: 5½ yards white, 7½ yards blue, 2½ yards red print.*

Fig. 3

Fig. 4

Four Doves in a Window

For a Double Size, 96 x 108 inches, make 56 stars set 7 x 8 before adding border. Use Best Six Cord, or Heavy Duty or Quilting Thread.

Only 1 unit is required.

Number of Each Color to Cut . . . See page 54 for making the pattern and cutting the units.

For 1 Star cut . . . *Harvest Sun*—8 polka dot, 16 yellow print, 24 red, 16 green print, 8 gold. *Ship's Wheel*—16 red print, 32 white, 24 blue print. *Four Doves In a Window*—16 blue, 16 red print, 40 white.

For Single Size multiply the above numbers by 40. For Double Size, multiply the above numbers by 56.

How to Combine Units to Form a Star . . . *Harvest Sun*—(Fig. 1) Make 8 sections as shown and join. *Ship's Wheel*—(Fig. 2) Make

8 sections as shown and join. *Four Doves In a Window*—(Fig. 3) Make 2 sections as shown. Make 2 more sections replacing blue with red print. Fig. 4—Make 4 sections. Join Fig. 3 and Fig. 4 alternately, as shown.

Setting the Quilt . . . For each quilt cut 67 squares each 4¾ inches, including seam allowance, in color shown, and join stars as in illustration. Cut 28 squares each 6½ inches including seam allowance and join as shown.

Allowing for seams, even all sides by cutting rectangles half the size of the large square and triangles half the size of small squares. Corners are one fourth of a large square.

Harvest Sun (Inside border): Join 6 Fig. 1 sections for each corner. Make 44 Fig. 1 sections and alternate them with triangles around the quilt. Cut 4 strips of polka dot 3 inches wide and long enough to fit between the stars. Complete corners as shown. *Ship's Wheel:* The widths of the strips are blue 2½ inches, white 1½ inches and red 3½ inches. Cut strips long enough to miter corners. *Four Doves In a Window:* Cut 2 strips of blue each 6½ x 72½ inches and 2 strips 6½ x 108½ inches. Sew to corresponding sides, mitering corners. Join 2 red and 2 white units together and appliqué to center of border just sewn on. Repeat around as shown.

Quilting . . . Quilt diamonds ⅛ inch away from seams. Quilt other squares as shown.

Hearts and Gizzards and Borrow and Return

Identical parts plus the magic of arrangement result in these two distinctive patterns . . . one, a beautiful geometrical design, the other a diagonal effect.

Allow for Seams

HEARTS and GIZZARDS

Materials: *For Single Size, 71 x 111 inches: 8½ yards of gold and 7 yards of white fabric. For Double Size, 95 x 111 inches: 10 yards of gold and 9 yards of white fabric. Use Best Six Cord, or Heavy Duty or Quilting Thread.*

BORROW and RETURN

Materials: *For Single Size, 72 x 104 inches: 4½ yards of fawn and 7 yards of white fabric. For Double Size, 88 x 104 inches: 5 yards of fawn and 9 yards of white fabric.*

See pages 54, 55 and 56 for general directions.

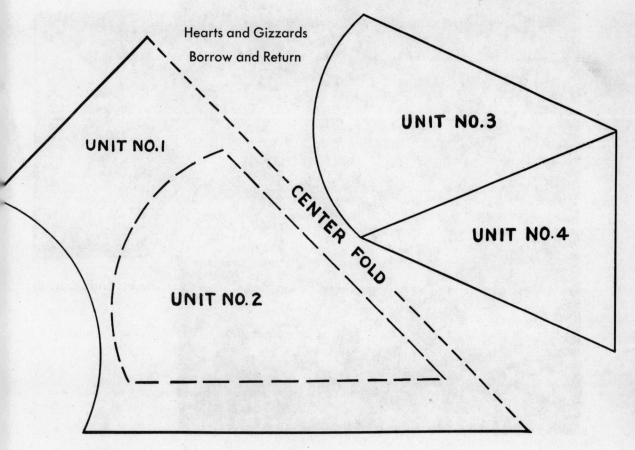

Hearts and Gizzards
Borrow and Return

UNIT NO.1

UNIT NO.2

CENTER FOLD

UNIT NO.3

UNIT NO.4

Number of Each Unit to Cut for 1 Block . . . Borrow and Return—Unit No. 1: 1 white, 1 fawn. **Unit No. 2:** 2 white, 2 fawn.

For Single Size, multiply the above numbers by 59; cut 58 white squares, each 8½ inches. For Double Size, multiply the above numbers by 72; cut 71 white squares, each 8½ inches.

Hearts and Gizzards—Unit No. 1: 1 white, 1 gold. **Unit No. 2:** 2 white, 2 gold.

For Single Size, multiply the above numbers by 104. For Double Size, multiply the above numbers by 143.

Each 8-inch block is made up of 2 units. Patterns are given for half of Unit No. 1 and for

Unit No. 2 (page 63). *For Hearts and Gizzards* the border consists of 2 units (No. 3 and No. 4) page 63.

How to Combine Units to Form a Block . . . Sew a contrasting color No. 1 unit to a white No. 1 unit across center. Sew 2 white No. 2 units to each side of contrasting color No. 1 unit. Sew 2 contrasting No. 2 units to each side of white No. 1 unit. Sew No. 2 units across center.

Setting the Quilt . . . *Borrow and Return—*For Single Size, set 9 x 13 blocks, alternating white and color. For Double Size, set 11 x 13 blocks, alternating white and color.

Hearts and Gizzards

Borrow and Return

Hearts and Gizzards—For Single Size, set 8 x 13 blocks as shown. For Double Size, set 11 x 13 blocks as shown.

Border . . . For Single Size, cut 168 white No. 3 units and 176 gold No. 4 units. For Double Size, cut 192 white No. 3 units and 188 gold No. 4 units. Alternate No. 3 and No. 4 units along all sides. Fill in corners with remaining units.

Quilting . . . *Borrow and Return*—Quilt all units ⅛ inch away from all seams. Quilt No. 1 units of colored blocks following the curved lines of No. 2 units. Quilt horizontal and diagonal lines in each white block, having each row of quilting 1 inch apart. Bind edges with fawn.

Hearts and Gizzards—Quilt all units ⅛ inch away from all seams. Quilt No. 1 units as desired. Place a white piping around scalloped edge of Border and then bind with gold.

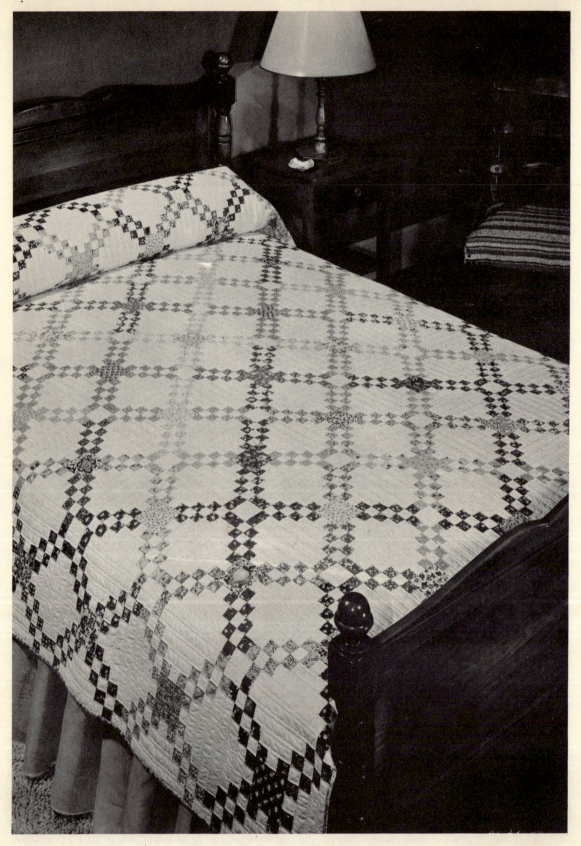

Double Irish Chain

Double Irish Chain

This variation of the most universally known quilt pattern, "Irish Chain," lends itself to the free use of gay colors. The white background accentuates the contrast. "Single" and "Triple Irish Chain" are other well known variations.

Allow for Seams

Materials: *For Single Size, 77 x 110 inches: 1 yard of light print, 9 yards each of dark and contrasting print, 11 yards of white fabric. For Double Size, 99 x 110 inches: 2 yards of light print, 12 yards each of dark and contrasting print, 14 yards of white fabric. Use Best Six Cord, or Heavy Duty or Quilting Thread. See pages 54, 55 and 56 for general directions.*

Number of Each Unit to Cut for 1 Block . . . **Unit No. 1:** 4 white. **Unit No. 2:** 4 white. **Unit No. 3:** 4 white. **Unit No. 4:** 20 white; 16 dark print; 16 contrasting print. **Unit No. 5:** 1 light print.

For Single Size, multiply the above numbers by 70. For Double Size, multiply the above numbers by 90.

How to Combine Units to Form a Block . . . Join 1 white and 2 print No. 4 units to each side of No. 5 unit. Join a white No. 1 unit to each corner. Complete block as shown.

Setting the Quilt . . . For Single Size, set 7 x 10 blocks. For Double Size, set 9 x 10 blocks.

Quilting . . . Quilt all units ⅛ inch away from all seams. Quilt center of No. 5 unit to form a nine patch. Bind all edges.

Each 11-inch block is made up of 5 units. Unit No. 1 is a rectangle 1 x 7 inches; Unit No. 2 is a rectangle 1 x 5 inches; Unit No. 3 is a rectangle 1 x 3 inches; Unit No. 4 is a 1-inch square and Unit No. 5 is a 3-inch square.

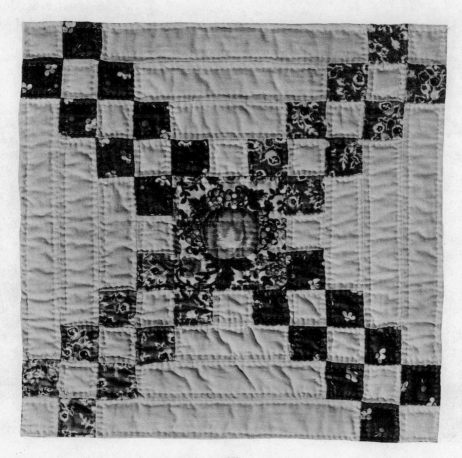

Red Cross

The cross unit is the basic feature of this beautiful but simple-to-make quilt. While it is the choice of the expert, it is easy enough for the beginner.

Allow for Seams

Materials: *For Single Size, 77 x 110 inches: 8½ yards of white polka dot and 4½ yards of red print fabric. For Double Size, 93½ x 110 inches: 10½ yards of white polka dot and 7 yards of red print fabric. Use Best Six Cord, or Heavy Duty or Quilting Thread.*

See pages 54, 55 and 56 for general directions.

Number of Each Unit to Cut for 1 Block . . . Unit No. 1: 8 print, 5 polka dot. **Unit No. 2:** 12 polka dot. **Unit No. 3:** 4 polka dot. **Unit No. 4:** 4 print.

For Single Size, multiply the above numbers by 35. For Double Size, multiply the above numbers by 42.

How to Combine Units to Form a Block . . . Make a nine patch with 5 polka dot and 4 print No. 1 units. Complete block as shown.

Setting the Quilt . . . For Single Size, make 5 strips each with 7 blocks divided by 5½-inch strips of polka dot. Join these strips together with 5½-inch polka dot strips (see quilt). For Double Size, make 6 strips each with 7 blocks and complete as for Single Size (see quilt).

Quilting . . . Quilt ⅛ inch away from all seams. Bind edges with red print.

Each 11-inch block is made up of 4 units. Unit No. 1 is a 2-inch square; Unit No. 2 is half of Unit No. 1; Unit No. 3 is a quarter of Unit No. 1; Unit No. 4 is a rectangle 2 x 6 inches.

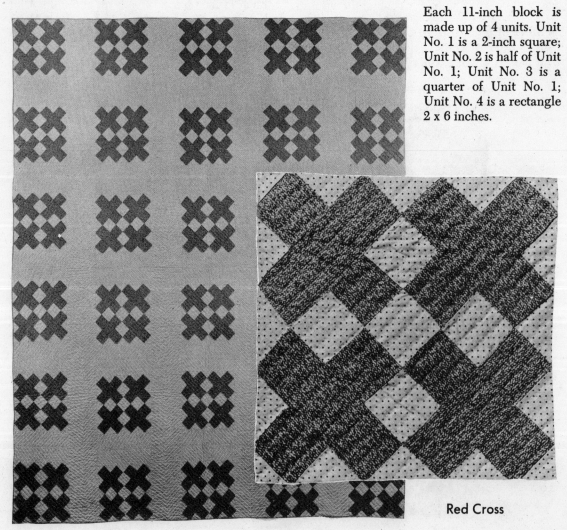

Red Cross

Star and Crescent

The Star and Crescent design was a favorite of Pennsylvania Dutch women who delighted to show their skill with the needle. The quilt illustrated was made in Franklin County, New York, over ninety years ago.

Materials: *For Single Size, 73 x 105 inches: 11 yards of white and 7 yards of blue polka dot. Use Best Six Cord, or Heavy Duty or Quilting Thread. Each block is made of 4 different kinds of units. Patterns are given for half of Unit No. 1, all of Unit Nos. 2 and 3 and half of Unit No. 4.*

See pages 54, 55 and 56 for general directions.

Number of Each Unit to Cut for 1 Block . . . Unit No. 1: (a diamond) 4 polka dot. **Unit No. 2:** (half diamond and first curved end) 4 white. **Unit No. 3:** (crescent) 4 polka dot. **Unit No. 4:** (corner piece) 4 white.

For a spread 73 x 105 inches make 5 x 7 blocks (illustration shows only 5 x 6 blocks—1 more row of blocks was added to the length to make it fit the standard size single bed).

How to Combine Units to Form a Block . . . Alternate No. 1 and No. 2 Units as shown. Sew a No. 3 Unit to each No. 2 Unit. Sew No. 4 Units to Nos. 1 and 3 Units as shown.

Setting the Quilt . . . See general directions on page 55.

Block—15 inches square

Quilting . . . Make 3 lines of quilting on each No. 2 Unit following the outline, spacing them evenly apart. Make 2 rows of quilting around each No. 3 Unit ¼ inch apart. Make a pattern of the small leaf shown, and quilt 9 in each corner. When quilting is completed, bind all edges with polka dot.

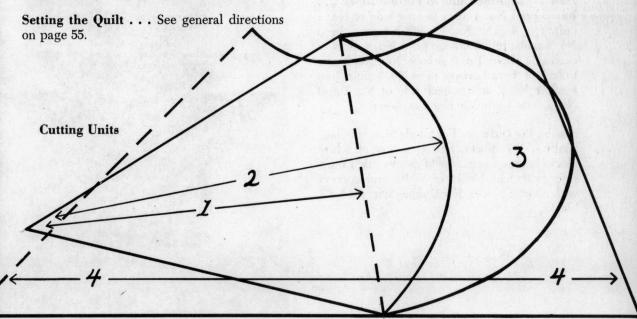

Cutting Units

Basket of Flowers

The basket pattern is another popular quilt pattern with several variations. Here, too, the design is most effective when colorful prints are used for the basket and plain white for the background.

Allow for Seams

Materials: *For Single Size, 72 x 114 inches: 3 yards of white, 2 yards of orange print and 4 yards of contrasting color printed fabrics. For Double Size, 100 x 114 inches: 5½ yards of white, 4 yards of orange print, 6 yards of contrasting color printed fabrics. Use Best Six Cord, or Heavy Duty or Quilting Thread.*

Note: Scraps may be used if desired.

See pages 54, 55 and 56 for general directions.

Number of Each Unit to Cut for 1 Block . . . Unit No. 1: 1 orange print. **Unit No. 2:** 2 white. **Unit No. 3:** 1 white. **Unit No. 4:** 2 orange print, 7 white, 16 print.

For Single Size, multiply the above numbers by 28. For Double Size, multiply the above numbers by 42. For Single Size, cut 28 white squares each 10½ inches. For Double Size, cut 42 white squares, each 10½ inches.

How to Combine Units to Form a Block . . . Join 3 print No. 4 units to long side of No. 1 unit. Join 4 print No. 4 units between the 3 No. 4 units. Join 2 orange print No. 4 units to each side of No. 1 unit at base. Join No. 3 unit to base of these 2 orange print No. 4 units. Join a white No. 2 unit to each side of No. 1 and No. 4 units. Complete block as shown.

Setting the Quilt . . . For Single Size, set diagonally 4 x 7 blocks, having a row of white blocks between each row of patchwork. Finish sides with half blocks of white and corners with quarter blocks. For Double Size, set 6 x 7 blocks.

First Border . . . Using No. 4 unit, piece border as shown to fit each side. Complete corners with white square.

Second Border . . . Cut a 2½-inch strip of white for each side, 4 inches longer than measurement of each side. Sew to First Border, mitering corners.

Quilting . . . Quilt ⅛ inch away from all seams. Quilt white blocks and triangles as desired. Bind all edges.

Each 10-inch block is made up of 4 units. Unit No. 1 is half of a 6-inch square; Unit No. 2 is a rectangle 2 x 6 inches; Unit No. 3 is half of a 4-inch square; Unit No. 4 is half of a 2-inch square.

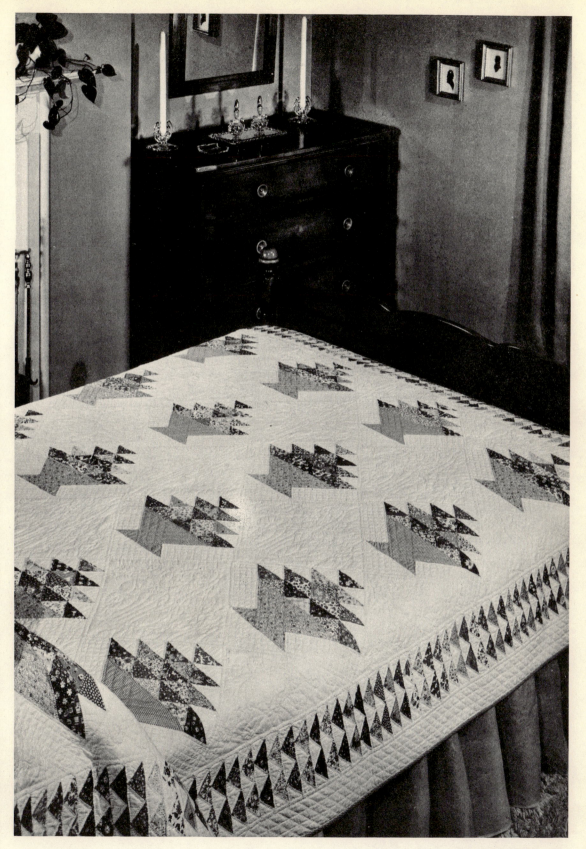

Basket of Flowers

Cross and Crown

The names and designs of the quilts were often expressions of the things which closely touched the daily lives of the makers. This is one of the most attractive designs for which religion furnished the inspiration.

Materials: *For Single Size, 72 x 108 inches: 7 yards of white, 5½ yards of royal blue, 4 yards of yellow print. For Double Size, 96 x 108 inches: make 72 blocks set 8 x 9. Use Best Six Cord, or Heavy Duty or Quilting Thread.*

Each block is made of 7 different units. Patterns are given for Unit Nos. 1, 2, 3 (inside each other) and 4. Unit Nos. 5, 6, and 7 are respectively a 2-inch square, a 2 x 4 inch rectangle, and a 2⅞-inch square.

See general directions on pages 54, 55 and 56.

Number of Each Unit to Cut for 1 Block . . .
Unit No. 1: (small triangle) 8 yellow print and 8 white. **Unit No. 2:** (medium triangle) 8 yellow print. **Unit No. 3:** (large triangle) 4 white. **Unit No. 4:** (point of cross) 4 royal blue. **Unit No. 5:** (2-inch square) 4 white.

Unit No. 6: (2 x 4 inch rectangle) 4 white.
Unit No. 7: (2⅞-inch square) 1 royal blue.

For Single Size, multiply the above numbers by 54. For Double Size, multiply above numbers by 72.

How to Combine Units to Form a Block . . .
Sew a No. 4 unit to each side of No. 7 unit. Sew a No. 3 unit between No. 4 units on each side. Sew No. 6 units to No. 3 units. Sew a white and a print No. 1 unit to a No. 2 unit to form a square. Sew one side of this square to a No. 6 unit and adjacent side to a No. 4 unit. Make 7 more squares like this and sew in place as shown. Complete block with No. 5 units.

Setting the Quilt . . . See general directions on page 55.

Quilting . . . Quilt No. 4 units in straight rows (quilting lines are carried across No. 7 unit). Quilt all other units ⅛ inch away from seams. Quilt a cross on all No. 3 and No. 5 units and 2 crosses on No. 6 units as shown. When completed bind edges with royal blue.

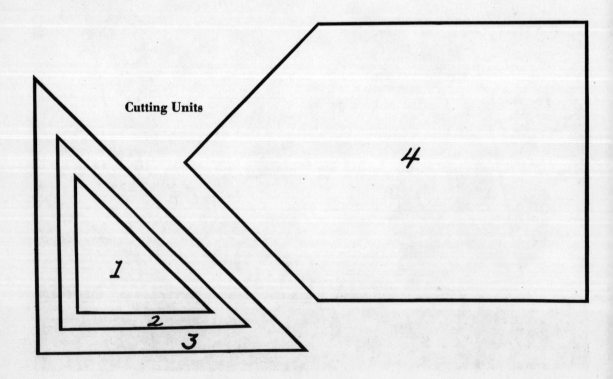

Cutting Units

1

2

3

4

Block—12 inches square

Cross and Crown

Sunflower

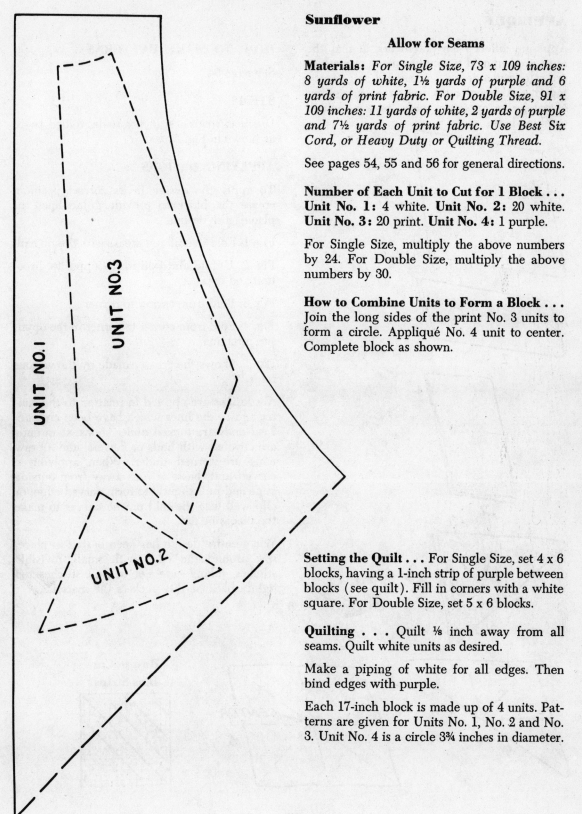

Sunflower

Allow for Seams

Materials: *For Single Size, 73 x 109 inches: 8 yards of white, 1½ yards of purple and 6 yards of print fabric. For Double Size, 91 x 109 inches: 11 yards of white, 2 yards of purple and 7½ yards of print fabric. Use Best Six Cord, or Heavy Duty or Quilting Thread.*

See pages 54, 55 and 56 for general directions.

Number of Each Unit to Cut for 1 Block . . . Unit No. 1: 4 white. **Unit No. 2:** 20 white. **Unit No. 3:** 20 print. **Unit No. 4:** 1 purple.

For Single Size, multiply the above numbers by 24. For Double Size, multiply the above numbers by 30.

How to Combine Units to Form a Block . . . Join the long sides of the print No. 3 units to form a circle. Appliqué No. 4 unit to center. Complete block as shown.

Setting the Quilt . . . For Single Size, set 4 x 6 blocks, having a 1-inch strip of purple between blocks (see quilt). Fill in corners with a white square. For Double Size, set 5 x 6 blocks.

Quilting . . . Quilt ⅛ inch away from all seams. Quilt white units as desired.

Make a piping of white for all edges. Then bind edges with purple.

Each 17-inch block is made up of 4 units. Patterns are given for Units No. 1, No. 2 and No. 3. Unit No. 4 is a circle 3¾ inches in diameter.

APPLIQUÉ

Appliqué differs from patchwork in that the units are hemmed to another piece of cloth in order to form a design, instead of being pieced together. Although most quilts are made either of patches or appliqué, there are some which combine both.

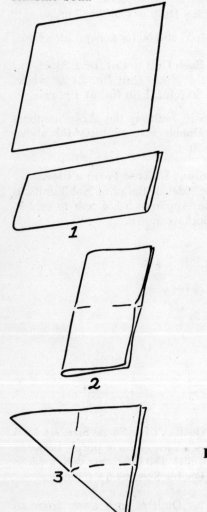

HOW TO MAKE PATTERNS

See page 54.

STEMS

Use bias strips, 1½ inches wide, folded twice as shown in Fig. A.

APPLYING DESIGNS

To apply the design in its correct position, crease the block to provide guide lines for placing the design.

Fig. 1. Fold in half and crease with thumb nail.

Fig. 2. Unfold and fold in the opposite direction and crease.

Fig. 3. Fold from corner to corner.

Fig. 4. Fold from corner to corner in the opposite direction.

Fig. 5. Shows the creases made by the various folds.

All designs are applied in relation to the center and to the lines which have been creased. Leaf ends are tucked under stems, stem ends are covered with buds or flowers, and all raw ends are turned under. When applying a curved unit, baste ⅛ inch away from outside edge and pull slightly to form curved edge; or clip well into the fold on the curves to make the pieces lie flat.

When entire design has been basted in place, sew around the edge with small, invisible stitches, taking care not to pull stitches too tightly because this puckers the material.

Fig. A

FOLD TWICE

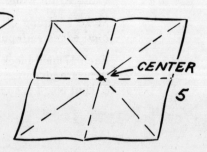

How to Cut Bias Strips

Rose of Sharon

Block—18 inches square

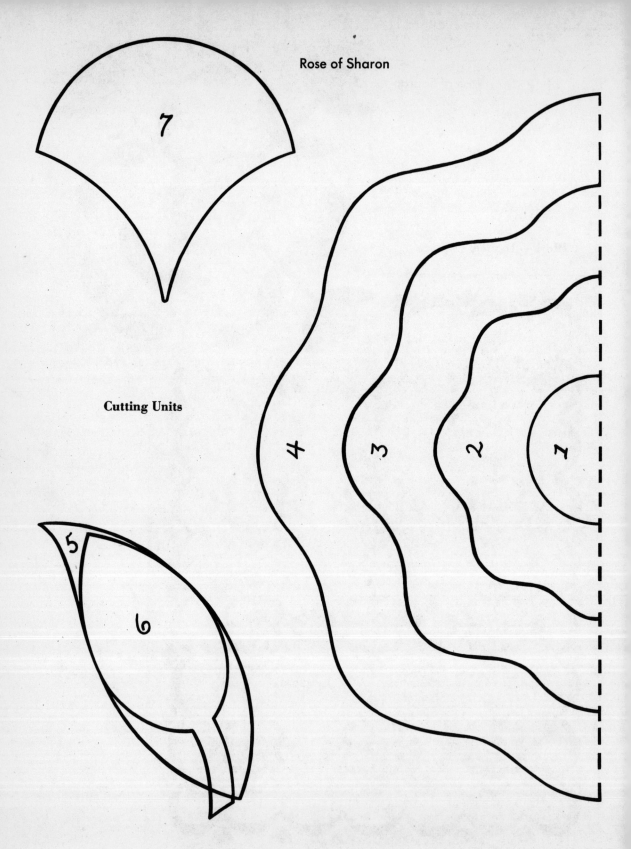

Rose of Sharon

Cutting Units

Rose of Sharon

The Rose of Sharon was a favorite bride's quilt. The name was taken from the Song of Solomon in the Bible.

I am the Rose of Sharon
And the lily of the valleys.
As the lily among the thorns
So is my love among the daughters.

97 x 121½ inches

Materials: *½ yard of rose print, 1 yard of rose, ½ yard of pink print, 7 yards of green print, ½ yard of gold and 11½ yards of white 39 inches wide. Use Best Six Cord, or Heavy Duty or Quilting Thread.*

Each block is made up of 7 units. Patterns are given for half of Unit Nos. 1, 2, 3 and 4; Unit Nos. 5 and 6 are inside each other. Unit No. 7 is complete.

See pages 54-56 and 78 for directions.

Number of Each Unit to Cut for 1 Block . . . **Unit No. 1:** (center of flower) 1 gold. **Unit No. 2:** (first petal) 1 rose print. **Unit No. 3:** (second petal) 1 pink print. **Unit No. 4:** (outside petal) 1 rose. **Unit No. 5:** (large leaf) 16 green print. **Unit No. 6:** (small leaf) 4 green print. **Unit No. 7:** (bud) 2 rose and 1 rose print. Cut 18 squares of white each 18½ inches. Cut 10 triangles (allowing for seams) half the size of white squares. Cut 4 pieces half the size of triangles for corners, allowing for seams.

To Apply Design . . . Place rose print bud 2¼ inches away from corner point.

Setting the Quilt . . . For border cut 2 strips of white 12½ x 97½ inches and 2 strips 12½ x 122 inches. Sew to corresponding sides mitering corners. Using green print, make five 12-inch scallops, 12 inches wide and 5½ inches deep for each short side, and 7 for each long side (use a plate or a victrola record 12 inches in diameter for making the pattern). Place center of one scallop to center of each side, then place the remainder of scallops adjacent to each other as shown. Make a scallop to fit each corner. Complete border with buds.

Quilting . . . Quilt as shown.

Turkey Track

Pioneer mothers, fearing that "Wandering Foot" suggested wanderlust, rechristened this beautiful quilt pattern "Turkey Track."

Allow for Seams

Materials: *For Single Size, 72 x 108 inches: 11 yards of red print and 9 yards of white fabric, 39 inches wide. For Double Size, 96 x 108 inches: 14½ yards of red print and 11 yards of white fabric, 39 inches wide. Use Best Six Cord, or Heavy Duty or Quilting Thread.*

See pages 54-56 and 78 for general directions.

Number of Each Unit to Cut for 1 Block . . . **Unit No. 1:** 1 red print. **Unit No. 2:** 12 red print.

For Single Size, multiply the above numbers by 28. For Double Size, multiply the above numbers by 42.

For Single Size, cut 28 white squares each 12½ inches. For Double Size, cut 42 white squares each 12½ inches.

To Apply Design . . . See page 78.

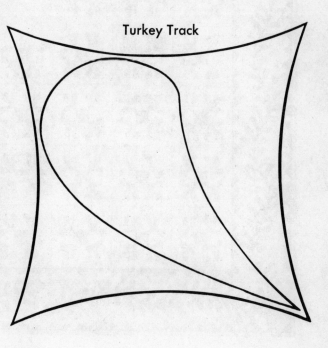

Turkey Track

Setting the Quilt . . . For Single Size, set 4 x 7 blocks. For Double Size, set 6 x 7 blocks.

Border . . . For Single Size, cut 2 strips of white 12½ x 108½ inches and 2 strips 12½ x 72½ inches. For Double Size, cut 2 strips 12½ x 108½ inches and 2 strips 12½ x 96½ inches. Sew to corresponding sides, mitering corners. Apply triangle borders as shown (triangles are half of a 2⅛-inch square). For stems, see page 78. Sew stems across center of each side of border as shown. Cut the necessary number of leaves and apply to stem.

Quilting . . . Quilt as desired.

Each 12-inch block is made up of 2 units. Patterns are given for Units No. 1 and No. 2.

Turkey Track

Hollyhock Wreath

Hollyhock Wreath

This colorful quilt, gay as a hollyhock border in old-time gardens, was copied in New York City in 1936. Pointed leaves are characteristic of many very old floral patterns.

Allow for Seams

Materials: *For Single Size, 73 x 115 inches: 7 yards of white and 3¼ yards of green fabric. For flowers, ½ yard each of solid and print fabric; ¼ yard each of solid yellow and yellow print fabric. For Double Size, 90 x 110 inches: 9 yards of white and 3½ yards of green fabric. For flowers, ½ yard each of solid and print fabric; ¼ yard each of solid yellow and yellow print fabric. Use Best Six Cord, or Heavy Duty or Quilting Thread.*

Note: Scraps of fabric may be used for flowers. See pages 54-56 and 78 for general directions.

Number of Each Unit to Cut for 1 Floral Block . . . Unit No. 1: 2 print, 2 solid. **Unit No. 2:** 4 green. **Unit No. 3:** 8 green. **Unit No. 4:** 2 solid yellow, 2 yellow print.

For Single Size, multiply the above numbers by 30. For Double Size, multiply the above numbers by 40. For Single Size, cut 60 white squares, each 11 inches. For Double Size, cut 80 white squares, each 11 inches.

To Apply Design . . . See page 78. Mark a circle 6½ inches in diameter in center of a white square. Sew units around circle as shown. Cut 4 bias strips (see page 78) and sew between flowers. For Single Size, make 29 more blocks like this. For Double Size, make 39 more blocks like this.

White Blocks . . . Appliqué 4 No. 3 units and 1 No. 4 unit to each remaining white square at center.

Setting the Quilt . . . For Single Size, set 6 x 10 blocks, alternating floral and white blocks. For Double Size, set 8 x 10 blocks, alternating floral and white blocks.

Border . . . Cut 4 strips of green (one for each side of quilt) 5½ inches wide and long enough to miter corners. Sew to corresponding sides, mitering corners.

Quilting . . . Quilt as shown, or as desired. Bind edges with green.

Each 11-inch floral block is made up of 4 units. Patterns are given for Units Nos. 1, 2, 3 and 4.

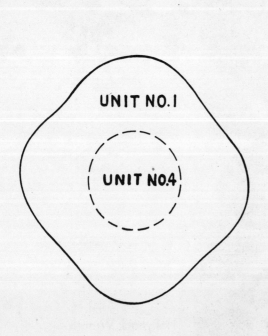

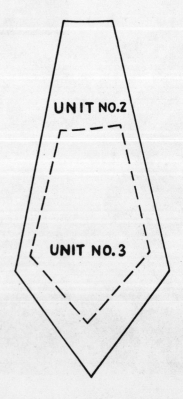

Rare Old Tulip

Block—18 inches square

Rare Old Tulip

This colorful design is very old. The first record we have of it is in a letter written early in the 1800's.

96 x 108 inches

Materials: *2 yards of red, 1 yard of yellow print, 1 yard of red polka dot, 5 yards of green print, and 9 yards of white 39 inches wide. Use Best Six Cord, or Heavy Duty or Quilting Thread.*

Each block is made of 6 units. Patterns are given for half of Unit Nos. 1, 2, and 3; Unit Nos. 4 and 5 are complete; Unit No. 6 is a circle 10 inches in diameter and is applied after 4 squares are joined. See pages 54-56 and 78 for general directions.

Number of Each Unit to Cut for 1 Block . . . 18½ inch white square. **Unit No. 1:** (tip of tulip) 3 red polka dot. **Unit No. 2:** (top petal of tulip) 3 yellow print. **Unit No. 3:** (base of tulip) 3 red. **Unit No. 4:** (small leaf) 2 green print. **Unit No. 5:** (large leaf) 2 green print. Cut a bias strip of green print 1½ inches wide and 12½ inches long for center stem. Cut 2 strips of green print 1½ x 6½ inches for short stems.

To Apply Design . . . Place center tulip 3 inches away from corner point. Make 16 blocks in all.

Setting the Quilt . . . When blocks are joined, appliqué a circle 10½ inches in diameter (allowing for seams) in center of every 4 blocks as shown. For the border, cut 2 strips of white 12½ x 72½ inches and 2 strips 18½ x 96½ inches. Sew one 12½-inch strip on each side. Then sew the remaining strips across top and bottom. Make a long bias strip as for stems and apply it as shown all around center of border. Appliqué 58 leaves and 4 tulips on border stem as shown.

Quilting . . . Follow the outline of design and quilt as shown, having quilting lines ¼ inch apart. Quilt ⅛ inch away from all joinings as shown. When quilting is completed, finish all edges.

Cutting Units

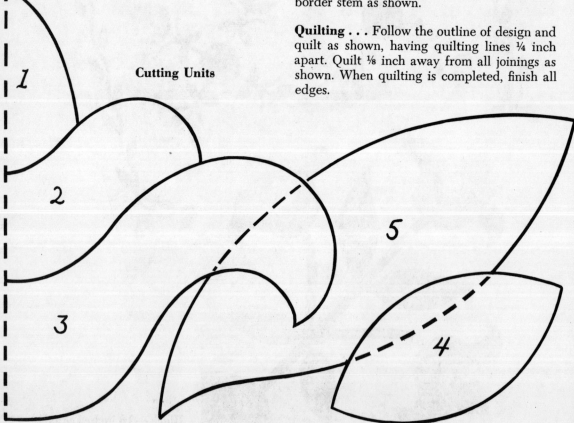

The President's Wreath

This pattern has the grace and elegance that made it popular for use as a bride's quilt. The coverlet in the picture was made near Harrisburg in the 1850's.

91½ x 103½ inches

Materials: *8½ yards of white 39 inches wide, 9½ yards of green, 3 yards of red. Use Best Six Cord, or Heavy Duty or Quilting Thread.*

Each block is made up of 5 different units. Patterns are given for half of Unit Nos. 1, 2 and 3; Unit No. 4 is complete; Unit No. 5 is made by drawing 2 circles inside each other, the larger circle 16¼ inches in diameter and the smaller circle 14⅝ inches in diameter. Patterns are also given for half of Unit Nos. 6 and 7; these are used for border. See pages 54-56 and 78 for general directions.

Number of Each Unit to Cut for 1 Block . . .
Unit No. 1: (tip of bud) 8 red. **Unit No. 2:** (base of bud) 8 green. **Unit No. 3:** (flower) 4 red. **Unit No. 4:** (leaf) 24 green. **Unit No. 5:** (circle) 1 green. Cut 9 squares of white 23 inches square.

To Apply Design . . . Place circle so that it is the same distance away from center on all sides. See page 78 for Applying Design.

Setting the Quilt . . . See general directions on pages 54-56. For border cut 2 strips of white 12½ x 68 inches. Sew one on each side. Then cut 2 strips 18½ x 92 inches and sew one across top and bottom. Using green, make six 12-inch scallops, 12 inches wide and 5½ inches deep for each short side, and seven for each long side (use a plate or a victrola record 12 inches in diameter to make the pattern). Place scallops 4 inches in from all edges and adjacent to each other. Make a scallop to fit each corner. Complete border by appliquéing a Unit No. 6 between each scallop and a Unit No. 7 in each scallop.

Quilting . . . Quilt as shown or as desired.

Block—22½ inches square

The President's Wreath

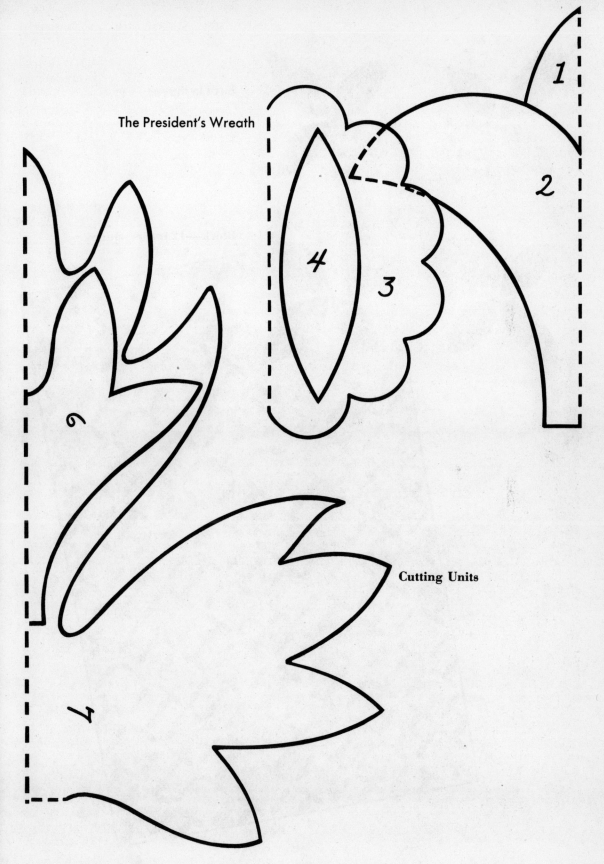

The President's Wreath

Cutting Units

1

2

3

4

6

7

89

Birds in the Air

Block—12 inches square

Birds in the Air

The originator of this quilt took much pleasure in the world about her, if we are to judge from the name she chose. She combined the familiar nine patch with appliqué to illustrate her pleasant fancy.

Materials: *8 yards of white, 3 yards of rust, 2 yards of gold, 2 yards of brown print, 2 yards of yellow print. Use Best Six Cord, or Heavy Duty or Quilting Thread.*

Each block is made up of 5 units. Patterns are given for Unit Nos. 1 and 2. Unit Nos. 3, 4, and 5 are respectively 2 inches square, 3 inches square, and a rectangle 3 x 6 inches.

See pages 54-56 and 78 for general directions.

Number of Each Unit to Cut for 1 Block . . .
Unit No. 1: 8 brown print. **Unit No. 2:** 2 gold, 2 rust. **Unit No. 3:** 5 yellow print and 4 white. **Unit No. 4:** 4 white. **Unit No. 5:** 4 white. For Single Size, multiply the above numbers by 54. For Double Size, multiply above numbers by 72.

How to Combine Units to Form a Block . . .
Make a nine patch as shown with No. 3 units. Sew a Unit No. 5 to each side of the nine patch. Complete block with Units No. 4. Appliqué a Unit No. 2 on each Unit No. 4, having the 2 gold and 2 rust opposite each other. Appliqué Units No. 1 on each side of Units No. 2 as shown.

Setting the Quilt . . . See general directions on page 55.

Quilting . . . Quilt appliqué leaves and yellow print squares of nine patch ¼ inch away from seams. Quilt white square of nine patch as shown.

When quilting is completed, bind all edges with rust.

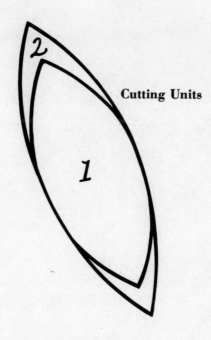

Cutting Units

91

CHAPTER III

KNITTING ... *makes fine fashion sense for you and your family*

SOMETIMES IT SEEMS that one should add the title of Financial Genius to the designation of mother and homemaker. No matter how thrifty or ingenious she is, there comes a point at which the budget balks and refuses to stretch another penny's worth. That is why mothers all over America are *knitting two*, *purling two*, trying to keep the budget balanced and the whole family in sartorial splendor.

Mothers and daughters who knit will find plenty of attractive reasons in the section that follows for keeping their needles clicking. Daughters will go for the plaid skirt with matching stole, the three color jerkin; mother for the pearl-fastened cardigan, the long torso beaded blouse. Then there is an argyle pullover for a young athletic star, a sleeveless pullover for the man of the house, an adorable pinafore for a very young miss and something wonderful afoot for every member of the household.

HOW TO KNIT

PRACTICE PIECES . . . Whenever a gauge appears in a direction, it is wise to make a practice piece to be sure that you have the same gauge as that specified before you proceed with your work. **BECAUSE**—if your gauge is different, your article when finished will *not* be the same as the one shown in the picture. **If you have fewer stitches to the inch, use a smaller needle. If you have more stitches to the inch, use a larger needle.**

Guide to Right-Handed Knitters

If you work with your Right Hand, the following steps show you the position in which your hands should be.

CASTING ON . . . The First Step in Knitting

Putting the first stitches on the needle is called casting on.

1. To cast on 20 stitches in the material suggested, it will be necessary to measure off 16 inches of yarn (Fig. 1).

2. Make a slip loop 16 inches from the end of the yarn (Figs. 1, 2, 3 and 4).

3. Place the loop on the needle and gently pull the ends of the yarn (not too tight, Fig. 5). The ball end of the yarn is to the right and the free end of the yarn is to the left.

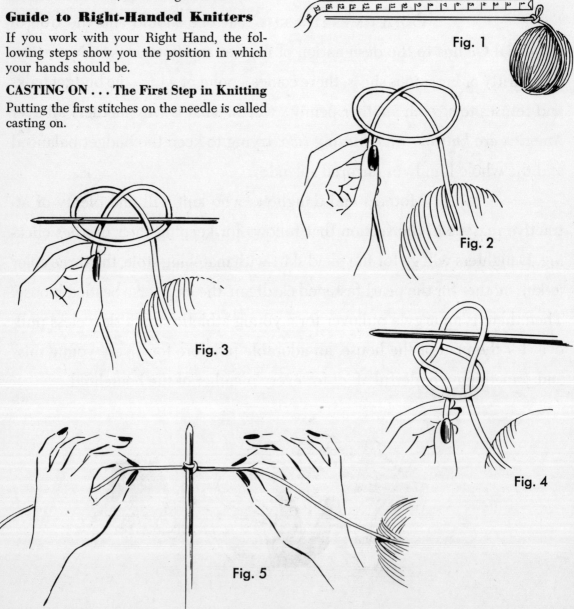

Fig. 1

Fig. 2

Fig. 3

Fig. 4

Fig. 5

WHAT TO DO WITH THE RIGHT HAND

1. Place the needle between the thumb and first finger, as if you were holding a pencil (Fig. 6).

2. Be sure that the loop is near the pointed end of the needle (Fig. 6).

3. Using the ball end of the yarn, place the yarn loosely over the first finger, under the second, over the third, under the fourth above middle joint (Fig. 6). The second and third fingers are very important because they keep the flow of yarn even, not too tight or not too loose, that is, they regulate the correct tension.

WHAT TO DO WITH THE LEFT HAND

1. Grasp the free end of the yarn lightly against the left hand with the second, third, and fourth fingers (Fig. 7).

2. Place the yarn near the needle around and under the thumb (Fig. 8).

NOW YOU ARE READY FOR WORK

Bring the hands close together and adjust the yarn. For position see Fig. 9.

1. Notice that the yarn makes a loop around the left thumb.

2. Insert your needle through the underside of the loop (Figs. 9 and 10).

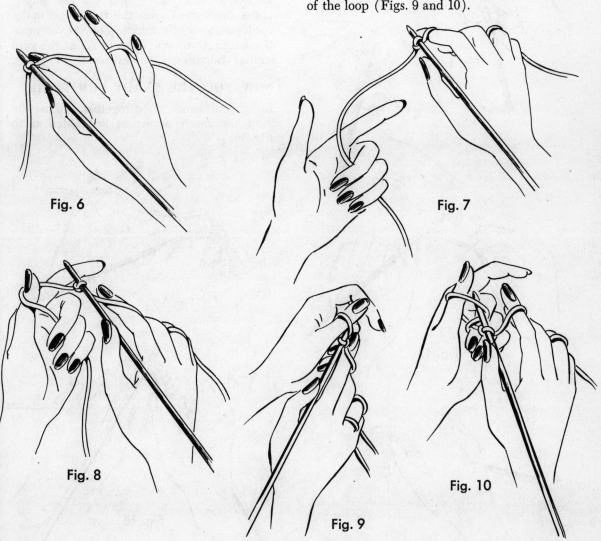

Fig. 6

Fig. 7

Fig. 8

Fig. 9

Fig. 10

3. Bring the yarn in the right hand over the point of the needle from the back (Fig. 11).

4. Draw it through the loop (Fig. 12).

5. Gently pull the free end of the yarn with the left hand to tighten the stitch (Fig. 13).

6. Place the yarn around thumb as directed before and repeat Steps 2 to 5 inclusive until you have 20 stitches.

The Knit Stitch

Plain Knitting or Garter Stitch

WHAT TO DO WITH THE LEFT HAND

1. In the left hand, hold the needle with the stitches just cast on. For position see Fig. 14.

2. The first stitch is held lightly by the index finger near the tip of the needle (Fig. 14).

WHAT TO DO WITH THE RIGHT HAND

1. Hold the needle between the thumb and the index finger, as if you were holding a pencil (Fig. 15).

2. The yarn is placed over the first finger, under the second, over the third, and under the fourth above the middle joint. As you practice knitting, you will learn to adjust the yarn so that you will get the best results (Fig. 15).

NOW YOU ARE READY FOR WORK

Bring your hands close together. Adjust the yarn and insert needle in first stitch as in Fig. 16.

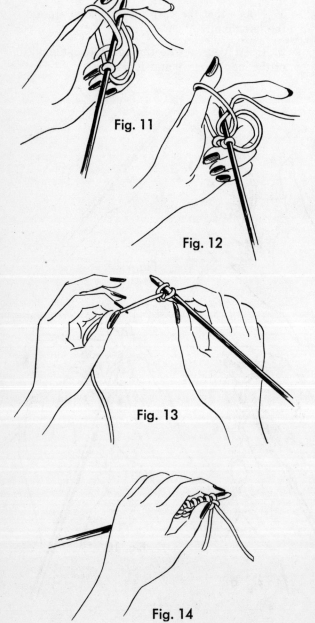

Fig. 11

Fig. 12

Fig. 13

Fig. 14

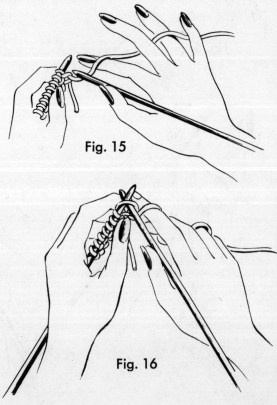

Fig. 15

Fig. 16

FIRST ROW

1. Insert the right needle into the front of the first stitch on the left needle from the left side (Fig. 17).

2. Steady the right needle against the forefinger of the left hand. Keep your yarn to the back of your work.

3. With the right hand bring the yarn over the point of the right needle (Fig. 18).

4. Draw the yarn through the stitch (Fig. 19).

5. Slip the old stitch off the left needle, thus completing the first stitch. A new row is being formed on the right needle (Fig. 20).

6. Always keep pushing your work up so that the stitch on which you are working is near the tip of the needle.

7. Repeat Steps 1 to 5 inclusive until all the stitches have been knitted off the left needle. An easy way to remember these steps is to repeat to yourself: "In"—(Step 1—Fig. 17)—"Over"—(Step 2—Fig. 18)—"Through"—(Step 3—Fig. 19)—"Off"—(Step 4—Fig. 20).

8. Now you have knitted one row. You should have 20 stitches on the needle.

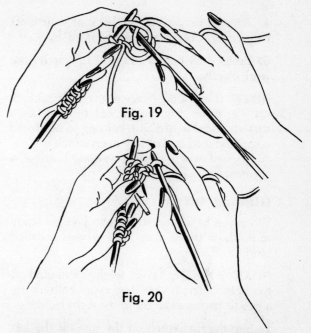

Fig. 19

Fig. 20

SECOND ROW and SUCCEEDING ROWS

1. Change the needle with the stitches into the left hand.

2. The empty needle is in the right hand. The yarn is over the first finger, under the second, over the third, and under the fourth above the middle joint (Fig. 15).

NOTE: When using a long needle many knitters tuck one end of the right needle under the right arm. This relieves strain and enables you to knit faster.

3. Insert right needle into the front of the first stitch on the left needle from the right side and slip the first stitch off the left needle onto the right needle without knitting. Do this with the first stitch of each succeeding row and you will have a smooth edge known as a chain edge (Fig. 21).

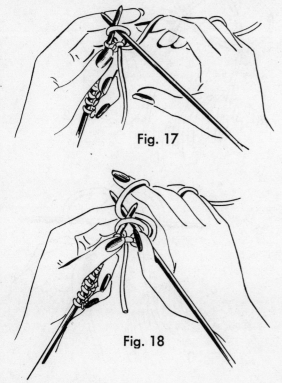

Fig. 17

Fig. 18

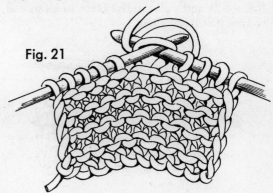

Fig. 21

4. Bring your yarn to the back of your work by passing it between the two needles.

5. Proceed as before (Fig. 21). Watch your work closely.

NOTE: It is not necessary or even desirable to use the chain edge in all cases. It makes a smooth edge on straight knitting. The closed edge produced by knitting every stitch is especially used when shaping various parts of a garment.

Binding Off

When you have worked 10 rows you are ready to finish off the swatch. This process is called binding off.

NOTE: Beginners have a tendency to bind off too tightly. To prevent this, many knitters use a needle two sizes larger in the right hand.

1. Slip the first stitch on the row off the left needle onto the right needle without knitting.

2. Knit the second stitch very loosely. (There are two stitches on the right needle).

3. Insert the left needle through the left side of the first stitch (Fig. 22).

4. Keep the yarn in the right hand very loose so that the second stitch remains loose.

5. Bring the first stitch forward over the second stitch and over the tip of the needle so that one stitch remains on the needle (Fig. 22).

6. Knit the next stitch loosely. There are two stitches on the right needle.

7. Repeat Steps 3 to 6 inclusive (Fig. 22).

8. When you come to the last stitch, clip your yarn about three inches from the needle. Bring the loose end through the stitch remaining on the needle and pull tightly. Darn in loose end so that it will not show.

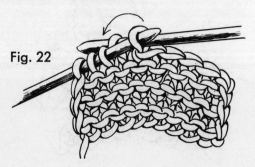

Fig. 22

HOW TO KNIT

Guide to Left-Handed Knitters

If you work with your Left Hand, the following steps show you the position in which your hands should be.

CASTING ON . . . The First Step in Knitting

Putting the first stitches on the needle is called casting on.

1. To cast on 20 stitches in the material suggested, it will be necessary to measure off 16 inches of yarn (Fig. 1).

2. Make a slip loop 16 inches from the end of the yarn (Figs. 1, 2, 3 and 4).

3. Place the loop on the needle and gently pull the ends of the yarn (not too tight, Fig. 5). The ball end of the yarn is to the left and the free end of the yarn is to the right.

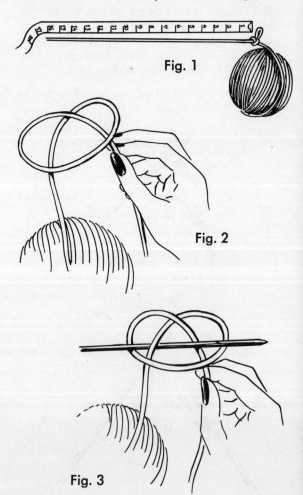

Fig. 1

Fig. 2

Fig. 3

WHAT TO DO WITH THE LEFT HAND

1. Place the needle between the thumb and first finger, as if you were holding a pencil (Fig. 6).

2. Be sure that the loop is near the pointed end of the needle (Fig. 6).

3. Using the ball end of the yarn, place the yarn loosely over the first finger, under the second, over the third, under the fourth above middle joint (Fig. 6). The second and third fingers are very important because they keep the flow of yarn even, not too tight or not too loose, that is, they regulate the correct tension.

WHAT TO DO WITH THE RIGHT HAND

1. Grasp the free end of the yarn lightly against the right hand with the second, third, and fourth fingers (Fig. 7).

2. Place the yarn near the needle around and under the thumb (Fig. 8).

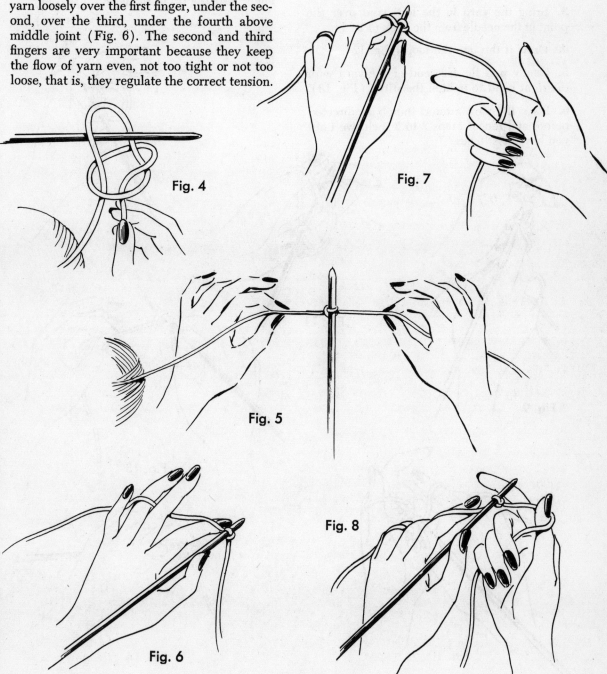

Fig. 4

Fig. 7

Fig. 5

Fig. 8

Fig. 6

NOW YOU ARE READY FOR WORK

Bring the hands close together and adjust the yarn. For position see Fig. 9.

1. Notice that the yarn makes a loop around the right thumb.

2. Insert your needle through the underside of the loop (Figs. 9 and 10).

3. Bring the yarn in the left hand over the point of the needle from the back (Fig. 11).

4. Draw it through the loop (Fig. 12).

5. Gently pull the free end of the yarn with the right hand to tighten the stitch (Fig. 13).

6. Place the yarn around thumb as directed before and repeat Steps 2 to 5 inclusive until you have 20 stitches.

The Knit Stitch

Plain Knitting or Garter Stitch

WHAT TO DO WITH THE RIGHT HAND

1. In the right hand, hold the needle with the stitches just cast on. For position see Fig. 14.

2. The first stitch is held lightly by the index finger near the tip of the needle (Fig. 14).

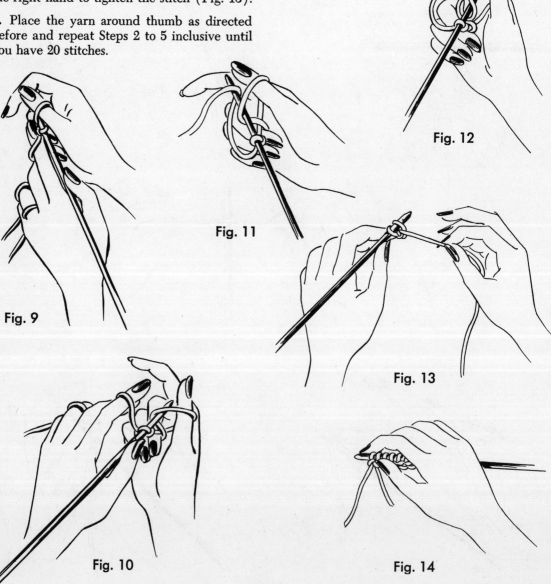

Fig. 9

Fig. 10

Fig. 11

Fig. 12

Fig. 13

Fig. 14

WHAT TO DO WITH THE LEFT HAND

1. Hold the needle between the thumb and the index finger, as if you were holding a pencil (Fig. 15).

2. The yarn is placed over the first finger, under the second, over the third, and under the fourth above the middle joint. As you practice knitting, you will learn to adjust the yarn so that you will get the best results (Fig. 15).

NOW YOU ARE READY FOR WORK

Bring your hands close together. Adjust the yarn and insert needle in first stitch as in Fig. 16.

FIRST ROW

1. Insert the left needle into the front of the first stitch on the right needle from the right side (Fig. 17).

2. Steady the left needle against the forefinger of the right hand. Keep your yarn to the back of your work.

3. With the left hand bring the yarn over the point of the left needle (Fig. 18).

4. Draw the yarn through the stitch (Fig. 19).

5. Slip the old stitch off the right needle, thus completing the first stitch. A new row is being formed on the left needle (Fig. 20).

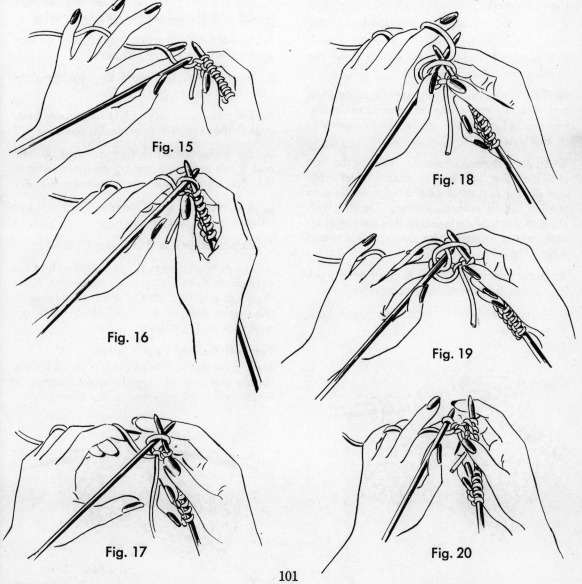

Fig. 15

Fig. 16

Fig. 17

Fig. 18

Fig. 19

Fig. 20

6. Always keep pushing your work up so that the stitch on which you are working is near the tip of the needle.

7. Repeat Steps 1 to 5 inclusive until all the stitches have been knitted off the right needle. An easy way to remember these steps is to repeat to yourself: "In"—(Step 1—Fig. 17)—"Over"—(Step 2—Fig. 18)—"Through"—(Step 3—Fig. 19)—"Off"—(Step 4—Fig. 20).

8. Now you have knitted one row. You should have 20 stitches on the needle.

SECOND ROW and SUCCEEDING ROWS

1. Change the needle with the stitches into the right hand.

2. The empty needle is in the left hand. The yarn is over the first finger, under the second, over the third, and under the fourth above the middle joint (Fig. 15).

NOTE: When using a long needle many knitters tuck one end of the left needle under the left arm. This relieves strain and enables you to knit faster.

3. Insert left needle into the front of the first stitch on the right needle from the left side and slip the first stitch off the right needle onto the left needle without knitting. Do this with the first stitch of each succeeding row and you will have a smooth edge known as a chain edge (Fig. 21).

4. Bring your yarn to the back of your work by passing it between the two needles.

5. Proceed as before (Fig. 21). Watch your work closely.

NOTE: It is not necessary or even desirable to use the chain edge in all cases. It makes a smooth edge on straight knitting. The closed edge produced by knitting every stitch is especially used when shaping various parts of a garment.

Binding Off

When you have worked 10 rows you are ready to finish off the swatch. This process is called binding off.

NOTE: Beginners have a tendency to bind off too tightly. To prevent this, many knitters use a needle two sizes larger in the left hand.

1. Slip the first stitch on the row off the right needle onto the left needle without knitting.

2. Knit the second stitch very loosely. (There are two stitches on the left needle).

3. Insert the right needle through the right side of the first stitch (Fig. 22).

4. Keep the yarn in the left hand very loose so that the second stitch remains loose.

5. Bring the first stitch forward over the second stitch and over the tip of the needle so that one stitch remains on the needle (Fig. 22).

6. Knit the next stitch loosely. There are two stitches on the left needle.

7. Repeat Steps 3 to 6 inclusive (Fig. 22).

8. When you come to the last stitch, clip your yarn about three inches from the needle. Bring the loose end through the stitch remaining on the needle and pull tightly. Darn in loose end so that it will not show.

For Left-Handed Pupils only:

Place a pocket mirror to the left of each illustration and you will see the exact position in which you work reflected in the mirror.

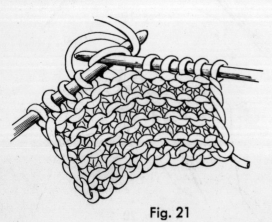

Fig. 21

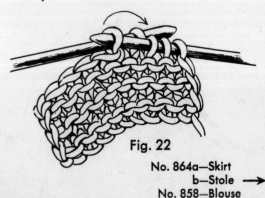

Fig. 22

No. 864a—Skirt
b—Stole →
No. 858—Blouse

No. 864a . . . . Skirt
Size 14 or 16

Materials: SOCK AND SWEATER YARN, SHRINK-RESIST FINISH, *3 Ply (1 oz. skeins): 12 skeins of Dark Green, 8 skeins of Dryad Green and 3 skeins each of Daffodil and Scarlet . . . 29-inch Steel Circular Knitting Needle No. 3 (3 mm. size).*

GAUGE: 7½ sts make 1 inch; 10 rows make 1 inch.

BLOCKING MEASUREMENTS:

Length of skirt—32 inches.
Width of skirt at hem—85 inches. .

Note: When changing from one color to another always twist the unused color around the other to prevent making holes.

With Dark Green cast on 640 sts loosely. **1st row:** * Knit 10 Dark Green, attach a ball of Dryad Green and (with Dryad Green k 2; k 2 Dark Green) twice; k 2 Dryad Green. Repeat from * across, ending with k 2 Dryad Green. Turn. **2nd row:** * (P 2 Dryad Green, p 2 Dark Green) twice; p 2 Dryad Green, p 10 Dark Green. Repeat from * across. Starting at 3rd row knit, following chart across (20 sts worked). Repeat these 20 sts to end of row. On following row purl, following chart across (20 sts worked). Repeat these 20 sts to end of row. Continue in this manner until top of chart is reached (40 rows). Repeat these 40 rows until piece measures 33 inches in all, or length desired. Bind off.

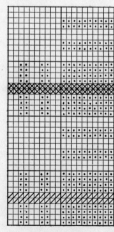

☑ DARK GREEN
☐ DRYAD GREEN
☒ DAFFODIL
☒ SCARLET

VERTICAL STRIPES . . . Starting at lower edge of skirt, with crochet hook and Daffodil, make a row of chain sts along each of the two center sts of first Dryad Green sections to waistline (a stripe completed). With Scarlet, work a stripe along next Dryad Green sections to waistline. Alternate these 2 stripes around entire skirt (see illustration).

Sew edges neatly together to form back seam. Make a narrow hem all around lower edge of skirt. Work a rnd of sc at top of skirt. Join, then make a beading as follows:

BEADING . . . * Ch 6, skip 3 rows of knitting and make an sc in next st, ch 6, skip 3 sc at top of skirt and make sc in next sc. Repeat from * around. Join and break off.

Run elastic through beading and sew ends securely together.

No. 864b . . . . Jacket
Sizes 12, 14 and 16

Materials: SOCK AND SWEATER YARN, SHRINK-RESIST FINISH, *3 Ply (1 oz. skeins): 11 skeins of Dark Green for Sizes 12 and 14; 13 skeins for Size 16 . . . Plastic or Aluminum Knitting Pins, 1 pair No. 3 (3 mm. size) . . . Buttons . . . Small shoulder pads.*

GAUGE: 7½ sts make 1 inch; 10 rows make 1 inch.

BLOCKING MEASUREMENTS:

Sizes	12	14	16
Bust	32"	34"	36"
Width across back at underarm	16"	17"	18"
Width across each front at underarm	10¼"	10¾"	11¼"
Width across back above armhole shaping	13"	13¾"	14½"
Length of side seam	13½"	14½"	15½"
Length from shoulder to lower edge	20½"	22"	23"
Length of sleeve seam	19"	19½"	20"
Width across sleeve at upperarm	13"	13½"	13½"

864

RIGHT LOWER BACK . . . Cast on

| 62 sts | 66 sts | 70 sts |

and work in stockinette st (k 1 row, p 1 row), decreasing 1 st at side edge every 3rd row until there remain

| 55 sts | 57 sts | 59 sts |

On Sizes 12 and 14 only, work without decreasing until piece measures 3 inches, ending with a k row.

On next row, bind off 6 sts and p across. Then k 1 row. Place on a stitch holder these

| 49 sts | 51 sts | 53 sts |

LEFT LOWER BACK . . . Work as for Right Lower Back, reversing shapings (keeping center edge straight), until there remain, ending with a p row,

| 55 sts | 57 sts | 59 sts |

On next row, bind off 6 sts, k across, then p 1 row and p across sts on stitch holder. There are on needle

| 98 sts | 102 sts | 106 sts |

On Sizes 12 and 14 only, dec 1 st at both ends of next row and every 3rd row thereafter until there remain

| 90 sts | 98 sts | — |

Continue in stockinette st without decreasing until piece measures in all

| 5″ | 5½″ | 6″ |

Inc 1 st at both ends of next row and every

| | 5th row | 6th row | 6th row |

thereafter until there are on needle

| 120 sts | 128 sts | 136 sts |

Work without increasing until piece measures in all

| 13½″ | 14½″ | 15½″ |

To Shape Armholes: Bind off

| | 6 sts | 7 sts | 8 sts |

at beginning of next 2 rows. Dec 1 st at end of each row until there remain

| 98 sts | 104 sts | 110 sts |

Work without decreasing until piece measures from 1st row of armhole shaping

| 3″ | 3½″ | 3½″ |

Inc 1 st at both ends of next row and every

| | 6th row | 10th row | 14th row |

thereafter until there are on needle

| 108 sts | 112 sts | 116 sts |

Work without increasing until piece measures from 1st row of armhole shaping

| 7″ | 7½″ | 7½″ |

To Shape Shoulders: Bind off 13 sts at beginning of each row until there remain

| 30 sts | 34 sts | 38 sts |

Bind off.

LEFT FRONT . . . Cast on

| 70 sts | 74 sts | 78 sts |

Work in stockinette st, decreasing 1 st at side edge on every 3rd row until there remain

| 61 sts | 67 sts | 69 sts |

Work in stockinette st without decreasing until piece measures in all, ending with a p row

| 5″ | 5½″ | 6″ |

Inc 1 st at side edge on next row and at side edge every 3rd row thereafter until there are on needle

| 87 sts | 91 sts | 95 sts |

Work without increasing until piece measures in all, ending with a p row

| 13½″ | 14½″ | 15½″ |

To Shape Armhole: Bind off at beginning of next row

| | 6 sts | 7 sts | 8 sts |

Dec 1 st at armhole edge every other row until there remain

| 76 sts | 79 sts | 82 sts |

Work without decreasing until piece measures from 1st row of armhole shaping

| 3″ | 3½″ | 3½″ |

Inc 1 st at armhole edge on next row and every

| | 6th row | 8th row | 12th row |

thereafter until there are on needle

| 81 sts | 83 sts | 85 sts |

Piece measures from 1st row of armhole shaping

| 5½″ | 6″ | 6″ |

To Shape Neck: Bind off

| | 26 sts | 27 sts | 27 sts |

and complete row. Work 1 more row. Then bind off 2 sts at neck edge on next row and every other row 3 times in all. Then dec 1 st at neck edge each row until there remain

| 42 sts | 42 sts | 45 sts |

Piece measures from 1st row of armhole shaping, ending at armhole edge

| 7″ | 7½″ | 7½″ |

To Shape Shoulder: Bind off

14 sts	14 sts	15 sts

at beginning of next row and every other row thereafter until all sts are worked off.

RIGHT FRONT . . . Work exactly as for Left Front, reversing shapings and making a set of buttonholes when piece measures in all

4½″	5½″	6½″

To make a set of buttonholes, work as follows:
1st row: *Starting at front edge, k 2, bind off next 4 sts, k 8, bind off next 4 sts, knit to end of row.* **2nd row:** *P across, casting on 4 sts to replace those bound off in previous row.* Make a set of buttonholes every 1½ inches thereafter, always measuring from center of previous buttonhole, until

10	10	11

sets of buttonholes in all have been made.

SLEEVES . . . Cast on

72 sts	76 sts	76 sts

Work in stockinette st for

4″	4½″	4½″

Inc 1 st at both ends of next row and every 11th row thereafter until there are on needle

98 sts	102 sts	102 sts

Work without increasing until piece measures in all

19″	19½″	20″

To Shape Top: Bind off

6 sts	7 sts	8 sts

at beginning of next 2 rows. Dec 1 st at end of each row until there remain

40 sts	34 sts	30 sts

Dec 1 st at both ends of each row until 22 sts remain. Bind off remaining sts.

COLLAR . . . Cast on 98 sts and work in stockinette st for ½ inch. Inc 1 st at both ends of next row and every 4th row thereafter, until there are 108 sts on needle. Work without increasing until piece measures 2½ inches in all, ending with a knit row. Knit 1 row (half of collar is completed). Continue in stockinette st until piece measures ½ inch from half way mark. Dec 1 st at both ends of next row and every 4th row thereafter until 98 sts remain. Work without decreasing until piece measures 5 inches in all. Bind off.

Block to measurements. Sew underarm and shoulder seams. Sew sleeve seams and sew in sleeves. Fold center front edges back on wrong side, having buttonholes overlap each other. Sew buttonhole edges together. Sew other edges in place. Sew Collar to neck edge. Sew on buttons to correspond with buttonholes. Make a 1-inch hem around lower edges and sleeves. Sew the bound-off edges at opening of back on wrong side.

No. 864c . . . . Stole

Materials: Sock and Sweater Yarn, Shrink-Resist Finish, *3 Ply (1 oz. skeins): 6 skeins of Dark Green, 5 skeins of Dryad Green and 2 skeins each of Scarlet and Daffodil . . . Plastic or Aluminum Knitting Pins, 1 pair No. 3 (3 mm. size).*

GAUGE: 7½ sts make 1 inch; 10 rows make 1 inch.

With Dark Green, cast on 180 sts loosely. Starting at 11th row on chart, work as for No. 864-A, beginning and ending each row with 5 Dark Green sts and working until piece measures 60 inches. Bind off.

STRIPES . . . Work as for No. 864-A, beginning and ending with a Scarlet Stripe.

FRINGE . . . Cut 4 strands of Dark Green, each 12 inches long. Double these strands to form a loop. Insert hook in end of Stole and draw loop through. Draw loose ends through loops and pull up tightly. Make a fringe closely across each short end, matching stripes with the same color. Trim ends evenly.

No. 858 . . . . Blouse
Sizes 14, 16 and 18

Materials: Sock and Sweater Yarn, Shrink-Resist Finish, *3 Ply (1 oz. skeins): 8 skeins for Size 14; 9 skeins for Sizes 16 and 18 . . . Plastic or Aluminum Knitting Pins, 1 pair No. 2 (2¾ mm. size) and 1 pair No. 3 (3 mm. size) . . . 3 buttons.*

GAUGE: 7½ sts make 1 inch; 10 rows make 1 inch.

BLOCKING MEASUREMENTS:

Sizes	14	16	18
Bust	34″	36″	38″

858

Width across back or front at underarm
17″	18″	19″

Length from shoulder to lower edge
20″	20½″	21½″

Length of side seam
13″	13½″	14″

Length of sleeve seam (finished)
10″	10½″	11″

Width across sleeve at upperarm
13″	13″	13½″

BACK ... With No. 2 needles, cast on loosely
112 sts	120 sts	128 sts

Work in ribbing of k 2, p 2, for 2½ inches.

Change to No. 3 needles and work in pattern as follows: **1st and 2nd rows:** * P 2, k 2. Repeat from * across. **3rd and 4th rows:** * K 2, p 2. Repeat from * across. The last 4 rows constitute pattern. Work in pattern until piece measures 4 inches in all.

Keeping continuity of pattern, inc 1 st at both ends of next row and every
11th row	11th row	14th row

thereafter until there are on needle
128 sts	136 sts	142 sts

Continue in pattern without increasing until piece measures in all
13″	13½″	14″

To Shape Armholes: Bind off 9 sts at beginning of next 2 rows. Dec 1 st at end of every row until there remain
100 sts	106 sts	112 sts

Continue in pattern without decreasing until piece measures from 1st row of armhole shaping
3″	3″	3½″

Keeping continuity of pattern, inc 1 st at both ends of next row and every
6th row	8th row	10th row

thereafter until there are on needle
112 sts	116 sts	120 sts

Work without increasing until piece measures from 1st row of armhole shaping
7″	7″	7½″

To Shape Shoulders: Bind off
13 sts	13 sts	14 sts

at beginning of next 6 rows.

Bind off remaining
34 sts	38 sts	36 sts

FRONT ... Work exactly as for Back until there remain after armhole shaping
100 sts	106 sts	112 sts

LEFT FRONT ... Work in pattern across
50 sts	53 sts	56 sts

Cast on
18 sts	19 sts	20 sts

Turn and work over this set of sts only, keeping continuity of pattern, until piece measures from 1st row of armhole shaping
3″	3″	3½″

Now work in pattern, increasing 1 st at armhole edge on next row and every
6th row	8th row	10th row

thereafter, until 6, 5, 4 increases in all are made

BUT

when piece measures 4 inches from cast on sts, shape neck as follows: **1st row:** Starting at front edge, bind off
28 sts	31 sts	31 sts

work across in pattern. Work 1 row without increasing. Bind off 2 sts at beginning of next row and every other row twice. Dec 1 st at neck edge each row 3 times in all (this completes neck shaping). Continue with increases at armhole edge until there are on needle
39 sts	39 sts	42 sts

Work without increasing until piece measures from 1st row of armhole shaping, ending at armhole edge
7″	7″	7½″

To Shape Shoulder: Bind off
13 sts	13 sts	14 sts

at beginning of next row and every other row thereafter until all sts are bound off.

RIGHT FRONT ... Cast on
18 sts	19 sts	20 sts

and, starting where sts were divided, work in pattern across remaining
50 sts	53 sts	56 sts

to correspond with opposite side, reversing shapings and making a set of buttonholes when piece measures ½ inch from cast-on sts and every 1½ inches thereafter, always measuring from center of previous buttonhole, until 3 sets of buttonholes in all are made—*to make a set of buttonholes work as follows:*

1st row: *Starting at front edge, work in pattern across 3 sts, bind off next 6 sts, work in pattern across 6 sts, bind off next 6 sts, and work in pattern to end of needle.* **2nd row:** *Work in pattern, casting on 6 sts to replace each set bound off.*

SLEEVES . . . With No. 3 needles, cast on

| 74 sts | 78 sts | 82 sts |

Work in pattern for 2½ inches. Keeping continuity of pattern, inc 1 st at both ends of next row and every

| 5th row | 6th row | 7th row |

thereafter until there are on needle

| 98 sts | 98 sts | 102 sts |

Work in pattern without increasing until piece measures in all

| 11" | 11½" | 12" |

To Shape Top: Bind off

| 7 sts | 8 sts | 9 sts |

at beginning of next 2 rows. Dec 1 st at end of each row until there remain

| 40 sts | 36 sts | 34 sts |

Dec 1 st at both ends of each row until 22 sts remain. Bind off.

COLLAR . . . With No. 3 needles, cast on loosely

| 132 sts | 136 sts | 140 sts |

Work in pattern, decreasing 1 st at both ends of every other row until there remain

| 112 sts | 116 sts | 120 sts |

Work 1 more row.

Dec 1 st at beginning of next row. Work in pattern across 13 sts (14 sts on right hand needle); bind off the next

| 82 sts | 88 sts | 92 sts |

(1 st remains on right hand needle), work in pattern across, decreasing 1 st at end of row. Turn and work in pattern over these sts only, decreasing 1 st at both ends of every other row until 6 sts remain. Dec 1 st at outside edge every other row until all sts are worked off. Attach yarn where sts were bound off on opposite side and work to correspond.

Block pieces to measurements. Sew side and shoulder seams. Sew sleeve seams and sew in sleeves. Line collar and sew in place. Fold right front flap under and sew, matching buttonholes. Overcast buttonholes. Sew left flap back. Sew on buttons to correspond with buttonholes. If desired, sew in shoulder pads. Make a 1-inch hem around lower edges of sleeve.

No. 1312 . . . . Jerkin
Sizes 12, 14 and 16

Materials: WOOL FLOSS, 2 Ply, 3 balls (1 oz. balls) each of Cherry Red, Blue Jewel and Black for Sizes 12 and 14; 4 balls of each color for Size 16 . . . Knitting Pins, 1 pair No. 2 (2¾ mm. size) . . . Bone Crochet Hook No. 1 . . . 1 small black button . . . Narrow leather belt . . . Shoulder pads.

GAUGE: 7½ sts make 1 inch; 10 rows make 1 inch.

BLOCKING MEASUREMENTS:

Sizes	12	14	16
Bust	32"	34"	36"
Width across front or back at underarm	16"	17"	18"
Length from shoulder to lower edge	18½"	20"	21½"
Length of side seam	12"	13"	14"

BACK . . . Starting at lower edge, with Blue, cast on

| 37 sts | 40 sts | 43 sts |

Drop Blue, attach Black and cast on

| 40 sts | 42 sts | 44 sts |

Drop Black, attach Cherry and cast on

| 37 sts | 40 sts | 43 sts |

1st row: Purl with Cherry

| 37 sts | 40 sts | 43 sts |

Drop Cherry, pick up Black **(when changing colors always twist the unused color around the other to prevent making a hole)** and purl

| 40 sts | 42 sts | 44 sts |

Drop Black, pick up Blue and purl

| 37 sts | 40 sts | 43 sts |

2nd row: With Blue, knit

| 37 sts | 40 sts | 43 sts |

Drop Blue, pick up Black and knit

| 40 sts | 42 sts | 44 sts |

Drop Black, pick up Cherry and knit

| 37 sts | 40 sts | 43 sts |

Repeat the last 2 rows alternately until piece measures ½ inch. Dec 1 st at both ends of the next row and every 6th row thereafter until there remain

| 102 sts | 110 sts | 118 sts |

1312

Work without decreasing until piece measures in all   5″   5½″   6½″

Inc 1 st at both ends of the next row and every 6th row thereafter until there are on needle   **120 sts**   **128 sts**   **136 sts**

Work without increasing until piece measures in all   **12″**   **13″**   **14″**

To Shape Armholes: Bind off at the beginning of the next 2 rows   **6 sts**   **6 sts**   **7 sts**
Dec 1 st at both ends of every other row until there remain   **96 sts**   **104 sts**   **108 sts**

Inc 1 st on the next row and every 6th row thereafter until there are on needle   **102 sts**   **110 sts**   **114 sts** (piece should measure 3½ inches from 1st row of armhole shaping). On the next row, work across next   **51 sts**   **55 sts**   **57 sts** turn. Work over this set of sts only, increasing 1 st at armhole edge every 6th row until there are on needle   **60 sts**   **64 sts**   **68 sts**

Work straight until piece measures from 1st row of armhole shaping, ending at armhole edge   **6½″**   **7″**   **7½″**

To Shape Shoulder: Bind off at the beginning of every other row

	10 sts	**10 sts**	**11 sts**
	4 times	**once**	**twice**

Bind off at the beginning of every other row

	—	**11 sts**	**12 sts**
	—	**3 times**	**twice**

Bind off the remaining sts for back of neck.

Attach yarn at base of piece just made and work other side to correspond.

FRONT . . . Work same as for Back to underarm.

To Shape Armholes: Bind off at the beginning of the next 2 rows   **6 sts**   **6 sts**   **7 sts**
Dec 1 st at both ends of every other row until there remain   **96 sts**   **104 sts**   **108 sts**

Inc 1 st on the next row and every 6th row thereafter until there are on needle   **120 sts**   **128 sts**   **136 sts**

Work without increasing until piece measures from 1st row of armhole shaping, ending with a p row   **6″**   **6½″**   **7″**

On next row, work across the first   **49 sts**   **52 sts**   **58 sts**
Bind off for neck the next   **22 sts**   **24 sts**   **20 sts**
Work across the remaining   **49 sts**   **52 sts**   **58 sts**

Work over the last set of sts only, binding off 3 sts at neck edge every other row   **3 times**   **3 times**   **4 times**

But, at the Same Time,

when piece measures from 1st row of armhole shaping, ending at armhole edge   **6½″**   **7″**   **7½″** shape shoulder as for Back. Attach yarn to opposite side of neck edge and work other side to correspond.

LEFT POCKET . . . Starting at lower edge with Cherry, cast on 38 sts. Work straight in stockinette st (k 1 row, p 1 row) for 2¼ inches, ending with a purl row. Bind off 8 sts at beginning of next row, then dec 1 st at decreased edge every other row until 12 sts remain. Bind off. Make a rnd of sc all around edges, making 3 sc in each corner.

RIGHT POCKET . . . Work as for Left Pocket, using Blue and reversing all shaping.

Block all pieces to measurements. Sew underarm and shoulder seams. Make a row of sc around all edges, using matching color yarn. Sew pockets in place, having lower edges of pockets in line with lower edge of sweater. Sew in shoulder pads. Make a ch-6 buttonloop at top of right center back opening. Sew button opposite buttonloop. Make a ch-6 loop on both sides of waistline, using matching color yarn. Draw belt through loops.

No. 871 . . . . **Beaded Blouse**
Sizes 14, 16 and 18

Materials: SCOTCH FINGERING YARN, *3 Ply (1 oz. skeins): 9 skeins of Caribou for Sizes 14 and 16; 10 skeins for Size 18 . . . Plastic or Aluminum Knitting Pins, 1 pair No. 2 (2¾ mm. size) and 1 pair No. 3 (3 mm. size) . . . Gold beads . . . 3 buttons.*

GAUGE: 7½ sts make 1 inch; 10 rows make 1 inch.

BLOCKING MEASUREMENTS:

Sizes	14	16	18
Bust	34″	36″	38″
Width across back or front at underarm	17″	18″	19″
Length from shoulder to lower edge	24″	24½″	25½″
Length of side seam	17″	17½″	18″
Length of sleeve seam	17½″	18″	18″
Width across sleeve at upperarm	13″	13″	13½″

BACK . . . With No. 2 needles, cast on loosely

| 128 sts | 136 sts | 144 sts |

Work in ribbing of k 2, p 2 for 2 inches.

Change to No. 3 needles and work in stockinette st (k 1 row, p 1 row) until piece measures 2½ inches in all.

Dec 1 st at both ends of next row and every 6th row thereafter until there remain

| 112 sts | 120 sts | 128 sts |

Work without decreasing until piece measures 8 inches in all.

Inc 1 st at both ends of next row and every

| **9th row** | **10th row** | **11th row** |

thereafter until there are on needle

| 128 sts | 136 sts | 144 sts |

Work without increasing until piece measures in all

| 17″ | 17½″ | 18″ |

To Shape Armholes: Bind off 9 sts at beginning of next 2 rows. Dec 1 st at end of each row until there remain

| 106 sts | 110 sts | 114 sts |

Work without decreasing until piece measures from 1st row of armhole shaping, ending with a purl row

| 3½″ | 4″ | 4½″ |

Knit across

| 53 sts | 55 sts | 57 sts |

Turn and work over this set of sts only, increasing 1 st at armhole edge on next row and every 5th row thereafter until there are on needle

| 55 sts | 58 sts | 60 sts |

Work without increasing until piece measures from 1st row of armhole shaping, ending with a purl row

| 7″ | 7″ | 7½″ |

To Shape Shoulder: Bind off

| 7 sts | 9 sts | 9 sts |

at beginning of next row and every other row thereafter until there remain

| 20 sts | 22 sts | 24 sts |

Bind off remaining sts for back of neck.

Attach yarn where sts were divided and work opposite side to correspond, reversing shapings.

FRONT . . . Work exactly as for Back until ribbing measures 2 inches. Change to No. 3 needles and work as follows: **1st row:** Knit across. **2nd row:** Purl

| 91 sts | 95 sts | 99 sts |

place a marker on right hand needle, k 4, place another marker on right hand needle, purl

| 33 sts | 37 sts | 41 sts |

Work in stockinette st, keeping the 4 sts between markers in garter st (knit each row) and making decreases and increases exactly as for Back until piece measures in all, ending with a knit row

| 16½″ | 17″ | 17½″ |

There are on needle

| 128 sts | 136 sts | 144 sts |

Now work as follows: **1st row:** Purl

| 33 sts | 37 sts | 41 sts |

place a marker on right hand needle, knit

| 58 sts | 58 sts | 58 sts |

remove marker, k 4, slip other marker, then purl

| 33 sts | 37 sts | 41 sts |

2nd row: Knit across. **3rd row:** Purl

| 33 sts | 37 sts | 41 sts |

slip marker, knit

| 62 sts | 62 sts | 62 sts |

slip marker, purl

| 33 sts | 37 sts | 41 sts |

871

4th and 5th rows: Repeat 2nd and 3rd rows. **6th row:** Knit 33 sts 37 sts 41 sts remove marker, knit

58 sts 58 sts 58 sts

place a marker on right hand needle, k 4, slip marker, knit 33 sts 37 sts 41 sts

Continue as for Back, keeping the 4 sts between markers in garter st and working until piece measures from 1st row of armhole shaping (omitting opening), ending with a knit row 5″ 5″ 5½″

There are on needle

110 sts 116 sts 120 sts

To Shape Neck: Purl

20 sts 19 sts 17 sts

knit 4 sts, purl 21 sts 25 sts 29 sts Bind off 20 sts; purl

45 sts 48 sts 50 sts

Work over the last set of sts only, binding off 2 sts at neck edge each purl row until there remain 35 sts 36 sts 36 sts

Work without decreasing until piece measures from 1st row of armhole shaping, ending at armhole edge 7″ 7″ 7½″

To Shape Shoulder: Bind off at beginning of next row and every other row thereafter

7 sts 9 sts 9 sts

until all sts are bound off.

Attach yarn to opposite side of neck edge and work other side to correspond, reversing shapings and keeping sts between markers in garter st.

SLEEVES . . . Starting at lower edge with No. 3 needles, cast on loosely

54 sts 56 sts 58 sts

Work in stockinette st for 1 inch. Inc 1 st at both ends of next row and every 7th row thereafter until there are on needle

98 sts 98 sts 102 sts

Work without increasing until piece measures in all 17½″ 18″ 18″

To Shape Top: Bind off 9 sts at beginning of next 2 rows. Dec 1 st at end of every row until there remain 44 sts 44 sts 46 sts

Dec 1 st at both ends of each row until 22 sts remain. Bind off.

CUFF . . . With No. 3 needles, cast on

54 sts 56 sts 58 sts

1st row: Knit across. **2nd row:** P 3, k 4, purl across to last 7 sts, k 4, p 3. **3rd row:** Knit across, increasing 1 st at both ends of row. Repeat the last 2 rows until there are on needle 68 sts 70 sts 72 sts

Now work as follows: **1st row:** P 3, knit across to last 3 sts, p 3. **2nd row:** Knit across, increasing 1 st at both ends of row. **3rd to 6th rows incl:** Repeat 1st and 2nd rows alternately. **7th row:** Purl across. **8th row:** Repeat 2nd row. **9th, 10th and 11th rows:** Purl across. **12th row:** Knit across, decreasing 1 st at both ends of row. **13th row:** Purl across. Repeat last 2 rows alternately until there remain

54 sts 56 sts 58 sts

Bind off loosely.

COLLAR (Make 2) . . . With No. 3 needles, cast on loosely 49 sts 51 sts 52 sts and work exactly as for Cuff until there are on needle 63 sts 65 sts 66 sts

Now work as follows: **1st row:** P 3, knit across to last 3 sts, p 3. **2nd row:** Knit across, increasing 1 st at both ends of row. **3rd to 6th rows incl:** Repeat 1st and 2nd rows alternately. **7th row:** Purl across. **8th row:** Repeat 2nd row. **9th, 10th and 11th rows:** Purl across. **12th row:** Knit across, decreasing 1 st at both ends of row. **13th row:** Purl across. Repeat last 2 rows alternately until there remain

49 sts 51 sts 52 sts

Bind off loosely.

Block pieces to measurements. Sew up shoulder and underarm seams. Sew up sleeve seams and sew in sleeves. Fold collar at ridge and sew edges to neck edge. Finish sleeves in same way. Embroider with gold beads. Work a row of sc along back opening, making three ch-5 button loops spaced evenly on right side. Sew on buttons to correspond.

678

No. 678 . . . . . . Cardigan

Materials: SOCK AND SWEATER YARN, *4 Ply (2 oz. balls): 7 balls for Size 14; 8 balls for Size 16; 9 balls for Size 18; 10 balls for Size 20 . . . Knitting Pins, 1 pair No. 2 (2¾ mm. size) and 1 pair No. 4 (3½ mm. size) . . . 1 yard of heavy cotton lace . . . 12 pearl studs . . . Shoulder pads.*

GAUGE: 6½ sts make 1 inch; 9 rows make 1 inch.

BLOCKING MEASUREMENTS:

Sizes	14	16	18	20
Bust	34″	36″	38″	40″
Width across back at underarm	17″	18″	19″	20″
Width across each front at underarm	9½″	10″	10½″	11″
Length from shoulder to lower edge	21″	22″	23″	24″
Length of side seam	14″	14½″	15″	15½″
Length of sleeve seam	18″	18½″	19″	19½″
Width across sleeve at upperarm	13″	13½″	14″	14½″

BACK . . . Starting at lower edge with No. 4 needles, cast on

113 sts	113 sts	127 sts	127 sts

1st row: (K 1, p 1) twice; * k 7, (p 1, k 1) 3 times; p 1. Repeat from * across, ending with (p 1, k 1) twice. **2nd row:** (P 1, k 1) twice; * p 7, (k 1, p 1) 3 times; k 1. Repeat from * across, ending with (k 1, p 1) twice. **3rd row:** (K 1, p 1) twice, * k 1, inc 4 sts in next st— *to inc 4 sts in 1 st, knit in front and back of same st twice, knit in front of same st again,* k 5, (p 1, k 1) 3 times; p 1. Repeat from * across, ending with (p 1, k 1) twice. **4th row:** (P 1, k 1) twice, * p 5, bind off 4 sts, p 1 more st, (k 1, p 1) 3 times; k 1. Repeat from * across, ending with (k 1, p 1) twice. **5th row:** (K 1, p 1) twice, * k 3, inc 4 sts in next st, k 3, (p 1, k 1) 3 times; p 1. Repeat from * across, ending with (p 1, k 1) twice. **6th row:** (P 1, k 1) twice, * p 3, bind off 4 sts, p 3 more sts, (k 1, p 1) 3 times; k 1. Repeat from * across, ending with (k 1, p 1) twice. **7th row:** (K 1, p 1) twice, * k 5, inc 4 sts in next st, k 1, (p 1,

k 1) 3 times; p 1. Repeat from * across, ending with (p 1, k 1) twice. **8th row:** (P 1, k 1) twice, * p 1, bind off 4 sts, p 5 more sts, (k 1, p 1) 3 times; k 1. Repeat from * across, ending with (k 1, p 1) twice.

The last 8 rows constitute the pattern. Work in pattern until piece measures in all

4″	4″	4½″	4½″

Change to No. 2 needles and work in pattern until piece measures in all

7″	7″	7½″	7½″

Change to No. 4 needles and work in pattern until piece measures in all

14″	14½″	15″	15½″

To Shape Armholes: Bind off at the beginning of the next 2 rows

6 sts	6 sts	8 sts	8 sts

Dec 1 st at armhole edge every other row until there remain

91 sts	91 sts	97 sts	97 sts

Work without decreasing until piece measures from 1st row of armhole shaping

7″	7½″	8″	8½″

To Shape Shoulders: Bind off 6 sts at the beginning of the next

10 rows	10 rows	6 rows	6 rows

On Sizes 18 and 20 only, bind off 7 sts at the beginning of the next 4 rows. Bind off remaining sts for back of neck.

LEFT FRONT . . . Starting at lower edge with No. 4 needles, cast on

57 sts	71 sts	71 sts	85 sts

Work in pattern, changing needles exactly as for Back, until piece measures in all, ending at side edge

14″	14½″	15″	15½″

To Shape Armhole: Bind off

6 sts	6 sts	8 sts	8 sts

Dec 1 st at armhole edge every other row until there remain

46 sts	60 sts	56 sts	70 sts

Work without decreasing until piece measures from 1st row of armhole shaping, ending at center front edge

5″	5½″	6″	6½″

To Shape Neck: Bind off once

| 6 sts | 14 sts | 12 sts | 18 sts |

Bind off 2 sts at neck edge every other row until there remain

| 30 sts | 30 sts | 32 sts | 32 sts |

Work without decreasing until piece measures from 1st row of armhole shaping, ending at armhole edge

| 7″ | 7½″ | 8″ | 8½″ |

To Shape Shoulder: Bind off 6 sts at armhole edge every other row

| 5 times | 5 times | 3 times | 3 times |

Bind off 7 sts at armhole edge every other row

| — | — | twice | twice |

RIGHT FRONT . . . Same as Left Front, reversing all shaping.

SLEEVES . . . Starting at lower edge with No. 2 needles, cast on 57 sts. Work in pattern as for Back until piece measures 3 inches.

Change to No. 4 needles. Inc 1 st at both ends of the next row and every

| 8th row | 8th row | 6th row | 6th row |

thereafter until there are on needle

| 85 sts | 89 sts | 91 sts | 95 sts |

Work without increasing until piece measures in all

| 18″ | 18½″ | 19″ | 19½″ |

To Shape Top: Bind off at the beginning of the next 2 rows

| 6 sts | 6 sts | 8 sts | 8 sts |

Dec 1 st at both ends of every other row until there remain

| 63 sts | 67 sts | 61 sts | 65 sts |

Dec 1 st at both ends of every 4th row until there remain

| 51 sts | 53 sts | 45 sts | 49 sts |

Bind off 2 sts at the beginning of the next 8 rows. Bind off remaining sts.

Block pieces to measurements. Sew shoulder and side seams. Sew sleeve seams and sew in sleeves. Make a row of sc around center front edges and neck edge, holding neck edge in to fit. On following row, make sc around, having twelve ch-4 buttonholes evenly across right front edge. On next row, make sc around, making 4 sc in each ch-4 loop. Sew lace up right front edge and around neck edge. Sew in shoulder pads. Place studs opposite buttonholes.

No. 7-106 . . . Man's Sleeveless Pullover

Materials: SCOTCH FINGERING YARN, 3 Ply (1 oz. skeins): 10 skeins for Sizes 36 and 38; 12 skeins for Sizes 40 and 42 . . . Knitting Pins, 1 pair No. 2 (2¾ mm. size) and 1 pair No. 4 (3½ mm. size).

GAUGE: (Pattern blocked) 7 sts make 1 inch; 9 rows make 1 inch.

BLOCKING MEASUREMENTS:

Sizes	36	38	40	42
Chest	36″	38″	40″	42″

Width across back or front at underarm

| 18″ | 19″ | 20″ | 21″ |

Width across back above armhole shaping (including bands)

| 13½″ | 14″ | 14½″ | 15″ |

Length from shoulder to lower edge

| 26″ | 26″ | 27″ | 27″ |

Length of side seam (without band)

| 15½″ | 15½″ | 16″ | 16″ |

BACK . . . Starting at lower edge, with No. 2 needles, cast on

| 129 sts | 136 sts | 143 sts | 150 sts |

Work tightly in ribbing of k 1, p 1 for 4 inches. Change to No. 4 needles and work in pattern as follows: **1st row:** K 2, * p 2, k 2, p 2, k 1. Repeat from * across to last st, k 1. **2nd row:** K 1, p 1, * k 2, p 2, k 2, p 1. Repeat from * across to last st, k 1. **3rd row:** K 2, * slip next 2 sts onto a double-pointed needle and hold at back of work, knit next st, purl the 2 sts from double-pointed needle, slip the next st onto double-pointed needle and hold in front of work, purl next 2 sts, knit the st from double-pointed needle, k 1. Repeat from * to last st, k 1. **4th row:** K 1, p 2, * k 4, p 3. Repeat from * across, ending with p 2, k 1. **5th row:** K 3, * p 4, k 3. Repeat from * across. **6th row:** Repeat 4th row. **7th row:** K 2, * slip next st onto double-pointed needle and hold in front of work, purl next 2 sts, knit the st from double-pointed needle, slip next 2 sts onto double-pointed needle and hold in back of work, knit next st, purl the 2 sts from double-pointed needle, k 1. Repeat from * to last st, k 1. **8th row:** Repeat 2nd row.

The last 8 rows constitute the pattern. Repeat

pattern until piece measures in all

15½″	15½″	16″	16″

To Shape Armholes: Bind off at beginning of next 2 rows

8 sts	8 sts	9 sts	9 sts

Bind off 3 sts at beginning of next 8 rows. Dec 1 st at end of each row until there remain

81 sts	84 sts	87 sts	90 sts

Work without decreasing until piece measures from 1st row of armhole shaping

10″	10″	10½″	10½″

To Shape Shoulders: Bind off 6 sts at beginning of next 6 rows. Bind off at beginning of next 2 rows

5 sts	6 sts	7 sts	8 sts

Bind off for back of neck remaining

35 sts	36 sts	37 sts	38 sts

FRONT . . . Work same as Back until there remain on needle

81 sts	84 sts	87 sts	90 sts

To Shape Front: Work in pattern across

39 sts,	42 sts,	42 sts,	45 sts
k 2 tog		k 2 tog	

Turn and work over the last set of sts only, keeping armhole edge straight and decreasing 1 st at front edge on next row and every 4th row thereafter until there remain

23 sts	24 sts	25 sts	26 sts

Work without decreasing until piece measures from 1st row of armhole shaping

10″	10″	10½″	10½″

To Shape Shoulder: Starting at armhole edge, bind off 6 sts on every other row 3 times. Starting at same edge, bind off remaining

5 sts	6 sts	7 sts	8 sts

Attach yarn where sts were divided and work remaining

40 sts	42 sts	43 sts	45 sts

to correspond.

Press pieces through a damp cloth. Sew right shoulder seam.

NECKBAND . . . With right side facing and No. 2 needles, pick up and knit evenly from left shoulder to center front

67 sts	67 sts	71 sts	71 sts

insert a marker on needle and pick up and knit evenly the same number of sts from center front to right shoulder, pick up and knit across back of neck

40 sts	42 sts	44 sts	46 sts

There are on needle

174 sts	176 sts	186 sts	188 sts

Work as follows: **1st row:** P 1, * k 1, p 1. Repeat from * to marker, slip marker, p 1, ** k 1, p 1. Repeat from ** across remaining sts. **2nd row:** Work in ribbing to 2 sts before marker, sl 1, k 1, p.s.s.o., slip marker, k 2 tog and continue in ribbing to end of row. Continue in ribbing, decreasing 1 st on each side of marker (k 2 tog or p 2 tog according to pattern) on each row until band measures ⅞ inch. Bind off in ribbing. Sew left shoulder seam.

ARMBANDS . . . With right side facing and No. 2 needles, pick up and knit around armhole edge

188 sts	188 sts	198 sts	198 sts

Work in ribbing of k 1, p 1 for ⅞ inch. Bind off in ribbing. Sew side seams. Block to measurements given.

No. 7-102 . . Argyle Sleeveless Pullover

Materials: SOCK AND SWEATER YARN, *4 Ply (2 oz. balls): 3 balls of Smoke Blue for Sizes 10 and 12; 4 balls for Size 14; and 1 ball each of Red and White for each size . . . Knitting Pins, 1 pair No. 2 (2¾ mm. size) and 1 pair No. 4 (3½ mm. size).*

GAUGE: 6½ sts make 1 inch; 8 rows make 1 inch.

BLOCKING MEASUREMENTS:

Sizes	10	12	14
Chest	30″	32″	34″
Width across back or front at underarm			
	15″	16″	17″
Width across back above armhole shaping (including armbands)			
	11¼″	12″	12¾″
Length from shoulder to lower edge			
	20″	21″	22″
Length of side seam (including armband)			
	13″	13½″	14″

7-106

7-102

BACK . . . Starting at lower edge with No. 2 needles and Blue, cast on

99 sts	**105 sts**	**111 sts**

Work in ribbing of k 1, p 1 for

3″	**3½″**	**4″**

Note: When changing color always twist the unused color around the other to prevent making a hole. *Measure off several 2-yard strands of both White and Red and attach a new strand each time the color changes on 1st row.*

Change to No. 4 needles. **1st row:** Work as follows: Knit

4 B	**1 B, 1 W,**	**4 B, 1 W,**
	5 B	**5 B**

* 1 W, 9 B, 1 R, 5 B, 1 R, 9 B, 1 W, 5 B. Repeat from * across, ending with

4 B	**1 W, 1 B**	**1 W, 4 B**

2nd row: Purl

3 B	**2 B, 1 W,**	**5 B, 1 W,**
	3 B	**3 B**

* 1 W, 11 B, 1 R, 3 B, 1 R, 11 B, 1 W, 3 B. Repeat from * across, ending with

—	**1 W, 2 B**	**1 W, 5 B**

3rd row: Knit

—	**3 B**	**6 B**

* 1 W, 1 B, 1 W, 13 B, 1 R, 1 B, 1 R, 13 B. Repeat from * across, ending with

1 W, 1 B,	**1 W, 1 B,**	**1 W, 1 B,**
1 W	**1 W, 3 B**	**1 W, 6 B**

4th row: Purl

1 B	**4 B**	**7 B**

* 1 W, 15 B, 1 R, 15 B. Repeat from * across, ending with

1 W, 1 B	**1 W, 4 B**	**1 W, 7 B**

Starting with the 5th row, follow chart to top, changing colors as indicated by symbols (28 rows of pattern completed). The last 28 rows

constitute the pattern. Work in pattern until piece measures in all

12″	**12½″**	**13″**

To Shape Armholes: Keeping continuity of pattern, bind off 7 sts at beginning of next 2 rows. Dec 1 st at both ends of each row until there remain

65 sts	**69 sts**	**73 sts**

Work without decreasing until piece measures from 1st row of armhole shaping

7″	**7½″**	**8″**

To Shape Shoulders: Bind off 6 sts at beginning of next 4 rows. Bind off at beginning of next 2 rows

6 sts	**7 sts**	**8 sts**

Bind off for back of neck remaining

29 sts	**31 sts**	**33 sts**

FRONT . . . Work same as Back until there remain on needle

65 sts	**69 sts**	**73 sts**

Next row: With right side facing, work in pattern across

31 sts	**33 sts**	**35 sts**

k 2 tog for beginning of front shaping. Turn.

Work over the last set of sts only, decreasing 1 st at front edge on every 3rd row until there remain

18 sts	**19 sts**	**20 sts**

Work without decreasing until piece measures from 1st row of armhole shaping

7″	**7½″**	**8″**

To Shape Shoulder: Starting at armhole edge, bind off 6 sts on every other row twice. Starting at same edge bind off remaining

6 sts	**7 sts**	**8 sts**

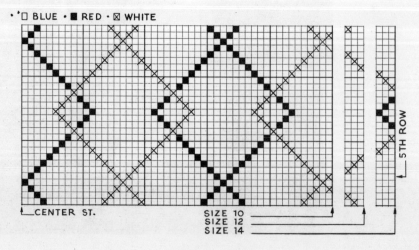

• '□ BLUE • ■ RED • ⊠ WHITE

CENTER ST. 5TH ROW

SIZE 10
SIZE 12
SIZE 14

Attach yarn where sts were divided and work other side to correspond.

BACK NECKBAND . . . With right side facing, using Blue and No. 2 needles, pick up and knit across back of neck

30 sts   32 sts   34 sts

Work in ribbing of k 1, p 1 for ¾ inch. Bind off loosely in ribbing.

FRONT NECKBAND . . . With right side facing, using Blue and No. 2 needles, pick up and knit from left shoulder to center front

56 sts   60 sts   64 sts

insert a marker on needle and pick up the same number of sts from center front to right shoulder. There are on needle

112 sts   120 sts   128 sts

1st row: * P 1, k 1. Repeat from * across to marker, slip marker, ** k 1, p 1. Repeat from ** across. **2nd row:** * K 1, p 1. Repeat from * across to 2 sts before marker, k 2 tog, slip marker, k 2 tog, complete row in ribbing.

Continue in ribbing, decreasing 1 st on each side of marker (k 2 tog or p 2 tog, according to pattern) on each row until ribbing measures ¾ inch. Bind off in ribbing.

ARMBANDS . . . Sew shoulder and neckband seams. With right side facing, using Blue and No. 2 needles pick up and knit around armhole edge   108 sts   116 sts   124 sts

Work same as Back Neckband.

Press pieces through damp cloth. Sew side seams.

7-114

No. 7-114 . Classic Cardigan for Boy or Girl

Materials: SCOTCH FINGERING YARN, 3 *Ply (1 oz. skeins): 8 skeins for Sizes 4 and 6; 10 skeins for Size 8 . . . Knitting Pins, 1 pair No. 2 (2¾ mm. size) and 1 pair No. 4 (3½ mm. size) . . . 5 buttons for each size.*

GAUGE: 6 sts make 1 inch; 8 rows make 1 inch.

BLOCKING MEASUREMENTS:

Sizes	4	6	8
Chest (cardigan buttoned)	25″	27″	29″
Width across back at underarm	12½″	13½″	14½″
Width across each front at underarm (including band)	7″	7½″	8″
Length from shoulder to lower edge	15″	16½″	18″
Length of side seam	10″	11″	12″
Length of sleeve seam	14½″	15″	15½″
Width across sleeve at upperarm	9″	10″	11″

BACK . . . Starting at lower edge with No. 2 needles, cast on **76 sts   80 sts   88 sts**

Work in ribbing of k 1, p 1 for
2″   2¼″   2½″

Change to No. 4 needles and work as follows: **1st and 2nd rows:** P 1, k 1 alternately across. **3rd and 4th rows:** K 1, p 1 alternately across. The last 4 rows constitute the pattern. Work in pattern until piece measures in all
10″   11″   12″

To Shape Armholes: Keeping continuity of pattern, bind off 3 sts at beginning of next 2 rows. Dec 1 st at end of each row until there remain **56 sts   64 sts   68 sts**

Work without decreasing until piece measures from 1st row of armhole shaping
5″   5½″   6″

Bind off for shoulder
18 sts   20 sts   21 sts
place a marker; bind off for back of neck next
20 sts   24 sts   26 sts

place a marker; bind off for other shoulder the remaining
18 sts   20 sts   21 sts

LEFT FRONT . . . Starting at lower edge cast on **36 sts   40 sts   44 sts**
and work as for Back until piece measures in all, ending at side edge
10″   11″   12″

To Shape Armhole: Bind off 3 sts at beginning of next row. Dec 1 st at armhole edge every other row
3 times   3 times   once
—at the same time—
decreasing 1 st at neck edge every
3rd row   3rd row   2nd row
until there remain
18 sts   20 sts   21 sts

Work without decreasing until piece measures in all   **5″   5½″   6″**
Bind off.

RIGHT FRONT . . . Work exactly as for Left Front (this stitch is reversible).

SLEEVES . . . With right side facing and No. 4 needles, pick up and knit around armhole edge   **56 sts   64 sts   68 sts**

Work in pattern until piece measures from picked-up sts   **1″   1½″   1½″**

Dec 1 st at both ends of next row and every
8th row   7th row   6th row
thereafter until there remain
36 sts   40 sts   40 sts

Work without decreasing until piece measures from picked-up sts
12½″   12¾″   13″

Change to No. 2 needles, and work in ribbing of k 1, p 1 for   **2″   2¼″   2½″**
Bind off loosely in ribbing.

Block pieces to measurements. Sew shoulder seams. Sew underarm and sleeve seams in one continuous seam.

BUTTON BAND . . . With No. 2 needles, cast on 10 sts. Work in ribbing of k 1, p 1 for 1 inch. **Next row:** K 1, p 1, k 1, bind off the next 4 sts, k 1, p 1. **Following row:** K 1, p 1, k 1, cast on 4 sts, p 1, k 1, p 1 (buttonhole made). Always measuring from 1st row of last buttonhole, make buttonholes every

2¼″	2¾″	2¾″

until 5 buttonholes in all are made.

Continue in ribbing until ribbing is long enough to go across front edge, around neck and down other front edge. Bind off.

Sew Button Band around edges of front and neck, having buttonholes on left front for boy's or on right front for girl's. Sew on buttons.

POCKET (Make 2) . . . With No. 4 needles cast on 20 sts. Work in pattern until piece is square. Bind off.

Sew pockets in place.

No. 702 . Long-Sleeved Pullover

Materials: Sock and Sweater Yarn, Shrink-Resist Finish, *3 Ply (1 oz. skeins): 10 skeins for Size 38; 11 skeins for Size 40; 12 skeins for Size 42; 13 skeins for Size 44 . . . Knitting Pins, 1 pair No. 1 (2½ mm. size) and 1 pair No. 3 (3 mm. size) . . . Double-pointed Bone Sock Needles No. 1 (2½ mm. size).*

GAUGE: 8 sts make 1 inch; 10 rows make 1 inch.

BLOCKING MEASUREMENTS:

Sizes	38	40	42	44
Chest	38″	40″	42″	44″
Width across back or front at underarm				
	19″	20″	21″	22″
Width across back above armhole shaping				
	14½″	15″	15½″	16″
Length from shoulder to lower edge				
	23″	23½″	24″	25″
Length of side seam				
	14½″	15″	15″	15½″
Length of sleeve seam				
	19″	19½″	20″	20½″
Width across sleeve at upperarm				
	14½″	15″	15½″	16″

BACK . . . Starting at lower edge with No. 3 needles, cast on

152 sts	160 sts	168 sts	176 sts

Change to No. 1 needles and work in ribbing of k 2, p 2 for 4 inches. Change to No. 3

needles. **1st row:** Knit across (right side of work). **2nd row:** P 3, * k 2, p 6. Repeat from * across, ending with k 2, p 3. The last 2 rows constitute pattern. Work in pattern until piece measures in all

14½″	15″	15″	15½″

To Shape Armholes: Keeping continuity of pattern throughout all shaping, bind off 8 sts at the beginning of next 2 rows. Dec 1 st at end of each row until there remain

116 sts	120 sts	124 sts	128 sts

Work without decreasing until piece measures from 1st row of armhole shaping

8½″	8½″	9″	9½″

To Shape Shoulders: Bind off

8 sts	10 sts	10 sts	11 sts

at the beginning of the next

6 rows	8 rows	8 rows	8 rows

On Size 38 only, bind off 7 sts at the beginning of the next 4 rows. Bind off for back of neck the remaining

40 sts	40 sts	44 sts	40 sts

FRONT . . . Work exactly as for Back until piece measures

14½″	15″	15″	15½″

To Shape Armholes: Keeping continuity of pattern, bind off 8 sts at beginning of next 2 rows. On next row, work in pattern across

66 sts	70 sts	74 sts	78 sts

k 2 tog, turn. Work in pattern over the last set of sts only, decreasing 1 st at armhole edge every other row

10 times	12 times	14 times	16 times
	at the same time		

dec 1 st at front edge (neck edge) every 3rd row until there remain

38 sts	40 sts	40 sts	44 sts

Work without decreasing until piece measures from 1st row of armhole shaping

8½″	8½″	9″	9½″

To Shape Shoulder: Starting at armhole edge bind off

8 sts	10 sts	10 sts	11 sts

every other row

3 times	4 times	4 times	4 times

On Size 38 only, bind off 7 sts every other row twice.

702

Attach yarn where sts were divided and work other side to correspond. Sew shoulder seams.

SLEEVES . . . Starting at cuff with No. 3 needles, cast on

80 sts **80 sts** **88 sts** **88 sts**

Change to No. 1 needles and work in ribbing of k 2, p 2 for 4 inches. Change to No. 3 needles and work in pattern as for Back, increasing 1 st at both ends of every 7th row until there are on needle

116 sts **120 sts** **124 sts** **128 sts**

Work without increasing until piece measures in all **19"** **19½"** **20"** **20½"**

To Shape Top: Bind off 2 sts at the beginning of each row until 32 sts remain. Bind off.

NECKBAND . . . Starting at center back of neck with double-pointed needles and right side facing, pick up and knit around to V

116 sts **116 sts** **124 sts** **124 sts**

Divide these sts on 2 needles, place a marker; with a 3rd needle pick up and knit to center back of neck

118 sts **118 sts** **126 sts** **126 sts**

Divide these sts onto 2 needles. There are on needles

234 sts **234 sts** **250 sts** **250 sts**

1st rnd: Work in ribbing of k 2, p 2 to marker, slip marker, * p 2, k 2. Repeat from * to end of rnd, ending with p 2. **2nd rnd:** K 2, p 2 alternately to 2 sts from marker, p 2 tog, slip marker, p 2 tog, work in ribbing to end of rnd. Repeat the last rnd, decreasing 1 st before and after marker on each rnd (p 2 tog or k 2 tog, whatever the case may be) until band measures 1 inch. Bind off loosely in ribbing.

Block pieces to measurements. Sew side and sleeve seams. Sew in sleeves.

No. 7-107 . . . . . . Pinafore

Materials: SCOTCH FINGERING YARN, 3 *Ply (1 oz. skeins): 8 skeins for Sizes 4 and 6; 10 skeins for Size 8 . . . Knitting Pins, 1 pair No. 2 (2¾ mm. size) and 1 pair No. 4 (3½ mm. size).*

GAUGE: 6 sts make 1 inch; 8 rows make 1 inch.

BLOCKING MEASUREMENTS:

Sizes	4	6	8
Waist	22½"	24"	25½"
Length from top of shoulder to lower edge of skirt	21½"	24½"	27½"
Width around lower edge of skirt	52"	54"	56"

BACK . . . Starting at lower edge of skirt with No. 4 needles, cast on

156 sts **162 sts** **168 sts**

Knit 1 row (wrong side). Work in stockinette st (k 1 row, p 1 row alternately), decreasing 6 sts evenly across every

6th row **7th row** **8th row**

until there remain

66 sts **72 sts** **78 sts**

Work without decreasing until piece measures in all **11½"** **13½"** **15½"** decreasing on last row to

64 sts **—** **76 sts**

Change to No. 2 needles and work in ribbing of k 2, p 2 for 1 inch, increasing evenly across last row to **72 sts** **76 sts** **80 sts**

Change to No. 4 needles and work in stockinette st until piece measures 1 inch from last row of ribbing.

To Shape Armholes: Bind off 4 sts at the beginning of the next 2 rows. Dec 1 st at both ends of each k row until there remain

58 sts **62 sts** **66 sts**

Work without decreasing until piece measures from 1st row of armhole shaping **2"** **2½"** **3"**

Inc 1 st at both ends of next row and every 6th row thereafter until there are on needle

72 sts **76 sts** **80 sts**

Work without increasing until piece measures from 1st row of armhole shaping **7½"** **8½"** **9½"**

To Shape Shoulders: Bind off at the beginning of the next **4 rows** **2 rows** **6 rows**

8 sts **8 sts** **9 sts**

Bind off at the beginning of the next

2 rows **4 rows** **—**

9 sts **9 sts** **—**

Bind off for back of neck the remaining

22 sts	**24 sts**	**26 sts**

FRONT . . . Work exactly as for Back to armhole shaping, ending with a purl row.

Next row: Bind off 4 sts, knit across the next

30 sts	**32 sts**	**34 sts**

k 2 tog (center front). Turn and work over the last set of sts only, decreasing 1 st at armhole edge each row 3 times.

Keeping armhole edge straight, dec 1 st at center front edge on next row and every 6th row thereafter until there remain

26 sts	**27 sts**	**28 sts**

Work 5 rows without decreasing. **Next row:** Dec 1 st at center front edge and inc 1 st at armhole edge. Repeat the last 6 rows 6 more times.

Keeping armhole edge straight and making 1 more dec at center front edge as before, work until piece measures from 1st row of armhole shaping **7½″   8½″   9½″**

To Shape Shoulder: Starting at armhole edge, bind off every other row

8 sts	**8 sts**	**9 sts**
twice	once	3 times

Bind off at armhole edge every other row

9 sts	**9 sts**	—
once	twice	—

Attach yarn where sts were divided and work over the remaining

36 sts	**38 sts**	**40 sts**

to correspond, reversing shapings.

POCKET (Make 2) . . . Starting at upper edge, cast on   **23 sts   25 sts   27 sts**

Knit 1 row (wrong side). Work in stockinette st for 3 inches. Dec 1 st at both ends of each row until 3 sts remain, k 3 tog. Break off.

Block pieces to measurements. Sew side and shoulder seams. Sew pockets 1 inch below waistband and ½ inch from side seams. Face armhole and neck edges. Trim pockets if desired.

No. 7-123 . . . . . Man's Vest

Materials: Scotch Fingering Yarn, *3 Ply (1 oz. skeins): 8 skeins for Sizes 38 and 40; 10 skeins for Size 42 . . . Knitting Pins, 1 pair No. 4 (3½ mm. size) . . . 5 buttons.*

GAUGE: 6½ sts make 1 inch; 9 rows make 1 inch.

BLOCKING MEASUREMENTS:

Sizes	38	40	42
Chest (vest buttoned)	36½″	38½″	40½″
Width across back at underarm	17½″	18½″	19½″
Width across each front at underarm	10″	10½″	11″
Width across back above armhole shaping	12½″	13″	13½″
Length from shoulder to lower edge	19″	19″	19″
Length of side seam	9″	9″	9″

BACK . . . Starting at lower edge, cast on   **90 sts   96 sts   102 sts**

Work 10 rows of garter st (k each row), increasing 10 sts evenly across last row. There are on needle   **100 sts   106 sts   112 sts**

Work in pattern as follows: **1st row:** Knit across. **2nd row:** P 4, * k 2, p 4. Repeat from * across. **3rd and 4th rows:** Repeat 1st and 2nd rows. **5th row:** Knit across. **6th row:** P 1, * k 2, p 4. Repeat from * across, ending with p 1. **7th and 8th rows:** Repeat 5th and 6th rows. The last 8 rows constitute the pattern. Work in pattern, increasing 1 st at both ends of next row and every 9th row thereafter until there are on needle

114 sts	**120 sts**	**126 sts**

Work without increasing until piece measures 9 inches in all.

To Shape Armholes: Bind off 6 sts at beginning of next 2 rows and 2 sts at beginning of following 6 rows. Dec 1 st at end of each row until there remain

80 sts	**84 sts**	**88 sts**

Work without decreasing until piece measures 9 inches from 1st row of armhole shaping.

To Shape Shoulders: Bind off 6 sts at beginning of next 6 rows. Bind off at beginning of next 2 rows

6 sts	7 sts	8 sts

Bind off for back of neck remaining

32 sts	34 sts	36 sts

LEFT FRONT . . . Starting at lower edge, cast on

40 sts	42 sts	46 sts

Work 10 rows of garter st, increasing 4 sts on last row. There are on needle

44 sts	46 sts	50 sts

7-123

7-107

Work in pattern as follows: **1st row:** Knit across to last 7 sts, k twice in next st, place a marker on needle, knit remaining 6 sts for front band. **2nd row:** K 6 sts of front band, slip marker, k twice in next st,

| p 2 | p 3 | p 2 |

* k 2, p 4. Repeat from * across.

3rd row: Repeat 1st row. **4th row:** K 6, slip marker, knit twice in next st,

| p 4 | k 1, p 4 | p 4 |

* k 2, p 4. Repeat from * across.

5th row: Repeat 1st row. **6th row:** K 6, slip marker, k twice in next st,

| p 3, k 2 | p 4, k 2 | p 3, k 2 |

* p 4, k 2. Repeat from * across, ending with p 1.

7th row: Repeat 1st row. **8th row:** K 6, slip marker, k twice in next st,

| k 1, p 4 | k 2, p 4 | k 1, p 4 |

* k 2, p 4. Repeat from * across, ending with p 1.

The pattern is now established. Continue in pattern, increasing 1 st inside the marker on each row until 14 sts **in all** have been increased

—at the same time—

inc 1 st at side edge on the next (9th) row. When front increases are completed there are on needle   **59 sts   61 sts   65 sts**

Keeping the 6 sts of front band in garter st, make a buttonhole 2 sts in from front edge on next row—*to make a buttonhole, on one row bind off 2 sts, then on next row cast on 2 sts to replace those bound off.* Continuing with side increases every 9th row until 7 sts in all are increased at this edge and measuring from 1st row of last buttonhole, make a buttonhole every 2 inches until 5 buttonholes in all are made

—at the same time—

when piece measures 3½ inches in all, work pocket opening as follows: Starting at front edge, work in pattern across next 24 sts, slip the next 28 sts on to a stitch holder to be worked later for Pocket Band, cast on 28 sts to replace those sts on stitch holder and complete row. Continue in pattern, shaping side edge and making buttonholes as directed.

When side shaping is completed, there are on needle   **66 sts   68 sts   72 sts**

Work without increasing until side edge measures 9 inches in all.

To Shape Armhole: Starting at side edge, bind off 6 sts once and 2 sts on every other row 3 times. Dec 1 st at armhole edge on every other row until there remain

| **48 sts** | **48 sts** | **52 sts** |

Keeping armhole edge straight, work until 5th buttonhole is completed.

To Shape Front: Dec 1 st inside the front band on next row and every 3rd row thereafter until there remain

| **30 sts** | **31 sts** | **32 sts** |

Work without decreasing until piece measures 9 inches from 1st row of armhole shaping.

To Shape Shoulder: Starting at armhole edge, bind off 6 sts on every other row 3 times. Starting at same edge, bind off

| **6 sts** | **7 sts** | **8 sts** |

Work without decreasing in garter st over remaining 6 sts of front band for 2½ inches. Bind off.

RIGHT FRONT . . . Work to correspond with Left Front, reversing shapings and omitting buttonholes.

POCKET BANDS . . . Slip the sts from stitch holder on to a needle, attach yarn and knit across, decreasing 4 sts. Work 6 rows of garter st. Bind off, knitting the sts.

POCKET LININGS . . . With right side facing, pick up and knit 28 sts along the 28 cast-on sts of pocket opening. Work in pattern for 2½ inches. Bind off.

Press pieces through damp cloth. Sew shoulder seams. Fit extensions of front band across back of neck and sew ends together; then sew in place.

ARMBANDS . . . With right side facing, pick up and knit 130 sts around armhole edge. Work 4 rows of garter st. Bind off, knitting the sts.

Sew side seams. Whip pocket linings in place. Sew ends of pocket bands in place. Sew on buttons. Block to measurements.

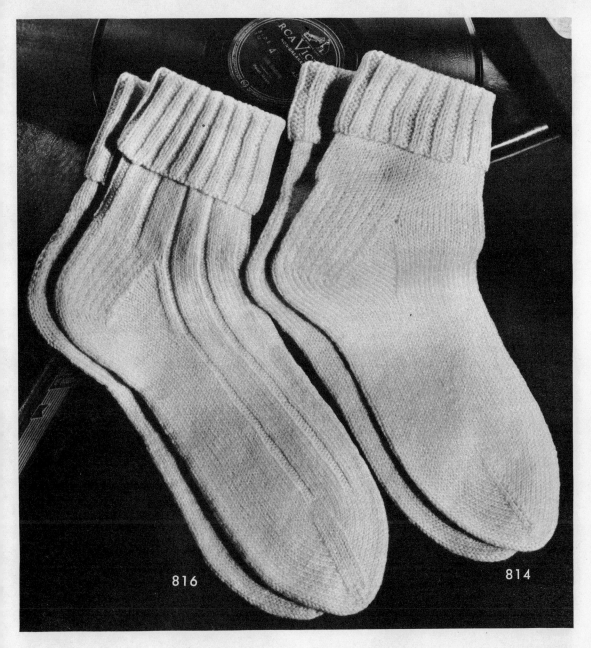

816

814

No. 816 . . . . . Men's Socks

Sizes 10½-12½—Slack Length

Materials: Sock and Sweater Yarn, Shrink-Resist Finish, 3 Ply (1 oz. skeins): 3 skeins for Sizes 10½ and 11½; 4 skeins for Size 12½ . . . Double-pointed Plastic Sock Needles, 1 set No. 2 (2¾ mm. size).

GAUGE: 8 sts make 1 inch; 11 rnds make 1 inch.

CUFF . . . Cast on 68 sts very loosely. Divide sts on 3 needles and join, being careful not to twist sts. Work in ribbing of k 2, p 2, for 2½ inches, decreasing evenly on last rnd to 64 sts.

Now work in ribbing of p 2, k 6, until entire piece measures 6 inches in all.

Divide sts for Heel as follows: With 4th needle, knit across 17 sts of **1st needle.** Slip 15 sts from **3rd needle** onto other end of 4th needle (there are 32 heel sts on 4th needle). Divide remaining sts on 2 needles for Instep.

See page 134 for Completion of Classic Socks.

131

No. 814 . . . . Women's Ribbed Cuff Anklet
Sizes 8½-11½

Materials: Scotch Fingering Yarn, 3 Ply (1 oz. skeins): 2 skeins for each size . . . Double-pointed Plastic Sock Needles, 1 set No. 2 (2¾ mm. size).

GAUGE: 8 sts make 1 inch; 11 rnds make 1 inch.

CUFF . . . Cast on 64 sts very loosely. Divide sts on 3 needles and join, being careful not to twist sts. Work in ribbing of k 2, p 2, for 3 inches for Cuff (1½ inches if Cuff is not desired). Now work in stockinette st (knit each rnd) for 2 more inches.

Divide sts for Heel as follows: With 4th needle, knit across 16 sts of **1st needle.** Slip 16 sts from **3rd needle** onto other end of 4th needle (there are 32 heel sts on 4th needle). Divide remaining sts on 2 needles for Instep.

See page 134 for Completion of Classic Socks.

No. 815 . Women's Cable Anklets
Sizes 10½-12½

Materials: Sock and Sweater Yarn, Shrink-Resist Finish, 3 Ply (1 oz. skeins): 2 skeins for each size . . . Double-pointed Plastic Sock Needles, 1 set No. 2 (2¾ mm. size).

GAUGE: 11 rnds make 1 inch.

CUFF . . . Cast on 64 sts very loosely. Divide sts on 3 needles and join, being careful not to twist sts. Work in ribbing of k 2, p 2, for 1½ inches.

Now work in pattern as follows: **1st to 5th rnds incl:** * P 2, k 6. Repeat from * around. **6th rnd:** * P 2, make a cable over next 6 sts—*to make a cable, slip next 3 sts onto a spare needle, hold in back of work, knit the next 3 sts, then knit the sts from spare needle. Repeat from * around. The last 6 rnds constitute pattern. Work in pattern until 16 rnds are completed.

Divide sts for Heel as follows: With 4th needle knit across 17 sts of **1st needle.** Slip

813

815

810

15 sts from **3rd needle** onto other end of 4th needle (there are 32 heel sts on 4th needle). Divide remaining sts on 2 needles for Instep.

See page 134 for Completion of Classic Socks.

No. 813 . . . . Cable Cuff Socks
Sizes 8½-11½

Materials: Scotch Fingering Yarn, *3 Ply (1 oz. skeins): 2 skeins for each size . . . Double-pointed Plastic Sock Needles, 1 set No. 2 (2¾ mm. size).*

GAUGE: 11 rnds make 1 inch.

CUFF . . . Cast on 64 sts very loosely. Divide sts on 3 needles and join, being careful not to twist sts. **1st to 5th rnds incl:** * K 2, p 1, k 4,

p 1. Repeat from * around. **6th rnd:** * K 2, p 1, make a cable over next 4 sts—*to make a cable, slip next 2 sts onto a spare needle and hold in back of work; knit next 2 sts, then knit the sts from spare needle,* p 1. Repeat from * around. Repeat the last 6 rnds until Cuff measures 2½ inches, ending with the 5th rnd.

Now work in ribbing of k 2, p 2, for 2 inches. Then reverse work by turning wrong side out.

Work in stockinette st (knit each rnd) for 1½ inches.

Divide sts for Heel as follows: With 4th needle, knit across 16 sts of **1st needle.** Slip 16 sts from **3rd needle** onto other end of 4th needle (there are 32 heel sts on 4th needle). Divide remaining sts on 2 needles for Instep.

See page 134 for Completion of Classic Socks.

133

No. 810 . . Women's Checkered Anklets

Sizes 9½-12½

Materials: SCOTCH FINGERING YARN, 3 *Ply (1 oz. skeins): 2 skeins of Woodland Green and 1 skein each of White and Melton Green . . . Plastic Knitting Pins, 1 pair No. 2 (2¾ mm. size) . . . Double-pointed Plastic Sock Needles, 1 set No. 2 (2¾ mm. size).*

GAUGE: 8 sts make 1 inch; 11 rows make 1 inch.

With Woodland Green and knitting pins, cast on 64 sts very loosely. Work in ribbing of k 2, p 2, for 1½ inches.

NOTE: When changing from one color to another, always twist the unused color around the other to prevent making holes.

Now work in pattern as follows: **1st row:** * K 2 Melton Green, k 2 Woodland Green. Repeat from * across. **2nd row:** * P 2 Woodland Green, p 2 Melton Green. Repeat from * across. **3rd row:** * K 2 Woodland Green, k 2 White. Repeat from * across. **4th row:** * P 2 White, p 2 Woodland Green. Repeat from * across. The last 4 rows constitute the pattern. Work in pattern until piece measures 3½ inches in all, ending with a knit row.

See page 135 for Completion of Argyle Socks.

Completion of Classic Socks

Work back and forth over the heel sts only as follows:

HEEL . . . 1st row: Sl 1, purl across. **2nd row:** * Sl 1, k 1. Repeat from * across. Repeat the last 2 rows alternately until piece measures 2¼ inches, ending with a purl row (Fig. 1).

To Turn Heel: 1st row: K 18, k 2 tog, k 1. Turn. **2nd row:** Sl 1, p 5, p 2 tog, p 1. Turn. **3rd row:** Sl 1, k 6, k 2 tog, k 1. Turn. **4th row:** Sl 1, p 7, p 2 tog, p 1. Turn. **5th row:** Sl 1, k 8, k 2 tog, k 1. Turn. **6th row:** Sl 1, p 9, p 2 tog, p 1. Turn. **7th row:** Sl 1, k 10, k 2 tog, k 1. Turn. **8th row:** Sl 1, p 11, p 2 tog, p 1. Turn. **9th row:** Sl 1, k 12, k 2 tog, k 1. Turn. **10th row:** Sl 1, p 13, p 2 tog, p 1. Turn. **11th row:** Sl 1, k 14, k 2 tog, k 1. Turn. **12th row:** Sl 1, p 15, p 2 tog, p 1. Turn. **13th row:** Sl 1, k 16, k 2 tog. Turn. **14th row:** Sl 1, p 16, p 2 tog. Turn. **15th row:** Knit across (18 sts remain on heel needle).

INSTEP . . . With a spare needle—**1st needle** —pick up and knit 16 sts along edge of heel (Fig. 2). With **2nd needle** knit across or work in pattern across Instep sts. With **3rd needle** pick up and knit 16 sts along other edge of heel; k 9 sts from heel needle. Slip other 9 sts of heel needle onto 1st needle. There are now

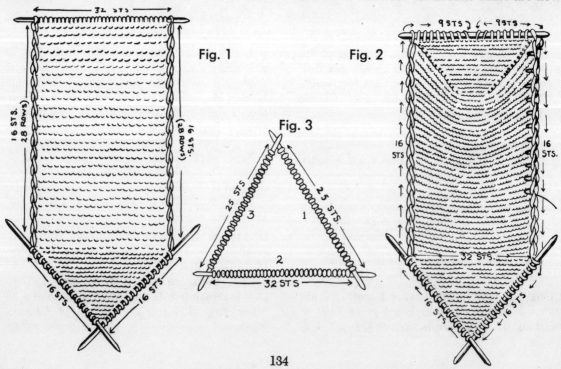

Fig. 1

Fig. 2

Fig. 3

25 sts on **1st and 3rd needles** and **32 sts on 2nd needle** (Fig. 3).

To Shape Instep: 1st rnd: Knit to last 3 sts on **1st needle**, k 2 tog, k 1. Knit across or **work in pattern across 2nd needle** (as the case may be). On **3rd needle** k 1, sl 1, k 1, p.s.s.o., knit to end of rnd. **2nd rnd:** Knit around, keeping in pattern across **2nd needle** if necessary. Repeat the last 2 rnds alternately until 16 sts remain on each of the **1st and 3rd needles.**

Work without decreasing until piece measures 6 inches for Size 8½; 7 inches for Size 9½; 8 inches for Size 10½; 9 inches for Size 11½; 10 inches for Size 12½, or 2¼ inches less than length desired.

To Shape Toe: 1st rnd: Knit to last 3 sts on **1st needle**, k 2 tog, k 1; **on 2nd needle**, k 1, sl 1, k 1, p.s.s.o., knit across to last 3 sts, k 2 tog, k 1; **on 3rd needle**, k 1, sl 1, k 1, p.s.s.o., knit to end of rnd. **2nd rnd:** Knit around. Repeat the last 2 rnds alternately until 16 sts remain. With 3rd needle knit across sts of 1st needle (8 sts on each of 2 needles). Break yarn, leaving 20 inches of yarn at end of needle. Weave sts together (see below).

How to Weave the Toe

WEAVING . . . Step 1: Thread the 20 inches of yarn onto a wool needle (Fig. 4).

Step 2: Hold the two needles with the stitches even and parallel, having the end of yarn at the right of back needle.

Step 3: Insert wool needle as if to purl in first stitch of front needle. Draw yarn through, leaving the stitch on needle.

Step 4: Insert wool needle as if to knit into first stitch of back needle. Draw yarn through, leaving the stitch on needle.

Step 5: Insert wool needle as if to knit into first stitch of front needle (same stitch as before), and slip this stitch off the needle. Insert needle in next stitch of front needle as if to purl. Draw yarn through, leaving the stitch on needle.

Step 6: Insert wool needle as if to purl into the stitch of back needle and slip this stitch off. Insert wool needle into next stitch of back needle as if to knit. Draw yarn through, leaving stitch on needle.

Repeat Steps 5 and 6 until all sts are worked off. Darn in end of yarn securely.

Completion of Argyle Socks

First Half of Heel . . . Attach another ball of matching color yarn and, with double yarn, purl across 16 sts. Turn. Work over this set of sts only as follows: **1st row:** * Sl 1, k 1. Repeat from * across. **2nd row:** Purl across. Repeat the last 2 rows alternately until heel measures 2¼ inches, ending with 1st row.

To Turn First Half of Heel: 1st row: P 1, p 2 tog, p 1. Turn. **2nd row:** Sl 1 st as if to purl, k 2. Turn. **3rd row:** P 2, p 2 tog, p 1. Turn. **4th row:** Sl 1 st as if to purl, k 3. Turn. **5th row:** P 3, p 2 tog, p 1. Turn. **6th row:** Sl 1 st as if to purl, k 4. Turn. **7th row:** P 4, p 2 tog, p 1. Turn. **8th row:** Sl 1 st as if to purl, k 5. Turn. **9th row:** P 5, p 2 tog, p 1. Turn. **10th row:** Sl 1 st as if to purl, k 6. Turn. **11th row:** P 6, p 2 tog, p 1. Turn. **12th row:** Sl 1 st as if to purl, k 7. Turn. **13th row:** P 7, p 2 tog, p 1. Turn. **14th row:** Sl 1 st as if to purl, k 8 (9 sts). **15th row:** P 9. Break off extra ball.

Attach a ball of yarn to match color at base of this half of heel and purl across, following chart or keeping in pattern as the case may be.

Second Half of Heel . . . Attach another ball of matching color yarn and, with double yarn, (sl 1, k 1) 8 times. Turn. Work over this set of sts only to correspond with First Half of Heel until heel measures 2¼ inches, ending with a purl row.

To Turn Second Half of Heel: 1st row: K 1, sl 1, k 1, p.s.s.o., k 1. Turn. **2nd row:** Sl 1, p 2. Turn. **3rd row:** K 2, sl 1, k 1, p.s.s.o., k 1. Turn. **4th row:** Sl 1, p 3. Turn. **5th row:** K 3,

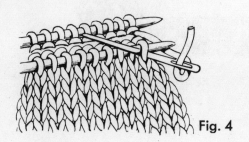

Fig. 4

135

sl 1, k 1, p.s.s.o., k 1. Turn. **6th row:** Sl 1, p 4. Turn. **7th row:** K 4, sl 1, k 1, p.s.s.o., k 1. Turn. **8th row:** Sl 1, p 5. Turn. **9th row:** K 5, sl 1, k 1, p.s.s.o., k 1. Turn. **10th row:** Sl 1, p 6. Turn. **11th row:** K 6, sl 1, k 1, p.s.s.o., k 1. Turn. **12th row:** Sl 1, p 7. Turn. **13th row:** K 7, sl 1, k 1, p.s.s.o., k 1. Turn. **14th row:** Sl 1, p 8 (9 sts). **15th row:** K 9. Break off extra ball.

INSTEP . . . With remaining ball of yarn, pick up and knit 16 sts down side of heel (see Fig. 5). Place a marker on right hand needle. Follow chart or work in pattern across. Place another marker on right hand needle. Pick up and knit 16 sts along other half of heel and knit across remaining heel sts.

To Shape Instep: 1st row: Purl across to marker, transfer marker, follow chart or work in pattern across to next marker, transfer marker and purl to end of row. **2nd row:** Knit to 3 sts before marker, then sl 1, k 1, p.s.s.o., k 1, transfer marker, follow chart or work pattern across to next marker, transfer marker, k 1, k 2 tog, knit to end of row. Repeat the last 2 rows alternately until the sts on the outside of each marker are reduced to one-half

the total number of stitches between markers at center. Work until top of chart is reached or until the same number of patterns are made as shown in photograph.

To Complete Foot: Work with main color only as follows: **1st rnd:** With double-pointed needle knit to marker—**this is 1st needle;** remove marker, **with 2nd needle** knit across center sts; remove marker; **with 3rd needle** knit remaining sts. **(The sts on the 1st and 3rd needles when added together should amount to the same number of sts as those on 2nd needle. If there is an odd stitch on second needle, then decrease 1 st on 3rd needle).**

Join and work in rnds (knit each rnd) until foot measures 2 inches less than desired length from back of heel.

To Shape Toe: 1st rnd: On 1st needle, knit across to last 3 sts, k 2 tog, k 1; **on 2nd needle,** k 1, sl 1, k 1, p.s.s.o., knit to last 3 sts from end of needle, k 2 tog, k 1; **on 3rd needle,** k 1, sl 1, k 1, p.s.s.o., knit to end of needle. **2nd rnd:** Knit around. Repeat the last 2 rnds until 16 sts remain. Weave sts together—see page 135.

Sew up back seam neatly, matching colors.

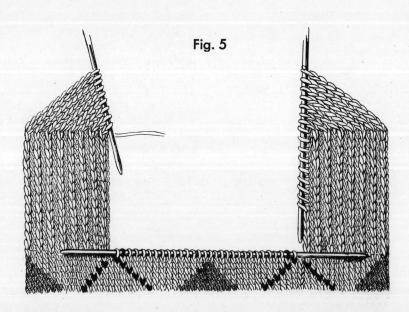

Fig. 5

CHAPTER IV

CROCHET ... *for connoisseurs of loveliness*

*I*F A POLL WERE TAKEN on hobbies, crochet would be found among the five top favorites. Certainly there are very few hobbies you can take with you to luncheons, picnics and Aunt Emma's tea party. It requires no elaborate equipment, a very modest investment. From a slender needle, thread and a page of instructions come forth rare and beautiful designs to ornament and enrich your home. Relaxing, soothing and strictly non-strenuous, crochet is a complete rest-cure to be taken in easy sittings.

For those of you who are novices, the crochet section begins with some small, useful and easy-to-make articles. These, we hope, will make your practice period pleasant and rewarding and whet your appetite for MORE. The experienced crocheter will find plenty of opportunity for displaying her skill on the variety of lacy doilies, handsome luncheon sets and exquisite tablecloths, while filet fans will delight in working on two of the most magnificent cloths ever to grace a dinner table.

139

HOW TO CROCHET

For Those Who Work With Their Right Hand

BEGIN BY MAKING A LOOP

1. Grasp thread near end between thumb and forefinger of left hand.

2. With right hand make loop by lapping long thread over short thread.

3. Hold loop in place between thumb and forefinger of left hand (Fig. 1).

4. Take hold of broad bar of hook as you would a pencil.

5. Put your hook through loop, catch long end of thread, draw it through (Fig. 2).

6. Do not remove hook from thread.

7. Pull short end and ball thread in opposite directions to bring loop close around the end of the hook, but not too tight (Fig. 3).

WHAT TO DO WITH THE LEFT HAND

1. Measure with your eye about 4 inches down ball thread from loop on needle.

2. At about this point insert thread between your ring and little fingers. (Palm of hand facing up, Fig. 4).

3. Bring thread toward back, under little and ring fingers, over the middle finger, and under the forefinger toward the thumb (Fig. 5).

4. Grasp needle and loop between thumb and forefinger of left hand.

5. Gently pull ball thread so that it lies around the fingers firmly but not tightly (Fig. 6).

6. Catch knot of loop between thumb and forefinger.

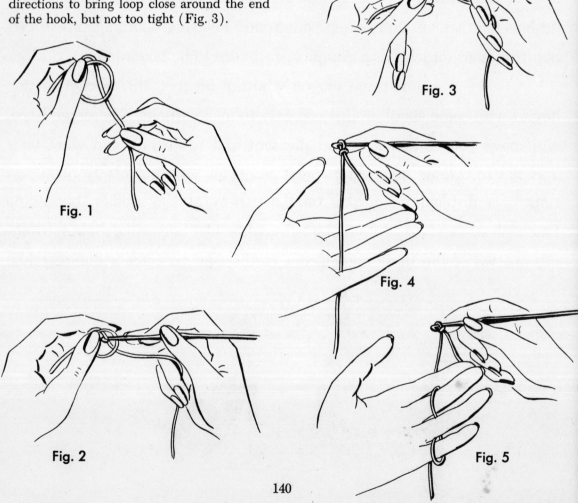

Fig. 1

Fig. 2

Fig. 3

Fig. 4

Fig. 5

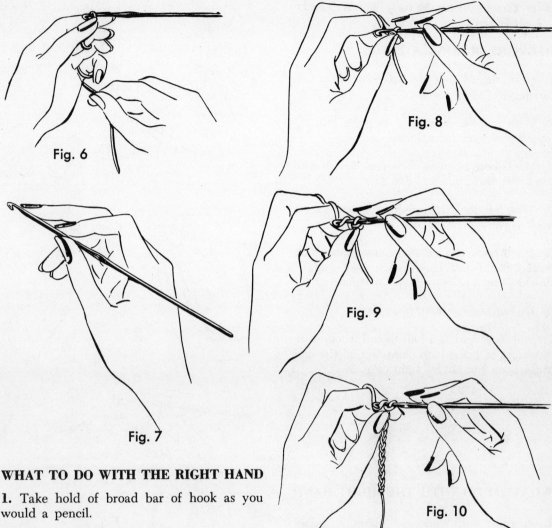

Fig. 6

Fig. 7

Fig. 8

Fig. 9

Fig. 10

WHAT TO DO WITH THE RIGHT HAND

1. Take hold of broad bar of hook as you would a pencil.

2. Bring middle finger forward to rest near tip of hook (Fig. 7).

BEFORE YOU BEGIN THE CHAIN STITCH

1. Adjust fingers of left hand as in Fig. 8. The middle finger is bent in such a way as to regulate the tension, while the ring and little fingers prevent the thread from moving too freely. As you practice you will become more familiar with the correct position.

Keep in mind that the motion of the hook in the right hand and the thread in the left hand should be easy and smooth. One of the most common faults of beginners is either to crochet too tightly or too loosely. Ease will come with practice.

Chain Stitch

1. Pass your hook under thread and catch thread with hook. (This is called "thread over" —Fig. 9).

2. Draw thread through loop on hook. This makes one chain (ch). (Do not work tightly).

3. Repeat Steps 1 and 2 until you have as many chain stitches as you need. One loop always remains on the hook (Fig. 10).

4. Always keep thumb and forefinger of your left hand near stitch on which you are working.

5. Practice making chains until they are even in size.

For Those Who Work With Their Left Hand

BEGIN BY MAKING A LOOP

1. Grasp thread near end between thumb and forefinger of right hand.

2. With left hand make a loop by lapping long thread over short thread.

3. Hold loop in place between thumb and forefinger of right hand (Fig. 1).

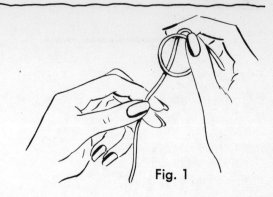

Fig. 1

4. With left hand take hold of broad bar of hook as you would a pencil.

5. Insert hook through loop and under long thread. With left hand catch long end of thread (Fig. 2). Draw loop through.

6. Do not remove hook from thread.

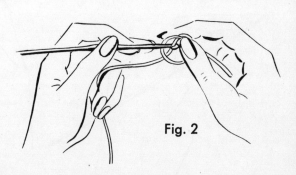

Fig. 2

7. Pull short end and ball thread in opposite directions to bring loop close around the end of the hook, but not too tight (Fig. 3).

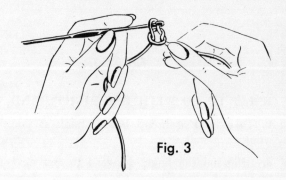

Fig. 3

WHAT TO DO WITH THE RIGHT HAND

1. Measure with your eye about 4 inches along ball thread from loop on hook.

2. At about this point insert thread between your ring and little fingers, having palm of hand facing up (Fig. 4).

3. Bring thread toward back, under little and ring fingers, over the middle finger, and under the forefinger toward the thumb (Fig. 5).

4. Grasp hook and loop between thumb and forefinger of right hand.

5. Gently pull ball thread so that it lies around the fingers firmly but not tightly (Fig. 6).

6. Catch knot of loop between thumb and forefinger.

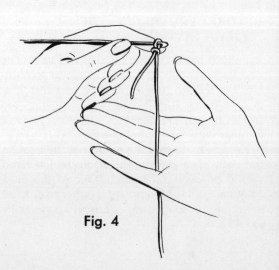

Fig. 4

WHAT TO DO WITH THE LEFT HAND

1. Take hold of broad bar of hook as you would a pencil.

2. Bring middle finger forward to rest near tip of hook (Fig. 7).

BEFORE YOU BEGIN THE CHAIN STITCH
Abbreviation—ch

1. Adjust fingers of right hand as in Fig. 8— the middle finger is bent to regulate the tension, the ring and little fingers control the thread. The *motion* of the *hook* in the *left hand* and the *thread* in the *right hand* should be free and even. Ease comes with practice.

CHAIN STITCH

1. Pass your hook under thread and catch thread with hook. This is called "thread over" (Fig. 9).

2. Draw thread through loop on hook. This makes one chain (ch).

3. Repeat Steps 1 and 2 until you have as many chain stitches (ch sts) as you need—1 loop always remains on the hook (Fig. 10).

4. Always keep thumb and forefinger of your right hand near stitch on which you are working.

5. Practice making chain stitches until they are even in size.

For Left Handed Pupils Only: Place a pocket mirror to the left of each illustration and you will see the exact position in which you work reflected in the mirror.

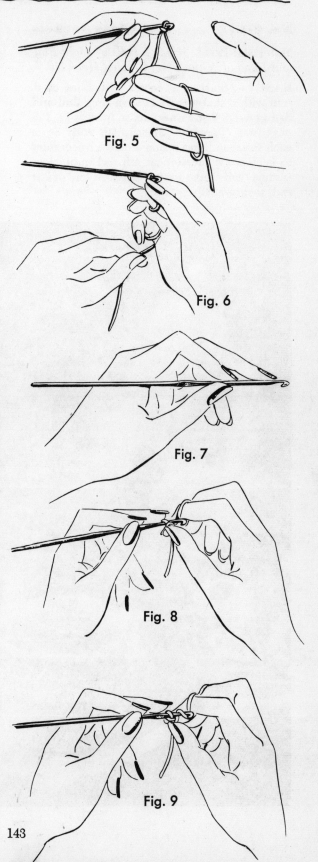

Fig. 5

Fig. 6

Fig. 7

Fig. 8

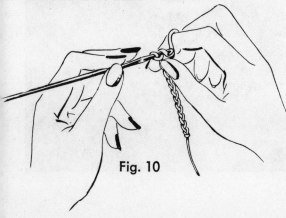

Fig. 10

Fig. 9

No. 6-147 . . . . Glass Jackets

Materials: PERLÉ, *Size 5: 5 balls of Light Blue and 1 ball of White. Steel Crochet Hook No. 7.*

BASE . . . Starting at center with Blue, ch 6. Join with sl st. **1st rnd:** 12 sc in ring. **2nd and 3rd rnds:** * 2 sc in next sc, sc in next sc. Repeat from * around (27 sc). **4th rnd:** Sc in each sc around, increasing wherever necessary to keep work flat. Repeat 4th rnd until piece is same diameter as base of glass. At end of last rnd, sl st in next sc.

SIDE . . . **1st rnd:** Ch 3, dc in each sc around, sl st in top of ch-3. **2nd rnd:** Ch 3, * dc around post of next dc, dc in next dc. Repeat from * around, sl st in ch-3, sl st in next dc. Repeat 2nd rnd 8 more times. On last rnd sl st in ch-3. Break off.

EDGING . . . Attach White. **Working through front loop only,** * ch 4, sc in next dc. Repeat from * around, sl st in first dc. Break off. Make 3 more glass jackets like this.

6-147

No. 7626 . . . . . . Glass Jackets

Materials: PEARL COTTON, *Size 5, 1 ball each of White and Light Blue and 5 balls of Dark Blue. Steel Crochet Hook No. 7.*

This amount of material is sufficient to make a set of 8 glass jackets.

GAUGE: 10 sts make 1 inch; 4 rnds make 1 inch.

BASE . . . Starting at center, with Dark Blue, ch 2. **1st rnd:** 7 sc in 2nd ch from hook. **2nd rnd:** 2 sc in each sc around (14 sts). Sl st in next sc. **3rd rnd:** Ch 3 (to count as 1 dc), dc in same place as sl st, 2 dc in each sc around (28 sts). Join with sl st in top st of starting chain. **4th, 5th and 6th rnds:** Ch 3, dc in each st around, increasing 14 dc evenly on each rnd.

Join (70 sts). Piece should measure about 2½ inches in diameter. Ch 1, turn. **Next rnd:** Work sl st in each st around. Join with sl st in first sl st. Ch 3, turn and work up the side as follows: **1st rnd:** Dc in each sl st around. Join (70 sts). Ch 3, turn. **2nd rnd:** Dc in each dc around. Join and break off Dark Blue. **3rd rnd:** Attach White in same place as sl st, ch 3, turn. Holding Light Blue along top of previous rnd, with White make dc in 3 dc (thus concealing Light Blue), thread over, insert hook in next st and pull loop through, thread over and draw through 2 loops, drop White, pick up Light Blue and draw through remaining 2 loops. **Always change color in this way.** * Holding White along top of previous row and working over it, make dc in next 5 dc, changing to White in last dc of this 5-dc

145

group; conceal Light Blue in the next 5 White dc and change to Light Blue as before. Repeat from * around. Join. With Light Blue, ch 3, turn. Fit this piece over a glass for size; it should fit snugly. Do this often while working.

4th rnd: Concealing unused color work Light Blue dc's in Light Blue dc's and White dc's in White dc's. Join and break off White. With Light Blue, ch 3, turn. **5th rnd:** Conceal Dark Blue in the first 4 Light Blue dc's changing to Dark Blue in the last dc of that group, concealing unused color work Dark Blue dc's over Light Blue dc's and Light Blue dc's over White dc's. Join. With Dark Blue, ch 3, turn. **6th rnd:** Work Dark Blue over Dark Blue and Light Blue over Light Blue. Join and break off Dark Blue. Attach White, ch 3, turn. **7th rnd:** Work White over Light Blue and Light Blue over Dark Blue. Join with Light Blue, ch 3, turn. **8th rnd:** Repeat 4th rnd. Join and break off both White and Light Blue. Attach Dark Blue, ch 3, turn. **9th, 10th and 11th rnds:** Dc in each dc around. Join, ch 3, turn. At end of 11th rnd break off. Make 7 more glass jackets same as this.

7716

No. 7716 . . . Hot Plate Mats

Materials: Knit-Cro-Sheen, *3 balls of White or Ecru, or 4 balls of any color. Steel Crochet Hook No. 6.*

These covers can be made in any size desired. Oval cover measures 7 x 9½ inches; round cover 8½ inches in diameter.

OVAL COVER . . . Starting at center, make a chain 3 inches long. **1st rnd:** Make 3 dc in 4th ch from hook, dc in each ch across, 7 dc in last ch; then, working along opposite side of starting chain, make dc in each ch across, 3 dc in same place where first 3 dc were made. Join with sl st in top st of starting chain. **2nd rnd:** Ch 3, dc in same place as sl st, 2 dc in each of next 3 dc, dc in each dc across to the 7 dc at other end, 2 dc in each of next 7 dc, dc in each dc to last 3 dc, 2 dc in each of last 3 dc. Join. **3rd rnd:** Ch 1, sc in same place as sl st.

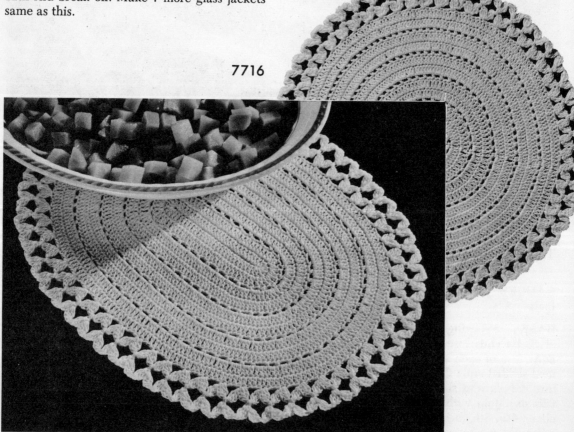

Increase across curve as follows: (Ch 2, skip next dc, sc in next dc) 4 times. Work along straight edge as follows: * Ch 2, skip next 2 dc, sc in next dc. Repeat from * across to the 14 dc at other end. Increase across curve as follows: (Ch 2, skip next dc, sc in next dc) 7 times. Work along straight edge as follows: ** Ch 2, skip next 2 dc, sc in next dc. Repeat from ** across to last 5 dc, increase across curve as follows: (Ch 2, skip 1 dc, sc in next dc) twice; ch 2, join with sl st in first sc made. **4th rnd:** Ch 3, (3 dc in next sp, dc in next sc) 4 times; * 2 dc in next sp, dc in next sc. Repeat from * across to curve at other end, (3 dc in next sp, dc in next sc) 7 times; ** 2 dc in next sp, dc in next sc. Repeat from ** across to last 3 sps, (3 dc in next sp, dc in next sc) twice; 3 dc in last sp. Join. **5th rnd:** Ch 3, dc in each dc around, increasing as necessary across curved ends to keep work flat. Join. Continue working 1 rnd of sps and 2 rnds of dc, increasing as necessary across curved ends to keep work flat until piece measures ½ inch smaller than desired size, ending with 2nd rnd of dc's.

Now work edging as follows: **1st rnd:** * Ch 3, holding back the last loop of each dc on hook make 2 dc in same place as sl st, thread over and draw through all loops on hook (2-dc cluster made), ch 4, make a 2-dc cluster in 4th ch from hook, skip 3 dc, sl st in next dc. Repeat from * around, joining last cluster with sl st in base of first cluster. **2nd rnd:** Sl st to top of first cluster, ch 1, sc between clusters, * (ch 4, 2-dc cluster in 4th ch from hook) twice; sc between next 2 clusters. Repeat from * around. Join and break off.

ROUND COVER . . . Starting at center, ch 4. **1st rnd:** 13 dc in 4th ch from hook. Join with sl st in 3rd st of starting chain. **2nd rnd:** Ch 3, dc in same place as sl st, 2 dc in each dc around. Join. **3rd rnd:** Ch 1, sc in same place as sl st, * ch 2, skip next dc, sc in next dc. Repeat from * around, joining last ch-2 with sl st in first sc. **4th rnd:** Ch 3, * 3 dc in next sp, dc in next sc. Repeat from * around. Join. **5th rnd:** Ch 3, dc in each dc around, increasing as necessary to keep work flat (about 14 dc). Join. Repeat 3rd, 4th and 5th rnds incl until piece measures ½ inch smaller than desired size, ending with 5th rnd. Work edging same as edging on Oval Cover. Break off. Starch lightly and press.

No. 7621 . . . . . **Bread Tray**

Materials: BEST SIX CORD MERCERIZED CROCHET, *Size 50, 3 balls of White only . . .* Steel Crochet Hook No. 12.

Doily measures 6¼ x 11½ inches

GAUGE: 6 sps make 1 inch; 6 rows make 1 inch.

Starting at bottom of chart, ch 14. **1st row:** Dc in 8th ch from hook, (ch 2, skip 2 ch, dc in next ch) twice. Ch 7, turn. **2nd row:** Dc in next dc (1 sp increased), (ch 2, dc in next dc) twice (2 sps made over 2 sps); ch 2, skip 2 sts of turning chain, dc in next ch, ch 5, dc in same place as last dc, turn, sl st in 3 ch (1 sp increased). Ch 7, do not turn. **3rd row:** Dc in same place as last sl st (inc made), make 5 more sps, ch 5, dc in same place as last dc, turn, sl st in 3 ch (inc made). Ch 7, do not turn. **4th row:** Inc a sp, make 3 more sps, 2 dc in next sp, dc in next dc (bl made over sp), make 3 sps, inc a sp. Ch 7, do not turn. Starting with 5th row, follow chart until the 43rd row is finished (when not increasing, ch 5 to turn). Do not ch at end of 43rd row, turn. **44th row:** Sl st in 2 ch, sl st in next dc (1 sp decreased), follow chart across to within last sp (another sp decreased). Ch 5, turn. Now follow chart to top. Break off.

EDGING . . . With right side facing, attach thread in the first sp on the 43rd row, ch 3,

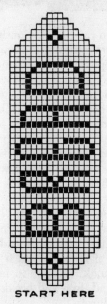

There are 10 spaces between heavy lines

START HERE

7621

sc in end sp on 44th row, ch 3. Continue thus to top. Then sl st across the end 3 sps and work down other side of point to correspond. Break off. With right side facing finish other end in same way, but do not break off. **1st rnd:** Ch 1, work 2 sc in each sp, sc in each dc and 5 sc in each loop along shaped ends. Join with sl st in first sc made. **2nd rnd:** Ch 5, tr in next sc, ch 1, * skip next sc, (tr in next sc, ch 1) twice. Repeat from * around. Join with sl st in 4th st of first ch-5. **3rd rnd:** Ch 4, tr in same place as sl st, * ch 2, 2 tr in next tr. Repeat from * around. Join. **4th to 7th rnds incl:** Ch 4, tr in next tr, * ch 3, tr in next 2 tr. Repeat from * around. Join. **8th rnd:** Ch 1, sc in same place as sl st, sc in next tr, * ch 5, sc in 3rd ch from hook, ch 2, sc in next 2 tr. Repeat from * around. Join and break off.

Starch lightly and press.

No. 7698 . . . . Luncheon Set

Materials: PEARL COTTON, Size 5, 10 balls of Ecru and 5 balls each of 3 contrasting colors (Blue, Red and Green) . . . Steel Crochet Hook No. 1.

Place Mat measures 11 x 14 inches

GAUGE: 1 shell measures 1 inch diagonally.

Use thread double throughout.

PLACE MAT (Make 4) . . . With Ecru make a chain about 18 inches long (6 ch sts to 1 inch). **1st row:** 3 dc in 4th ch from hook, * dc in next ch, skip 4 ch, sc in next ch (shell made), ch 3, 3 dc in same ch as last sc. Repeat from * across until row measures 14 inches, ending with 3 dc in same ch as last sc. Cut off remaining chain. Ch 3, turn. **2nd row:** * Sc in ch-3 of next shell, ch 3, 3 dc in same ch-3, dc

148

in next sc. Repeat from * across, ending with 3 dc in last ch-3. (There must be the same number of shells on each row.) Ch 3, turn. **3rd row:** Sl st in ch-3 of shell. Break off. Attach Red, ch 3, 3 dc in same ch-3, dc in next sc, sc in next ch-3. Continue working shells across row, ending with 3 dc in last ch-3. Ch 3, turn. Repeat 2nd and 3rd rows alternately, working 1 more row of Red, 2 rows of Blue, 2 rows of Green, then continue with Ecru until piece measures 8 inches in all. Now work stripes to correspond with beginning, reversing colors. Break off.

FRINGE . . . Cut two 4-inch strands of thread. Double these strands forming a loop. Insert hook in a stitch at edge of short side of Mat and pull loop through; now draw loose ends through loop and pull tightly. Make fringe closely together at both short ends, using corresponding colors. Trim fringe to measure 1½ inches.

7698

7743

No. 7743 . . . . Luncheon Set

Materials: BEST SIX CORD MERCERIZED CROCHET, *Size 30*, **Small Ball:** *20 balls of White or Ecru, or 23 balls of any color. . . . Steel Crochet Hook No. 10.*

Each doily measures 12½ x 17½ inches

GAUGE: Motif measures 2½ inches square.

DOILY (Make 3)—FIRST MOTIF . . . Starting at center, ch 10. Join with sl st. **1st rnd:** Ch 3, make 23 dc in ring. Sl st in top of ch-3. **2nd rnd:** Sc in same place as sl st, * ch 10, skip 2 dc, holding back on hook the last loop of each d tr, make 5 d tr in next dc, thread over and draw through all loops on hook (cluster made); ch 10, skip 2 dc, sc in next dc. Repeat from * around, ending with ch 10, sl st in first sc. **3rd rnd:** In ch-10 loop make 5 sc, ch 5 and 5 sc; * ch 5, (in next ch-10 loop make 5 sc, ch 5 and 5 sc) twice. Repeat from * around. Join. **4th rnd:** Sl st in next 4 sc, sl st in next ch and in next loop, ch 4, holding back on hook the last loop of each tr make 2 tr in same loop, thread over and draw through all loops on hook (tr-cluster made), * ch 7, in next ch-5 loop make (5-d tr cluster, ch 7) twice and 5-d tr cluster; ch 7, make 3-tr cluster in next 2 ch-5 loops. Repeat from * around. Join. **5th rnd:** Sc in same place as sl st, * ch 5, sc in next sp, ch 5, sc in tip of next cluster. Repeat from * around. Join and break off.

SECOND MOTIF . . . Work as for First Motif until 4 rnds are completed. **5th rnd:** Sc in same place as sl st, (ch 5, sc in next sp, ch 5, sc in tip of next cluster) twice; ch 2, sc in corresponding loop of First Motif, ch 2, sc in next sp on Second Motif, ch 2, sc in next loop on First Motif, ch 2, sc in tip of next cluster on Second Motif, and complete rnd, joining next 6 loops to adjacent loops of First Motif as before.

Make 5 rows of 7 motifs for each doily, joining adjacent sides as Second Motif was joined to First.

No. 7709 . . . . . Luncheon Set

Materials: BEST SIX CORD MERCERIZED CROCHET, *Size 30*. **Small Ball:** *10 balls of White or Ecru, or 12 balls of any color . . . Steel Crochet Hook No. 10 . . . ¾ yard of linen.*

Place Mats 11½ x 16½ inches; Runner 11½ x 22 inches; Napkins 11 inches square

PLACE MAT (Make 2)—Lace . . . Make a chain 1 yard long (14 ch sts to 1 inch). **1st rnd:** In 6th ch from hook make tr, ch 1 and tr, (ch 1, skip next ch, tr in next ch) 38 times; ch 1, skip next ch, in next ch make (tr, ch 1) twice and tr; (ch 1, skip next ch, tr in next ch) 74 times; ch 1, skip next ch, in next ch make (tr, ch 1) twice and tr; (ch 1, skip next ch, tr in next ch) 38 times; ch 1, skip next ch, in next ch make (tr, ch 1) twice and tr; (ch 1, skip next ch, tr in next ch) 74 times; ch 1, join with sl st in 4th st of turning chain at beginning of rnd. Cut off remaining chain. **2nd rnd:** Ch 5, ** in corner tr make (tr, ch 1) twice and tr; * ch 1, tr in next tr. Repeat from * across to next corner tr, ch 1. Repeat from ** around. Join. **3rd to 7th rnds incl:** Ch 5, * make tr in next tr, ch 1. Repeat from * across to next corner tr; in corner tr make (tr, ch 1) twice and tr. Continue thus around. Join. **8th rnd:** Ch 7, skip next tr, tr in next tr, (ch 3, skip next tr, tr in next tr) twice; ch 3, in corner tr make (tr, ch 1) twice and tr; ch 3, tr in next tr, (ch 3, skip next tr, tr in next tr) 21 times; (ch 1, tr in next tr) 3 times; (ch 3, skip next tr, tr in next tr) 21 times; ch 3, in corner tr make (tr, ch 1) twice and tr; ch 3, tr in next tr,

7709

(ch 3, skip next tr, tr in next tr) 12 times; (ch 1, tr in next tr) 3 times; (ch 3, skip next tr, tr in next tr) 12 times; ch 3, in corner tr make (tr, ch 1) twice and tr; ch 3, tr in next tr, (ch 3, skip next tr, tr in next tr) 21 times; (ch 1, tr in next tr) 3 times; (ch 3, skip next tr, tr in next tr) 21 times; ch 3, in corner tr make (tr, ch 1) twice and tr; ch 3, tr in next tr, (ch 3, skip next tr, tr in next tr) 12 times; (ch 1, tr in next tr) 3 times; (ch 3, skip next tr, tr in next tr) 8 times. Ch 3 and join with sl st in 4th st of starting chain.

9th and 10th rnds: Ch 7 and work in pattern as established on 8th rnd, making ch-3 sps over ch-3 sps and ch-1 sps over ch-1 sps and turning corners as before. Join. **11th rnd:** Ch 7, (tr in next tr, tr in next 3 ch, tr in next tr, ch 3) twice; tr in next tr, tr in 3 ch, tr in next tr, ch 3, in corner tr make (tr, ch 1) twice and tr; ch 3, (tr in next tr, tr in 3 ch, tr in next tr, ch 3) 12 times; (tr in next tr, tr in next ch) 3 times; tr in next tr, (ch 3, tr in next tr, tr in 3 ch, tr in next tr) 12 times; ch 3, in corner tr make (tr, ch 1) twice and tr; ch 3, (tr in next tr, tr in 3 ch, tr in next tr, ch 3) 15 times; tr in next tr, tr in 3 ch, tr in next tr, ch 3, turn corner as before and complete remaining two sides to correspond. Join. **12th rnd:** Ch 1, sc in same place as sl st, (ch 5, sc in 5th ch from hook—picot made—sc in 3 ch, sc in next tr, picot, sc in 4 tr) 3 times; sc in 3 ch, (picot, sc in tr, sc in ch-1) twice; picot, sc in tr, * sc in 3 ch, sc in next tr, picot, sc in next 4 tr, picot. Repeat from * around, turning corner as before. Join and break off. Press lace through damp cloth. Cut a paper pattern of the center area. Cut linen slightly larger than pattern (allowing for a narrow hem). Hem edges; then sew lace to linen.

RUNNER—Lace . . . Make a chain 1½ yards long (14 ch sts to 1 inch). **1st rnd:** In 6th ch from hook make tr, ch 1 and tr; (ch 1, skip next ch, tr in next ch) 38 times; ch 1, skip next ch, in next ch make (tr, ch 1) twice and tr; (ch 1, skip next ch, tr in next ch) 118 times; ch 1, skip next ch, in next ch make (tr, ch 1) twice and tr; (ch 1, skip next ch, tr in next ch) 38 times; ch 1, skip next ch, in next ch make (tr, ch 1) twice and tr; (ch 1, skip next ch, tr in next ch) 118 times; ch 1, join with sl st in 4th st of turning chain at beginning of rnd. Cut off remaining chain. **2nd to 7th rnds incl:** Work same as 2nd to 7th rnds incl of Place Mat. **8th rnd:** Ch 7, skip next tr, tr in next tr, (ch 3, skip next tr, tr in next tr) twice; ch 3, in corner tr make (tr, ch 1) twice and tr; ch 3, tr in next tr, (ch 3, skip next tr, tr in next tr) 12 times; (ch 1, tr in next tr) 3 times; (ch 3, skip next tr, tr in next tr) 12 times; ch 3, in corner tr make (tr, ch 1) twice and tr; ch 3, tr in next tr, (ch 3, skip next tr, tr in next tr) 32 times; (ch 1, tr in next tr) 3 times; (ch 3, skip next tr, tr in next tr) 32 times; ch 3, in corner tr make (tr, ch 1) twice and tr; ch 3, tr in next tr, (ch 3, skip next tr, tr in next tr) 12 times; (ch 1, tr in next tr) 3 times; (ch 3, skip next tr,

tr in next tr) 12 times; ch 3, in corner tr make (tr, ch 1) twice and tr; ch 3, tr in next tr, (ch 3, skip next tr, tr in next tr) 32 times; (ch 1, tr in next tr) 3 times; (ch 3, skip next tr, tr in next tr) 28 times. Ch 3 and join with sl st in 4th st of starting chain.

9th and 10th rnds: Work same as 9th and 10th rnds of Place Mat. **11th rnd:** Ch 7, (tr in next tr, tr in next 3 ch, tr in next tr, ch 3) twice; tr in next tr, tr in 3 ch, tr in next tr, ch 3, in corner tr make (tr, ch 1) twice and tr; (ch 3, tr in next tr, tr in 3 ch, tr in next tr) 8 times; ch 5, skip next 2 tr, (tr in next tr, tr in 3 ch, tr in next tr, ch 3) 8 times; in corner tr make (tr, ch 1) twice and tr; (ch 3, tr in next tr, tr in 3 ch, tr in next tr) 18 times; ch 5, skip 2 tr, (tr in next tr, tr in 3 ch, tr in next tr, ch 3) 18 times; turn corner and complete remaining two sides to correspond. Join. **12th rnd:** Work same as 12th rnd of Place Mat. Sew linen in center same as Place Mat.

NAPKIN (Make 2)—Lace . . . Make a chain 10 inches long (14 ch sts to 1 inch). **1st row:** Tr in 11th ch from hook, (ch 3, skip 3 ch, tr in next ch) 12 times; ch 3, skip next ch, in next ch make (tr, ch 1) twice and tr; ch 3, skip next ch, tr in next ch, (ch 3, skip 3 ch, tr in next ch) 13 times. Cut off remaining chain. Ch 7, turn. **2nd row:** (Tr in next tr, tr in 3 ch, tr in next tr, ch 3) 7 times; in corner tr make (tr, ch 1) twice and tr; (ch 3, tr in next tr, tr in 3 ch, tr in next tr) 7 times; ch 3, skip 3 sts of turning chain, tr in next ch. Break off.

Cut linen 11½ inches square. Cut out corner for lace. Roll entire edge and whip down. Sew lace to edge of cut-out corner. Attach crochet thread in top of last tr made, make a chain about 5 inches long. Attach another ball of thread in same tr, ch 1 and work sc in each st of chain just made. Whip the chain edge of this strip to edge of napkin. * Make 5 inches more of chain; work sc in each st of chain; then whip to edge of napkin. Repeat from * until other end of corner is reached. Break off the chain thread and continue with sc over lace edge as follows: * Ch 5, sc in 5th ch from hook (picot made), sc in 3 ch, sc in tr, picot, sc in 4 tr. Repeat from * to corner; sc in 3 ch, sc in tr, picot, (sc in ch 1, sc in tr, picot) twice; ** sc in 3 ch, sc in tr, picot, sc in 4 tr, picot. Repeat from ** across to end of lace. Break off.

3-43

No. 3-43 . . . . Doily

Materials: SIX CORD CORDICHET, *Size 50, 2 balls (small balls) of White only . . . Steel Crochet Hook No. 12 . . . A circle of linen about 5¼ inches in diameter.*

Doily measures 13½ inches in diameter

1st rnd: Roll edges and work sc closely around. Sl st in first sc made. **2nd rnd:** Ch 4 (to count as tr), tr in next 2 sc, * ch 11, skip about ⅜ inch, tr in next 3 sc. Repeat from * until there are 32 tr-groups on rnd. Join last ch-11 to top st of first ch-4. **3rd rnd:** Sl st in

next 2 tr and the following 5 ch, in next ch make sc, ch 3 and sc (picot made); * ch 13, in center st of next ch-11 make sc, ch 3 and sc (picot made). Repeat from * around, joining last ch-13 with sl st in first sc made. **4th rnd:** Sl st across to center st of next ch-13, picot in center st, * ch 13, picot in center st of next ch-13. Repeat from * around. Join. **5th rnd:** Sl st across to center st of next ch-13, picot in center st, * ch 5, in next picot make 4 d tr with ch-2 between, ch 5, picot in center st of next ch-13. Repeat from * around, ending with ch 5, sl st in first sc made. **6th rnd:** Sl st in next ch, * sc in picot, (ch 3, sc in next sp) 5

154

times; ch 3. Repeat from * around, joining last ch-3 with sl st in first sc made.

7th to 10th rnds incl: Sl st in next ch, sc in loop, * ch 3, sc in next loop. Repeat from * around. Join. **11th rnd:** Sl st in next ch, sc in loop, (ch 3, sc in next loop) 5 times; * ch 10, skip 2 loops, sc in next loop, (ch 3, sc in next loop) 9 times. Repeat from * around. Join. **12th rnd:** Sl st in next ch, sc in loop, (ch 3, sc in next loop) 3 times; * ch 3, skip 1 st of the ch-10 loop, dc in next ch, (ch 2, dc in next ch) 6 times; ch 3, skip 1 loop, sc in next loop, (ch 3, sc in next loop) 6 times. Repeat from * around. Join. **13th rnd:** Sl st in next ch, sc in loop, ch 3, sc in next loop, * (ch 3, dc in next dc) 7 times; ch 3, skip 1 loop, sc in next loop, (ch 3, sc in next loop) 3 times. Repeat from * around, ending with ch 1, half dc in first sc made. **14th rnd:** In loop formed by ch-1 and half dc, make sc, ch 3 and sc (picot made); * (ch 3, 2 dc in next dc) 7 times; ch 3, skip 1 loop, picot in center st of next loop. Repeat from * around. Join. **15th rnd:** Sl st in picot, ch 1, sc in same picot, * (ch 3, 2 dc in next dc, dc in next dc) 7 times; ch 3, sc in next picot. Repeat from * around. Join. **16th rnd:** Sl st in next 3 ch and in next dc, ch 4 (to count as tr) and complete a cluster as follows: Holding back the last loop of each tr on hook make tr in each of next 2 dc, thread over and draw through all loops on hook; * (ch 4, tr in each of next 3 dc) 5 times; ch 4, (make a 3-tr cluster over next 3 dc) twice. Repeat from * around, ending with a cluster, sl st in tip of first cluster made.

17th rnd: Ch 8, * (tr in each of next 3 tr, ch 5) 5 times; skip 1 cluster, dc in tip of next cluster, ch 4. Repeat from * around. Join last ch-4 to 3rd st of ch-7. **18th rnd:** Sl st in next 4 ch and in following tr, ch 4 and complete a cluster as before, * (ch 11, cluster over next 3 tr) 4 times; ch 3, cluster over next 3 tr. Repeat from * around. Join last ch-3 to tip of first cluster. **19th rnd:** Sl st in next 5 ch, picot in next st, * ch 13, picot in center st of next ch-11. Repeat from * around, joining last ch-13 with sl st in first sc made. **20th rnd:** Sl st across to center st of next ch-13, picot in center st, * ch 13, picot in center st of next ch-13. Repeat from * around. Join. **21st rnd:** Repeat last rnd, only making ch 15 (instead of ch-13) between picots. Break off.

Starch lightly and block to measurement.

No. 1-46 . . . . . . Vanity Set

Materials: Six Cord Cordichet, *Size 30, 3 balls (small balls) . . . Steel Crochet Hook No. 10.*

Large doily measures about 13 inches in diameter and 2 small doilies each about 8 inches in diameter.

GAUGE: 5 rows make 1 inch.

LARGE DOILY . . . Starting at center, ch 8. Join with sl st to form ring. **1st rnd:** Ch 3 (to count as 1 dc), 15 dc in ring. Join with sl st in top st of ch-3. **2nd rnd:** Ch 3, dc in same place as sl st (inc made), dc in each dc around, increasing 12 more dc in the rnd—*to inc a dc, make 2 dc in 1 dc* (29 dc in all). **3rd rnd:** Same as previous rnd (42 dc in rnd). **4th rnd:** Ch 5 (to count as dc and ch 2), * skip 1 dc, dc in next dc, ch 2. Repeat from * around, ending with sl st in 3rd st of ch 5 (21 sps). **5th rnd:** Ch 3, * 3 dc in next sp, dc in next dc, (2 dc in next sp, dc in next dc) twice. Repeat from * around (70 sts). Join. **6th and 7th rnds:** Ch 3, dc in each dc around, increasing 15 dc in the rnd (100 dc on 7th rnd). **8th rnd:** Ch 3, dc in next 2 dc, * ch 9, skip 7 dc, dc in next 3 dc. Repeat from * around. Join last ch-9 to top of ch-3 (10 sps on rnd). **9th rnd:** Ch 3, dc in next 2 dc, * ch 4, skip 3 ch, dc in next 3 ch, ch 4, dc in next 3 dc. Repeat from * around. Join last ch-4 to top st of ch-3. **10th to 20th rnds incl:** Same as previous rnd, having 1 additional ch between dc groups in each following rnd (ch 15 between dc groups on 20th rnd).

21st rnd: Ch 3, dc in next 2 dc, * ch 8, sc in 8th st of ch-15 below, ch 8, dc in next 3 dc. Repeat from * around. Join. **22nd rnd:** Ch 3, dc in next 2 dc, * ch 5, sc in 6th st of ch-8, ch 5, sc in 3rd st of next ch-8, ch 5, dc in next 3 dc. Repeat from * around. Join. **23rd rnd:** Ch 3, dc in next 2 dc, * (ch 5, sc in center st of next ch-5 loop below) 3 times; ch 5, dc in next 3 dc. Repeat from * around. Join. **24th to 27th rnds incl:** Work as for 23rd rnd, having 1 additional ch-5 loop in each following rnd. **28th rnd:** Ch 3, dc in next 2 dc, * ch 6, skip first ch-5, sc in center st of next loop, make five ch-5 loops, ch 6, dc in next 3 dc. Repeat from * around. Join. **29th rnd:** Ch 3, dc in next 2 dc, * ch 8, skip next ch, sc in center st of next loop,

1-46

make 4 loops, ch 8, dc in next 3 dc. Repeat from * around. Join. **30th rnd:** Ch 3, dc in next 2 dc, * ch 10, skip next ch, sc in center st of next loop, make 3 loops, ch 10, dc in next 3 dc. Repeat from * around. Join. **31st rnd:** Ch 3, dc in next 2 dc, * ch 12, skip next ch, sc in center st of next loop, make 2 loops, ch 12, dc in next 3 dc. Repeat from * around. Join.

32nd rnd: Ch 3, dc in next 2 dc, * ch 14, skip next ch, dc in center st of next loop, make 1 loop, ch 14, dc in next 3 dc. Repeat from * around. Join. **33rd rnd:** Ch 3, dc in next 2 dc, * ch 16, skip next ch, dc in center st of next loop, ch 16, dc in next 3 dc. Repeat from * around. Join and break off.

SMALL DOILY ... Ch 8. Join with sl st to form ring. **1st rnd:** Ch 3, 14 dc in ring. Join. **2nd rnd:** Ch 3, dc in same place as sl st, 2 dc in each st around (30 sts). Join. **3rd rnd:** Same as 4th rnd of Large Doily (15 sps). **4th rnd:** Ch 3, * (3 dc in next sp, dc in next dc) 4 times; 4 dc in next sp, dc in next dc. Repeat from * around (63 sts). **5th rnd:** Ch 3, dc in next 2 dc, * ch 9, skip 6 dc, dc in next 3 dc. Repeat from * around. Join. **6th to 13th rnds incl:** Same as 9th to 16th rnds incl of Large Doily (ch 11 between dc groups on 13th rnd). **14th rnd:** Ch 3, dc in 2 dc, * ch 6, sc in 6th st of ch-11, ch 6, dc in 3 dc. Repeat from * around. Join.

15th rnd: Ch 3, dc in 2 dc, * ch 5, sc in 4th st of ch 6, ch 5, sc in 3rd st of next ch 6, ch 5, dc in 3 dc. Repeat from * around. Join. **16th rnd:** Ch 3, dc in 2 dc, * (ch 5, sc in center st of ch-5 loop) 3 times; ch 5, dc in 3 dc. Repeat from * around. Join. **17th rnd:** Ch 3, dc in 2 dc, * (ch 5, sc in center st of next loop) 4 times; ch 5, dc in 3 dc. Repeat from * around. Join. **18th rnd:** Ch 3, dc in 2 dc, * ch 3, (sc in center st of next loop, ch 5) 4 times; sc in next loop, ch 3, dc in 3 dc. Repeat from * around. Join. **19th rnd:** Ch 3, dc in 2 dc, * ch 6, (sc in center st of next ch-5 loop, ch 5) 3 times; sc in next loop, ch 6, dc in 3 dc. Repeat from * around. Join. **20th rnd:** Ch 3, dc in 2 dc, * ch 8, (sc in center st of next ch-5 loop, ch 5) twice; sc in next loop, ch 8, dc in 3 dc. Repeat from * around. Join. **21st rnd:** Ch 3, dc in 2 dc, * ch 10, sc in center st of next ch-5 loop, ch 5, sc in center st of next loop, ch 10, dc in 3 dc. Repeat from * around. Join. **22nd rnd:** Ch 3, dc in 2 dc, * ch 12, sc in center st of ch-5 loop, ch 12, dc in 3 dc. Repeat from * around. Join and break off.

Starch lightly, pin out as in illustration and press until dry.

No. 7839 . . . . Doily

Materials: BEST SIX CORD MERCERIZED CROCHET, *Size 50, 3 balls (small balls) of White only ... Steel Crochet Hook No. 12 ... A hemstitched piece of linen (5¾ inches in diameter).*

Doily measures 15 inches in diameter.

1st rnd: Attach thread to edge of linen and make 315 sc around edge. Join. **2nd rnd:** Ch 5, * skip 2 sc, dc in next sc, ch 2. Repeat from * around. Join with sl st to 3rd ch of ch-5 (105 sps). **3rd rnd:** Ch 4, * (2 tr in next sp, tr in next dc) 3 times; ch 4, holding back on hook the last loop of each tr make 2 tr in last tr, thread over and draw through all loops on hook (cluster made), skip 1 dc, tr in next dc, ch 2, tr in same dc, ch 4, 2-tr cluster in last tr made, skip 1 dc, tr in next dc. Repeat from * around, ending with 2-tr cluster. Join to top of ch-4. **4th rnd:** Sl st in next tr, ch 4, tr in next 7 tr, * ch 4, 2-tr cluster in last tr, in next ch-2 sp make (tr, ch 2) twice and tr; ch 4, 2-tr cluster in last tr, skip next tr, tr in next 8 tr. Repeat from * around, ending with cluster. Join. **5th rnd:** Sl st in next tr, ch 4, tr in next 5 tr, * ch 4, 2-tr cluster in last tr, in next ch-2 sp make tr, ch 2 and tr; ch 2, tr in next tr, ch 2, in next ch-2 sp make tr, ch 2 and tr; ch 4, 2-tr cluster in last tr, skip next tr, tr in next 6 tr. Repeat from * around, ending with 2-tr cluster. Join. **6th rnd:** Sl st in next tr, ch 4, tr in next 3 tr, * ch 4, 2-tr cluster in last tr, (in next ch-2 sp make tr, ch 2 and tr) 4 times; ch 4, 2-tr cluster in last tr, skip next tr, tr in next 4 tr. Repeat from * around. Join. **7th rnd:** Sl st in next tr, ch 4, tr in next tr, * ch 4, cluster in last tr, (in next ch-2 sp make tr, ch 2, tr and ch 1) 3 times; in next ch-2 sp make tr, ch 2 and tr; ch 4, cluster in last tr, skip next tr, tr in next 2 tr. Repeat from * around. Join. **8th rnd:** Ch 4, cluster in same place as sl st, * ch 4, (in next ch-2 sp make tr, ch 2, tr and ch 2) 3 times; in next ch-2 sp make tr, ch 2 and tr; ch 4, cluster between next 2 tr. Repeat from * around. Join.

9th rnd: Ch 6, tr in tip of cluster, * ch 2, in next ch-2 sp make tr, ch 2 and tr; (ch 2, skip next ch-2, in next ch-2 sp make tr, ch 2 and tr) 3 times; ch 2, in tip of next cluster make tr, ch 2 and tr. Repeat from * around. Join. **10th rnd:** Sl st in sp, ch 6, in same sp make tr, ch 2 and tr; * (ch 2, skip next sp, in next sp make tr, ch 2 and tr) 4 times; ch 2, skip next sp, in next sp make (tr, ch 2) twice and tr. Repeat from * around. Join. **11th rnd:** Sl st in sp, ch 6, tr in same sp, * ch 2, in next sp make tr, ch 2 and tr; (ch 2, skip next sp, in next sp make tr, ch 2 and tr) 5 times. Repeat from * around. Join. **12th rnd:** Sl st in sp, ch 6, tr in same sp, * (ch 1, in next sp make tr, ch 2 and tr) twice; (ch 2, skip next sp, in next sp make tr, ch 2

7839

and tr) 5 times. Repeat from * around. Join. **13th rnd:** Sl st in sp, ch 6, tr in same sp, * ch 2, skip next sp, in next sp make tr, ch 2 and tr. Repeat from * around. Join. **14th rnd:** Sl st in sp, ch 6, tr in same sp, (in next sp make tr, ch 2 and tr) 4 times; * ch 2, (skip next sp, in next sp make tr, ch 2 and tr) 4 times; ch 2, skip next sp, (in next sp make tr, ch 2 and tr) 5 times. Repeat from * around. Join. **15th rnd:** Sl st in next sp, ch 6, tr in same sp, * (ch 1, skip 2 tr, in next sp make tr, ch 2 and tr) 4 times; ch 2, skip next sp, in next sp make tr, ch 2 and tr; skip next ch-2 sp, in sp between next 2 tr make tr, ch 2 and tr; skip next ch-2 sp, in next sp make tr, ch 2 and tr; ch 2, skip next sp, in next sp make tr, ch 2 and tr. Repeat from * around. Join. **16th rnd:** Sl st in next sp, ch 6, tr in same sp, * (ch 2, skip next sp, in next sp make tr, ch 2 and tr) 5 times; tr in next ch-2 sp, in next ch-2 sp make tr, ch 2 and tr; ch 2, skip next sp, in next sp make tr, ch 2 and tr. Repeat from * around. Join. **17th rnd:** Sl st in sp, ch 6, tr in same sp, * (ch 3, skip next sp, in next sp make tr, ch 2 and tr) 5 times; ch 2, skip 3 tr, in next sp make tr, ch 2 and tr; ch 3, skip next sp, in next sp make tr, ch 2 and tr. Repeat from * around. Join. **18th rnd:** Sl st in sp, ch 7, dc in 4th ch from hook, (tr in same sp as sl st, ch 4, dc in 4th ch from hook) twice; * tr in same sp, skip next sp, tr in next sp, ch 4, dc in 4th ch from hook, (tr in same sp as last tr, ch 4, dc in 4th ch from hook) twice. Repeat from * around. Join and break off.

No. 4-65 . . . . . Cluster Doily

Materials: SIX CORD CORDICHET, Size 50, 2 balls (small balls) of White only . . . Steel Crochet Hook No. 12.

Doily measures about 8½ inches in diameter.

Starting at center, ch 12. Join with sl st to form ring. **1st rnd:** Ch 1, 28 sc in ring. Join with sl st in first sc. **2nd rnd:** Ch 5, skip next sc, dc in next sc, * ch 2, skip next sc, dc in next sc. Repeat from * around. Join with sl st in 3rd st of starting chain (14 sps). **3rd rnd:** Ch 3, * 3 dc in sp, dc in dc. Repeat from * around. Join with sl st in 3rd st of starting chain (56 dc). **4th rnd:** Ch 1, sc in same place as sl st, * ch 4, skip next dc, sc in next dc. Repeat from * around, joining last ch-4 with sl st in first sc (28 loops). **5th rnd:** Sl st to center of next loop, ch 4, holding back on hook the last loop of each d tr make 2 d tr in same loop, thread over and draw through all loops on hook (a 2-d tr cluster made). * Ch 4, make a 3-d tr cluster in next loop. Repeat from * around, joining last ch 4 with sl st in first cluster (28 clusters). **6th rnd:** Sl st to center of next loop, ch 1, sc in same loop, * ch 5, sc in next loop. Repeat from * around. Join (28 loops). **7th rnd:** Sl st to center of next loop, ch 9, * dc in next loop, ch 5. Repeat from * around, joining last ch 5 with sl st in 3rd st of ch-9 (28 sps). **8th rnd:** Ch 1, sc in same place as sl st, * ch 4, sc in next sp, ch 4, sc in dc. Repeat from * around. Join (56 loops). **9th, 10th and 11th rnds:** Repeat 5th, 6th and 7th rnds. **12th rnd:** Ch 1, sc in same place as sl st, * ch 4, sc in next sp, ch 4, sc in dc, ch 4, sc in sp. Repeat from * around. Join (84 loops). **13th, 14th and 15th rnds:** Repeat 5th, 6th and 7th rnds. **16th and 17th rnds:** Repeat 7th rnd. **18th rnd:** Repeat 12th rnd (126 loops). **19th rnd:** Sl st to center of next loop, ch 4, make a 2-d tr cluster in same loop, * ch 6, sc in 3rd ch from hook, ch 2, make a 3-d tr cluster in next loop. Repeat from * around, ending with ch 6, sc in 3rd ch from hook, ch 2, sl st in top of first cluster. Break off. Starch lightly and press.

4-65

No. 7831 . . . . Doily

Materials: BEST SIX CORD MERCERIZED CRO-CHET, *Size 20*, **Small Ball:** *4 balls . . . Steel Crochet Hook No. 9.*

Doily measures 14 inches in diameter

Starting at center, ch 10. Join with sl st to form ring. **1st rnd:** Ch 3, 23 dc in ring. Join with sl st to top of ch-3. **2nd rnd:** Sc in same place as sl st, * ch 3, skip 1 dc, sc in next dc. Repeat from * around, ending with ch 1, half dc in first sc. **3rd rnd:** * Ch 4, sc in next loop. Repeat from * around. Join. **4th rnd:** Sl st in loop, ch 3, 4 dc in same loop, 5 dc in each loop around. Join. **5th rnd:** * Ch 3, skip 1 dc, sc in next dc. Repeat from * around, ending with ch 1, half dc in top of ch-3. **6th and 7th rnds:** Sc in loop just completed, * ch 3, sc in next loop. Repeat from * around, ending with ch 1, dc in first sc. **8th rnd:** Ch 8, * tr in next loop, ch 4. Repeat from * around. Join to 4th ch of starting ch-8. **9th rnd:** Sl st in sp, ch 4, 4 tr in same sp, 5 tr in each sp around. Join. **10th** rnd: Sc in same place as sl st, * ch 4, skip 2 tr, sc in next tr. Repeat from * around, ending with ch 1, dc in first sc. **11th and 12th rnds:** Sc in loop just completed, * ch 4, sc in next loop. Repeat from * around, ending as before. **13th rnd:** Ch 8, * tr in next loop, ch 4. Repeat from * around. Join.

14th rnd: Sl st in sp, * ch 4, holding back on hook the last loop of each tr make 4 tr in sp, thread over and draw through all loops on hook—cluster made; (ch 3, make a 5-tr cluster in next sp) 3 times; ch 3, make a 4-tr cluster in next sp, ch 4, sl st in same sp, sl st in next sp. Repeat from * around, ending with a 5-tr cluster in last sp. Turn. **15th rnd:** Sl st in next 3 ch, turn; ch 4, make a 4-tr cluster in sp, * ch 12, (5-tr cluster in next sp, ch 3) 3 times; cluster in next sp. Repeat from * around. Join, turn. **16th rnd:** Sl st in next 3 ch, turn; ch 4, make a 4-tr cluster in sp, * ch 8, dc in ch-12

7831

loop, ch 8, (cluster in next sp, ch 3) twice; cluster in next sp. Repeat from * around. Join, turn. **17th rnd:** Sl st in next 3 ch, turn; ch 4, 4-tr cluster in sp, * (ch 8, tr in next loop) twice; ch 8, cluster in next sp, ch 3, cluster in next sp. Repeat from * around. Join, turn. **18th rnd:** Sl st in next 3 ch, turn; ch 4, 4-tr cluster in sp, * (ch 8, tr in next loop) 3 times; ch 8, cluster in next sp. Repeat from * around, ending with ch 4, tr in tip of first cluster. **19th rnd:** * Ch 6, sc in 3rd ch from hook (picot), ch 10, sc in 3rd ch from hook (another picot), ch 3, sc in next loop. Repeat from * around. Join. **20th, 21st and 22nd rnds:** Sl st to center of first loop, sc in same loop, * ch 3, picot, ch 7, picot, ch 3, sc in next loop. Repeat from * around. Join. At end of 22nd rnd break off.

No. 7751 . . . . . Tablecloth

Materials: BEST SIX CORD MERCERIZED CROCHET, *Size 30*. **Big Ball:** *30 balls of White, Ecru or Cream . . . Steel Crochet Hook No. 10.*

Tablecloth measures 56 x 72 inches.

GAUGE: Motif measures 1⅛ inches in diameter.

FIRST MOTIF . . . Starting at center, ch 8. Join with sl st to form ring. **1st rnd:** Ch 7, in ring make (tr, ch 3) 7 times; join last ch-3 with sl st in 4th st of starting chain (8 sps). **2nd rnd:** Ch 1, 5 sc in each sp around. Sl st in first sc. **3rd rnd:** Ch 1, sc in same place as sl st, * ch 8, skip 4 sc, sc in next sc. Repeat from * around, joining last ch-8 to first sc. **4th rnd:** In each loop make 5 sc, ch 2 and 5 sc. Sl st in first sc. Break off.

SECOND MOTIF . . . Work same as First Motif until 3rd rnd is completed. **4th rnd:** * 5 sc in next loop, ch 1, sl st in corresponding ch-2 loop on First Motif, ch 1, 5 sc in same loop on Second Motif. Repeat from * once more; then complete 4th rnd same as for First Motif.

Make 49 rows of 61 motifs, joining them as Second Motif was joined to First Motif.

FILL-IN-MOTIF . . . Attach thread in a joining of motifs, ch 4, * skip 4 sc, tr in next sc, tr in next joining. Repeat from * around. Join with sl st in 4th st of starting chain. **Next rnd:** Work sc between first and next st, * sc between next and following st. Repeat from * around. Join and break off. Fill in all sps between joinings like this.

EDGING . . . 1st rnd: Attach thread in any joining on edge, ch 4, skip 4 sc, tr in next sc, * (ch 8, sc in next ch-2) twice; ch 8, skip 5 sc, holding back the last loop of each tr on hook make tr in next sc, tr in joining, skip 5 sc, tr in next sc, thread over and draw through all loops on hook (joined tr made). Repeat from * across to next corner motif, then (ch 8, sc in next ch-2) twice; (ch 8, skip 5 sc, dc in next sc, ch 8, sc in next ch-2) twice; ch 8, make joined tr. Continue thus around, joining last tr with sl st in 4th st of starting chain. **2nd rnd:** In each ch-8 loop make 5 sc, ch 2 and 5 sc. Join. **3rd rnd:** Sl st across to next ch-2, sc in same ch-2, * ch 8, sc in next ch-2. Repeat from * around, ending with ch 4, tr in first sc made. **4th rnd:** Ch 1, 5 sc over the tr just made, 5 sc in next loop, ch 8, turn, skip 9 sc, sc in next sc, ch 1, turn. Make 12 dc over last ch-8, sc in incompleted loop, ch 8, turn. Skip 3 dc, dc in next dc, (ch 1, dc in next dc) 4 times; ch 8, skip 3 dc, sc in next dc, ch 1, turn. Make 5 sc, ch 2 and 5 sc over loop, * (ch 5, sc in next ch-1 sp) 4 times; ch 5, make 5 sc, ch 2 and 5 sc over next loop. Make 5 sc over incompleted loop (scallop completed). Make 5 sc, ch 2 and 5 sc over next loop, 5 sc over following loop, ch 8, turn. Sc in last ch-2, ch 1, turn. Make 12 dc over last ch-8, sc in incompleted loop, ch 8, turn. Skip 3 dc, dc in next dc, (ch 1, dc in next dc) 4 times; ch 8, skip 3 dc, sc in next dc; ch 1, turn. Make 5 sc over loop, ch 1, sl st in corresponding ch-2 on previous scallop, ch 1, 5 sc over same loop. Repeat from * around. Join and break off.

BALL FRINGE . . . Starting at bottom, ch 5. Join with sl st to form ring. **1st rnd:** Ch 3, work 17 dc in ring. Join with sl st in 3rd st of starting chain. **2nd to 6th rnds incl:** Sc in each st around. Stuff this piece with cotton. **7th and 8th rnds:** Sc in each sc, decreasing 6 sc evenly around (6 sc remain). Ch 10, break off, leaving an end for sewing. Pull the ch-10 through center ch-5 loop on any scallop, thread needle with end of thread and close opening. Fasten securely.

7751

No. 7734 . . . . . Tablecloth

Materials: BEST SIX CORD MERCERIZED CRO-CHET, *Size 30.* **Big Ball:** *47 balls of White, Ecru or Cream . . . Steel Crochet Hook No. 10.*

Tablecloth measures 60 x 80 inches.

GAUGE: Motif measures 1⅝ inches square.

FIRST MOTIF . . . Starting at center, ch 12. Join with sl st. **1st rnd:** 24 sc in ring. Sl st in first sc. **2nd rnd:** Sc in same place as sl st, * ch 5, skip 1 sc, sc in next sc. Repeat from * around, ending with ch 2, dc in first sc (12 loops). **3rd rnd:** * Ch 5, in next loop make cluster, ch 5 and cluster—*to make a cluster, holding back on hook the last loop of each tr make 3 tr in same place, thread over and draw through all loops on hook;* (ch 5, sc in next loop) twice. Repeat from * around, ending with ch 2, dc in top of dc. **4th rnd:** Ch 4, 2-tr cluster in loop just made, * ch 5, sc in next loop, ch 5, in corner loop make cluster, ch 5 and cluster; ch 5, sc in next loop, ch 5, cluster in next loop. Repeat from * around, ending with ch 5, sl st in top of first cluster. Break off.

SECOND MOTIF . . . Work as for First Motif until 3 rnds are completed. **4th rnd:** Ch 4, 2-tr cluster in loop just made, ch 5, sc in next loop, ch 5, cluster in corner loop, ch 2, sl st in corner loop of First Motif, ch 2, cluster in same loop as last cluster on Second Motif; ch 2, sl st in corresponding loop of First Motif, ch 2, sc in next loop on Second Motif, complete rnd, joining next 4 loops to corresponding loops of First Motif as before.

Make 35 rows of 48 motifs, joining adjacent sides as Second Motif was joined to First Motif (where 4 corners meet, join 3rd and 4th corners to joining of previous 2 corners).

EDGING . . . 1st rnd: Attach thread to a corner loop, ch 4 and **complete a cluster,** ch 10, cluster in same loop, * ch 10, sc in next cluster. Repeat from * around, making cluster, ch 10 and cluster in each corner loop. Join. **2nd and 3rd rnds:** Sl st in next ch, sl st in same loop, ch 4 and complete cluster as before, ch 10, cluster in same loop, * ch 10, sc in next loop. Repeat from * around, making cluster, ch 10 and cluster in each corner loop. Join. Break off at end of 3rd rnd.

7734

No. 4-68 . . . . Curtains

Materials: EVERSHEEN, *400-yard balls: 21 balls of White or Ecru . . . Steel Crochet Hook No. 7 or 8.*

Each Panel measures about 40 x 81 inches.

GAUGE: 2 V sts make 1 inch; 2 rows make 1 inch.

Starting at bottom, make a chain 45 inches long (15 ch sts to 1 inch). **1st row:** Tr in 7th ch from hook, * skip 4 ch, in next ch make tr, ch 4 and tr (a V st made). Repeat from * across until there are 80 V sts, skip 4 ch, in next ch make tr, ch 2 and tr. Cut off remaining chain. Ch 4, turn. **2nd row:** * Tr in next tr, ch 4, tr in next tr. Repeat from * across, ending with tr in 3rd st of turning chain. Ch 6, turn. **3rd row:** Tr in next tr, * tr in next tr, ch 4, tr in next tr. Repeat from * across, ending with tr in next tr, ch 2, tr in 4th st of

turning chain. Ch 4, turn. Repeat 2nd and 3rd rows alternately until piece measures about 2 yards and 7 inches, or length desired. Break off.

BORDER . . . Attach thread in end of starting chain and work border along bottom and one long edge as follows: **1st row:** Ch 4, * 3 tr in next sp, tr between 2 tr's. Repeat from * across to corner, make 7 tr in corner st. ** 3 tr in next sp, tr in end of row. Repeat from ** to top of curtain. Ch 4, turn. **2nd and 3rd rows:** Tr in each tr and 5 tr in center st of corner. Ch 4, turn. At end of 3rd row, ch 1, turn and work sc in each tr across. Now work sc evenly across remaining 2 edges. Sl st in first sc. Break off.

Make another panel, being careful when working border to have panels correspond. Starch lightly if desired and block on a curtain stretcher.

4-68

4-68

5-121

No. 5-121 . . . . . . Chair Set

Materials: SIX CORD CORDICHET, *Size 50.*
Small Ball: *3 balls of White only . . . Steel*
Crochet Hook No. 12.

**Chair Back measures about 11 x 16 inches;
each Arm Piece about 7 x 11 inches.**

GAUGE: 6 sps make 1 inch; 6 rows make
1 inch.

CHAIR BACK . . . Starting at bottom of chart,
make a chain 21 inches long (18 ch sts to
1 inch). **1st row:** Dc in 8th ch from hook,
* ch 2, skip 2 ch, dc in next ch. Repeat from *
until 97 sps are made. Cut off remaining chain.
Ch 5, turn. **2nd row:** Dc in next dc (sp made
over sp), 2 dc in next sp, dc in next dc (bl
made over sp), ch 2, dc in next dc (another
sp made over sp), 1 bl, 1 sp, (2 bls, 1 sp, 1 bl,
1 sp) 18 times; 1 bl, ch 2, skip 2 ch of turning
chain, dc in next ch. Ch 5, turn. **3rd row:**
1 sp, dc in next 3 dc (bl made over bl), 1 sp,

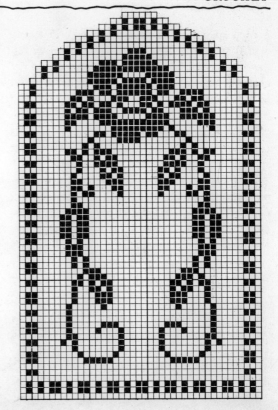

5-121

1 bl, 1 sp, (2 bls, 1 sp, 1 bl, 1 sp) 18 times; 1 bl, 1 sp. Ch 5, turn. Starting at 4th row, follow chart until 53 rows are completed. Do not chain to turn at end of 53rd row. **54th row:** Sl st in next 7 sts (2 sps decreased), ch 5 and follow chart to last 2 sps (2 more sps decreased). Turn. **55th row:** Sl st in next 4 sts (1 sp decreased), ch 5 and follow chart to last sp (another sp decreased). Ch 5, turn.

Now follow chart until 60 rows are completed. Do not chain to turn at end of 60th row. **61st row:** Dec 2 sps as before, ch 5, 2 sps, 1 bl, 1 sp, 1 bl, 12 sps, 1 bl, 1 sp, 1 bl, 2 sps,

turn. **62nd row:** Dec 2 sps; 1 bl, 1 sp, 1 bl, 8 sps, 1 bl, 1 sp, 1 bl, 2 sps, turn. Now follow chart to top to complete scallop. Break off. Make other two scallops to correspond with chart.

Attach thread to edge of Chair Back and work sc closely around all edges, making a p after every 8th sc—*to make a picot, ch 3, sl st in last sc.*

ARM PIECE (Make 2) . . . Make a chain 12 inches long (18 ch sts to 1 inch) and follow chart for Arm Piece, having 42 sps on first row. Finish as for Chair Back.

170

CHAPTER V

TATTING . . . *the perfect finishing touch for your possessions*

---

*I*F TATTING IS NEW TO YOU, you'll be surprised how easy —and enjoyable—it is to learn. In no time your shuttle will be flying through the thread, and your only problem will be in choosing from the myriad enchanting designs. There are gossamer doilies and place mats, a tablecloth of extraordinary delicacy and beauty . . . One edging is lovelier and more delicate than the next. There is no limit to the ways in which you will use them . . . on guest towels, pillow slips, to give a touch of luxury to a simple slip or night dress, or to add a handmade look to your tea napkins.

How to Tat

Shuttles . . . Shuttles are made of various materials, such as Bone, Tortoise Shell, and Steel. Some are shaped like the one shown in the illustrations. Others are made with a hook at the end, but the latter is not practical, for it hinders the worker in gaining speed.

Winding the Shuttle . . . Wind thread around the bobbin in center of shuttle. If there is a hole in center of bobbin, insert thread through the hole and tie a knot. In some instances the bobbin is removable. Do not wind thread beyond the edge of shuttle.

Tatting Threads . . . Tatting is made with fine thread. Tatting-Crochet comes in lovely colors and is especially suited to work of this type. For coarser work, use Best Six Cord Mercerized Crochet in Sizes 20 and 30.

Materials: BEST SIX CORD MERCERIZED CROCHET, *Size 20, 2 balls . . . One tatting shuttle with a pointed end.*
   With this thread you will be able to practice and then you can make the dainty towel edging shown on page 178.

LEARN HOW STEPS

WHAT TO DO WITH THE LEFT HAND

1. Grasp the free end of the thread between thumb and forefinger.

2. Spread the middle, ring and little fingers and encircle them with the thread.

3. Bring the thread around to make a circle and hold securely between the thumb and forefinger (Fig. 1).

4. Bend the little finger to catch the thread against the palm (Fig. 2).

5. Bend the middle finger back to catch the loose part of the circle (Fig. 3).

6. Adjust the thread so that the fingers do not feel strained.

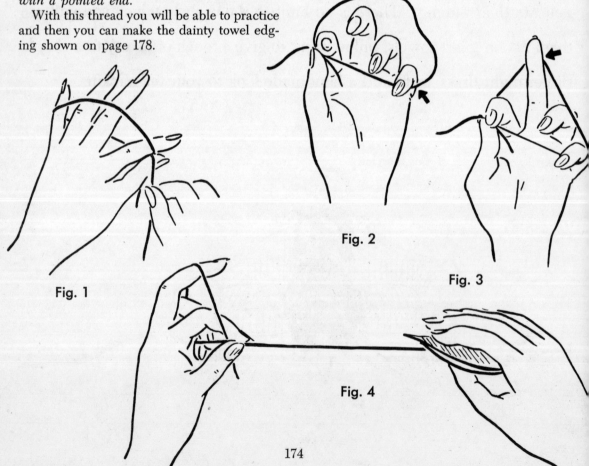

Fig. 1

Fig. 2

Fig. 3

Fig. 4

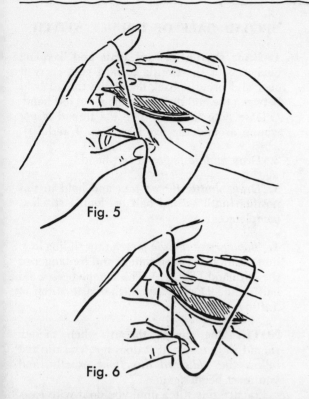

Fig. 5

Fig. 6

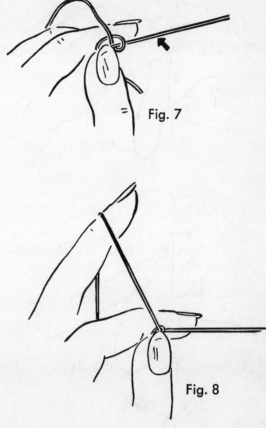

Fig. 7

Fig. 8

WHAT TO DO WITH THE RIGHT HAND

1. Unwind shuttle so that shuttle thread is about 12 inches long (Fig. 4).

2. Hold shuttle so that pointed end is facing the left hand and thread coming from back of bobbin (Fig. 4).

3. Grasp flat side between thumb and forefinger in a horizontal position, holding the other three fingers on a level with the forefinger (Fig. 4).

The Double Stitch—The Basic Stitch of Tatting

FIRST HALF OF THE DOUBLE STITCH

1. Draw shuttle thread out to its full length, keeping right and left hands at equal levels (Fig. 4).

2. Pass the shuttle thread under and then over the right hand below the top joint of fingers (Fig. 5).

3. With thread in this position, bring the shuttle forward and insert it *under* (Fig. 5) and bring it back *over* thread held between middle and forefinger of left hand (Fig. 6).

4. *Drop middle finger* of left hand.

5. *Draw shuttle thread taut* (Fig. 7) and hold it in this position until first half of double stitch is completed.

6. *Slowly raise middle finger of left hand,* thus sliding loop into position between thumb and forefinger (Fig. 8). This completes first half of a *double stitch.*

NOTE: Be careful to do *Steps 4, 5 and 6* exactly as directed. Notice as you work that the shuttle thread is encircled by a loose loop made by the circle of thread in left hand. The importance of keeping the shuttle thread taut until this loop is in position cannot be overemphasized.

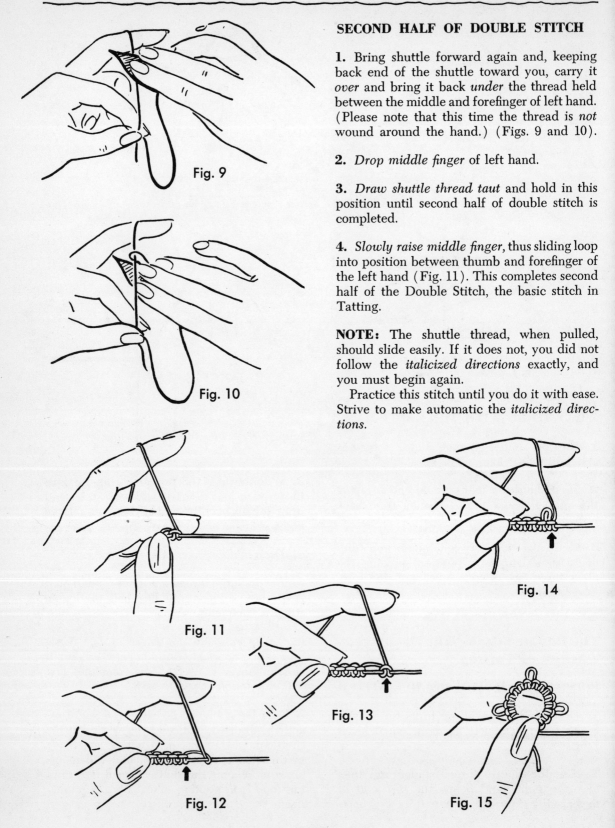

SECOND HALF OF DOUBLE STITCH

1. Bring shuttle forward again and, keeping back end of the shuttle toward you, carry it *over* and bring it back *under* the thread held between the middle and forefinger of left hand. (Please note that this time the thread is *not* wound around the hand.) (Figs. 9 and 10).

2. *Drop middle finger* of left hand.

3. *Draw shuttle thread taut* and hold in this position until second half of double stitch is completed.

4. *Slowly raise middle finger*, thus sliding loop into position between thumb and forefinger of the left hand (Fig. 11). This completes second half of the Double Stitch, the basic stitch in Tatting.

NOTE: The shuttle thread, when pulled, should slide easily. If it does not, you did not follow the *italicized directions* exactly, and you must begin again.

Practice this stitch until you do it with ease. Strive to make automatic the *italicized directions.*

Fig. 9

Fig. 10

Fig. 11

Fig. 12

Fig. 13

Fig. 14

Fig. 15

Rings, Picots and Joinings

All tatting designs contain rings and picots. The ring forms the basis of the design. The picots are used for decoration and for joining.

Practice the following directions. They give in detail the fundamentals of rings, picots and joinings. When your rings are even and your picots uniform in size, cut off your practice piece and begin again, because the same directions will make the attractive edging for the Guest Towel on page 178.

FIRST RING

NOTE: The working stitch always comes between the thumb and forefinger. In Figs. 12, 13 and 14 the fingers should come where the arrow points. The drawings are made in this manner so that all the steps may be clear.

1. Make four double stitches (ds). (Follow directions on page 178).

2. Next make the first half of a double stitch (ds), but as you slide it into position stop about ¼ inch from the preceding double stitch (ds) (Fig. 12).

3. Complete the double stitch (ds) (Fig. 13).

4. Draw the entire stitch close to the first four stitches (Fig. 14). The little loop formed from the space left between the stitches is a *picot* (p).

5. Make four more double stitches (ds).

6. Please note that Steps 2, 3, 4 and 5 should be written 1 picot (p) and 5 double stitches (ds). A picot refers only to the loop and does not include the double stitch which fastens the loop.

7. Make another picot and five double stitches (see Step 6).

8. Make a picot and four double stitches.

9. Holding the stitches securely between thumb and forefinger of left hand, draw the shuttle thread tight so that the first and last stitches meet, forming a ring (Fig. 15).

SECOND RING and JOINING

1. Wind the thread around the left hand in position for another ring.

2. Make 4 double stitches ¼ of an inch away from ring just made.

3. Insert pointed end of shuttle through the last picot of previous ring and catch the thread encircling the left hand.

4. Pull the thread through until there is a loop large enough to insert shuttle (Fig. 16).

5. Pull the shuttle through loop and draw the shuttle thread tight.

6. Slowly raise middle finger of left hand to draw up the loop. This joins the new ring to the old one and counts as the first half of the next double stitch.

7. Complete the double stitch.

8. Repeat Steps 5 to 9 under First Ring.

Continue in this manner for each succeeding ring, repeating Steps 1 to 8 under Second Ring and Joining.

The preceding directions have been given in detail so as to make the steps clear in your mind. Now you are ready to read the same directions as they would appear in a book. (The abbreviations are explained to make the directions easier for a beginner to read).

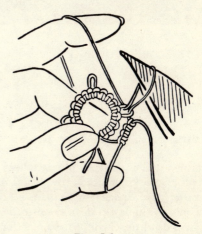

Fig. 16

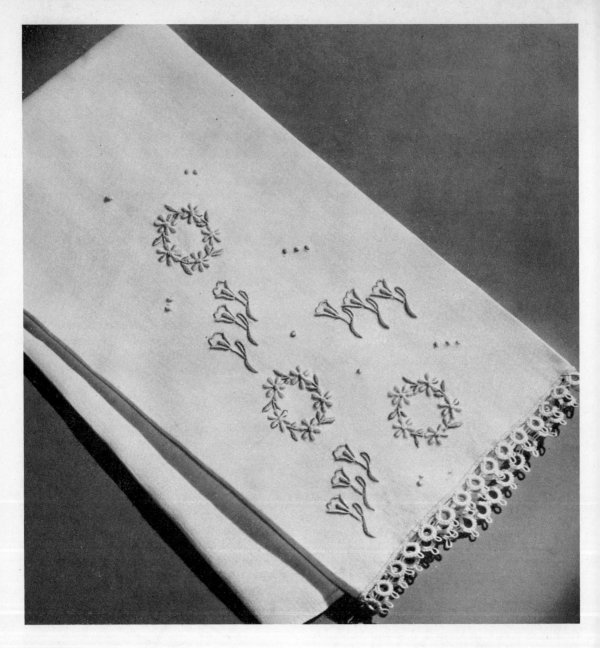

GUEST TOWEL EDGING

Edging . . . . For Guest Towel

R (ring) of 4 ds (double stitches), 3 p's (picots) sep (separated) by 5 ds, 4 ds, cl (close); * sp (space) of ¼ inch; r (ring) of 4 ds, join to the last p of previous r, 5 ds, 2 p's sep by 5 ds, 4 ds, cl. Repeat from * for length desired.

JOINING THE THREAD

When a new thread is required make a square knot close to the base of the last ring or chain, but do not cut off the ends, for the strain of the work may loosen the knot. If you make a knot in the thread, cut it off and tie the new thread close to last ring. Knots prevent the ring from being drawn up, for they will not pass through the double stitches. Cut off loose ends later.

178

REVERSING YOUR WORK

In tatting you have noticed that the rounded end of the loop on which you are working faces the top. However, you can produce an effect such as that shown in Handkerchief Edging by turning your work first up and then down. The directions will say rw (reverse work). To do this, the ring you have just worked is turned so that the base of the ring faces the top, and the new ring is worked as usual with the loop side up.

Handkerchief Edging

Reversing Your Work

Materials: TATTING-CROCHET, *Size 70, 2 balls. . . . A tatting shuttle.*

* R of 5 ds, p, 5 ds, cl. Rw, sp of ⅛ inch. R of 4 ds, 3 p's sep by 4 ds, 4 ds, cl. Rw, sp of ⅛ inch. Lr of 5 ds, join to p of first r, 2 ds, 5 p's sep by 2 ds, 5 ds, cl. Rw and make another r like 2nd, joining to 3rd p of 2nd r. Rw and make another r like first, joining to last p of 3rd r. Rw and make another r like 2nd, joining to adjacent r. Rw, sp. Repeat from * for length desired, joining to first p of lr.

HANDKERCHIEF EDGING

Using a Ball Thread and a Shuttle

Some tatting designs contain chains besides rings and picots. Rings can be made only with the shuttle thread wound in a complete circle around the left hand. Chains can be made only with a thread wound halfway around the hand (Fig. 17). When rings and chains appear in

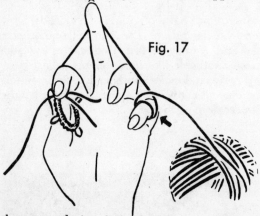

Fig. 17

the same design it is necessary to use two working threads (a shuttle thread and a ball thread). Tie end of ball thread to end of shuttle thread. When you are making a ring, use the shuttle thread in the regular manner.

When the ring is completed and you wish to make a chain, turn it so that the base of ring is held between the thumb and forefinger (see Fig. 17). Stretch the ball thread over the back of the fingers in same way as shuttle thread, but instead of making a complete circle, wind it twice around the little finger to control tension (Fig. 17). Work over the ball thread with the shuttle in the same manner as in making rings. (Picots and joinings are made in the same way as on rings.) When you have finished the chain, pull the stitches close together and put down the ball thread. Pick up the shuttle thread to make another ring.

Luncheon Set

Materials: BEST SIX CORD MERCERIZED CRO-CHET, *Size 20, 9 balls of White or Ecru . . . 3⅛ yards of linen, 36 inches wide.*

Mat 15 x 33 inches, place mats 11 x 16½ inches, and napkins, each about 16½ inches square.

PLACE MAT (Make 6) . . . Cut 6 pieces of linen, each 12½ x 18 inches. Make a ½-inch hem all around, with hemstitching.

CORNER MOTIF (Make 4 for each mat) . . . Use shuttle and ball of thread.

FLOWER . . . 1st rnd: With shuttle make r of 2 ds, 4 p's sep by 3 ds, 1 ds, cl. Tie ends securely and cut. **2nd rnd:** Tie shuttle and ball threads to one p of r. * Make a ch of 2 ds, p, 2 ds, p, 2 ds, join to next p of r. Repeat from * around. Tie ends and cut. **3rd rnd:** Tie threads to one p of previous rnd. * Make a ch of 3 ds, p, 3 ds, join to next p. Repeat from * around. Tie ends securely and cut off ball thread (8 scallops in rnd).

SPRAY . . . With shuttle, sp of ¼ inch. R of 4 ds, join to adjacent p of 3rd rnd, 8 ds, p, 4 ds, p, 8 ds, cl. Rw. Leave no sp. R of 4 ds, join to adjacent p of 3rd rnd, 8 ds, p, 4 ds, p, 8 ds, cl. Insert tip of shuttle in the sp to the right of the ¼ inch thread and fasten securely (as for joining to a p). One group of 2 rings is made.

* Rw, sp of ⅜ inch. R of 4 ds, join to first p of adjacent r, 8 ds, p, 4 ds, p, 8 ds, cl. Rw, no sp. R of 4 ds, join to first p of adjacent r, 8 ds, p, 4 ds, p, 8 ds, cl. Insert tip of shuttle in sp to the right of ⅜ inch thread and fasten securely (as for joining to a p). Repeat from * until 14 rings are made (7 groups of 2 rings each). Sp of ¼ inch. R of 4 ds, join to adjacent p, 8 ds, p, 8 ds, join to adjacent p of r at opposite side, 4 ds, cl. Tie securely and cut. A spray is now made on one side. Skip 2 scallops of flower, attach shuttle thread and make a 2nd spray at right angle to first spray, joining first 2 rings of spray to next 2 p's of flower. This completes one corner motif.

Baste corners to linen, having outer edges of corners ½ inch in from hemstitching. With a ruler and pencil, draw a line around tatted corner, touching the p's. With Mercerized Crochet (or matching embroidery thread), work buttonhole stitch around the tatted corners and over the penciled line as for cutwork, making a stitch into each p to join lace to linen. Cut away linen at back of lace.

CENTER MAT . . . Cut a piece of linen 18½ x 36 inches. Make a 1¼-inch hem all around with hemstitching. Work and insert 4 Corner Motifs as for Place Mats. Now make

LUNCHEON SET

2 more inserts as follows: Work as for Corner Motif until first Spray is completed. Skip 4 scallops of flower, attach shuttle thread: make a second Spray exactly opposite first Spray. Baste one insert at center of long side of runner, ½ inch in from hemstitching, and finish as for corners. Sew second insert at opposite long side to correspond.

NAPKIN (Make 6) . . . Cut 6 pieces of linen, each 18 inches square. Make a ½-inch hem all around with hemstitching.

NAPKIN INSERT . . . Work as for Corner Motif until first Spray is completed. Baste Insert on corner of napkin so that outer edge is ½ inch in from hemstitched edges, and finish as for other inserts.

JOSEPHINE KNOT . . . This is an ornamental ring, consisting of the first half of a double stitch made a specified number of times.

LONG PICOT . . . To make a long picot, make a longer space between double stitches.

TWO SHUTTLES . . . When you wish to work rings in two colors, two shuttles are used. The two colors (one in each shuttle) may be alternated. When this takes place you drop the shuttle which made the preceding ring, pick up the second shuttle and make a ring as before. When the rings are separated by a chain, hold the thread of the second shuttle like the ball thread in Fig. 17.

Collar Edging

Materials: TATTING-CROCHET, *2 balls*. . . . *A tatting shuttle*.

Tie shuttle and ball threads. ** With shuttle make r of 4 ds, 7 p's sep by 2 ds, 4 ds, cl. * R of 4 ds, join to last p of previous r, 2 ds, 6 p's sep by 2 ds, 4 ds, cl. Repeat from * 2 more times, joining the last r at both sides. Tie ends securely and cut (a flower made). Repeat from ** for desired length, joining center p of one r to center p of one r of previous flower.

EDGING . . . Attach threads to first free p of r opposite joining of flowers, and * make a ch of 6 ds, 7 p's sep by 2 ds, 6 ds, skip r, join to next p of next r, ch of 3 ds, 2 p's sep by 2 ds, 3 ds, join to next p of next r. Repeat from * across. Tie ends and cut.

COLLAR EDGING

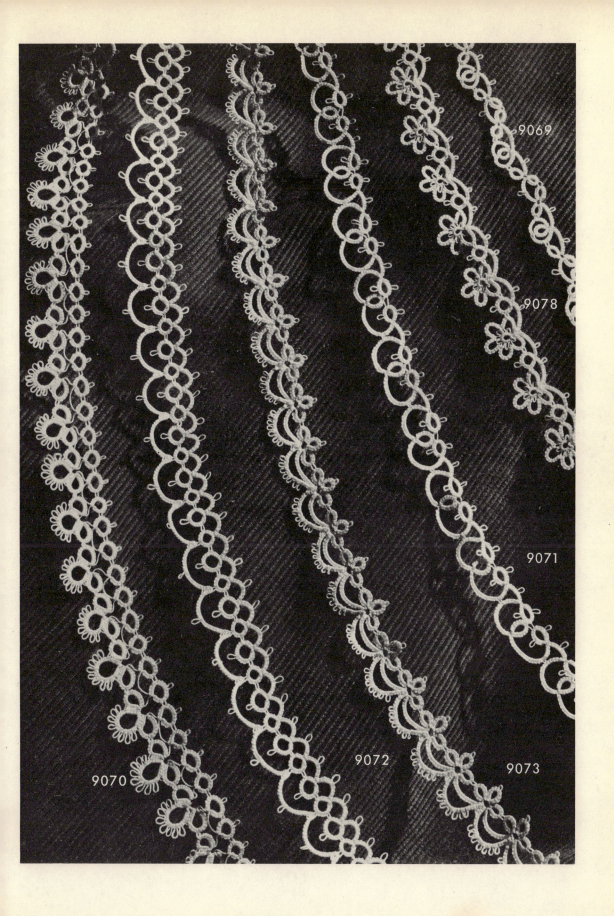

9069

9078

9071

9070

9072

9073

No. 9070 . . . . Edging

Materials: TATTING-CROCHET, *Size 70.*

Sr of 4 ds, 3 sm p's sep by 4 ds, 4 ds, cl. Rw, sp of ⅛ inch, r of 9 ds, sm p, 4 ds, sm p, 5 ds, cl. * R of 5 ds, join to last sm p of preceding r, 2 ds, 8 p's sep by 2 ds, 2 ds, sm p, 5 ds, cl. R of 5 ds, join to sm p of preceding r, 4 ds, sm p, 9 ds, cl (last 3 r's constitute a clover). Rw, sp of ⅛ inch, r of 4 ds, join to last sm p of last sr, (4 ds, sm p) twice, 4 ds, cl. Sp of ⅜ inch, sr of 4 ds, join to last sm p of preceding r, (4 ds, sm p) twice, 4 ds, cl. Rw, sp of ⅛ inch, r of 9 ds, join to sm p of last r of clover, 4 ds, sm p, 5 ds, cl. Repeat from * for length desired. Tie and cut.

No. 9072 . . . . Edging

Materials: TATTING-CROCHET, *Size 70.*

1st row: Tie ball and shuttle threads together. Sr of 4 ds, 3 sm p's sep by 4 ds, 4 ds, cl. * Rw, ch of 5 ds, p, 5 ds. Rw, lr of 4 ds, join to last sm p of preceding r, 6 ds, p, 6 ds, sm p, 4 ds, cl. Rw, ch of 5 ds, p, 5 ds. Rw, sr of 4 ds, join to sm p of preceding r, 4 ds, 2 sm p's sep by 4 ds, 4 ds, cl. Repeat from * for desired length, ending with a sr. **2nd row:** Fasten ball and shuttle threads to 2nd p of first r of 1st row. Ch of 2 ds, sm p, 9 ds, p, 9 ds, sm p, 2 ds, * skip lr, join free p of next sr of 1st row. Ch of 2 ds, join to last p of preceding ch, 9 ds, p, 9 ds, sm p, 2 ds. Repeat from * across. Tie and cut.

No. 9073 . . . . Edging

Materials: TATTING-CROCHET, *Size 70.*

1st row: Tie ball and shuttle threads together. R of 6 ds, sm p, 5 ds, sm p, 1 ds, cl. * R of 1 ds, join to sm p of preceding r, (5 ds, sm p) twice, 1 ds, cl. R of 1 ds, join to sm p of preceding r, 5 ds, sm p, 6 ds, cl (shamrock made). Rw, ch of 16 ds. Rw, r of 6 ds, join to sm p of preceding r, 5 ds, sm p, 1 ds, cl. Repeat from * for desired length. Tie and cut. **2nd row:** Fasten ball and shuttle threads to sp at base of first shamrock of 1st row. Ch of 2 ds, sm p, * 4 ds, 7 p's sep by 2 ds, 4 ds, sm p,

2 ds, join to sp at base of next shamrock. Ch of 2 ds, join to last sm p of preceding ch. Repeat from * across. Tie and cut.

No. 9071 . . . . Edging

Materials: TATTING-CROCHET, *Size 70.*

Tie ball and shuttle threads together. R of 4 ds, 3 p's sep by 4 ds, 4 ds, cl. Rw, ch of 6 ds, sm p, 14 ds. * Rw, r of 8 ds, join to 2nd p of preceding r, 8 ds, cl. Rw, ch of 14 ds, sm p, 6 ds. Rw, r of 4 ds, p, 4 ds, join to 2nd p of next-to-last r, 4 ds, p, 4 ds, cl. Ch of 4 ds, p, 4 ds. R of 4 ds, 3 p's sep by 4 ds, 4 ds, cl. Rw, ch of 6 ds, join to sm p of next-to-last ch, 14 ds. Repeat from * for desired length, ending with rw, r of 4 ds, p, 4 ds, join to 2nd p of next-to-last r, 4 ds, p, 4 ds, cl. Tie and cut.

No. 9078 . . . . Edging

Materials: TATTING-CROCHET, *Size 70.*

Tie ball and shuttle threads together. Lr of 4 ds, sm p, 4 ds, p, 4 ds, sm p, 4 ds, cl. * Rw, ch of 3 ds, p, 7 ds, sm p, 1 ds. Rw, sr of 1 ds, 9 sm p's sep by 1 ds, 1 ds, cl. Ch of 6 ds, join to last sm p of last lr, 4 ds. Skip 1 p on last sr, join to next p. (Ch of 10 ds, skip next p on same sr, join to next p) 3 times. Ch of 4 ds, sm p, 6 ds, join to base of sr (flower made). Rw, ch of 1 ds, join to p on adjoining ch, 7 ds, p, 3 ds. Rw, lr of 4 ds, join to sm p of last ch of flower, 4 ds, p, 4 ds, sm p, 4 ds, cl. Repeat from * for length desired. Tie and cut.

No. 9069 . . . . Edging

Materials: TATTING-CROCHET, *Size 70.*

Tie ball and shuttle threads together. * Sr of 6 ds, sm p, 6 ds, cl. Rw, ch of 5 ds, p, 6 ds. Rw, lr of 7 ds, sm p, 7 ds, cl. Ch of 6 ds, join to sm p of sr, 6 ds, join to sm p of lr, 6 ds, sm p, 6 ds and fasten ball thread to sp at base of lr. Rw, ch of 6 ds, p, 5 ds. Rw, sr of 6 ds, join to sm p in next-to-last ch, 6 ds, cl. Rw, sr of 6 ds, sm p, 6 ds, cl. Rw, ch of 6 ds, p, 6 ds. Rw, r of 6 ds, join to sm p of preceding r, 6 ds, cl. Rw. Repeat from * for length desired. Tie and cut.

No. 9066 . . . . Edging

Materials: TATTING-CROCHET, *Size 70, 2 balls.*

Sr of (4 ds, p) twice, 4 ds, cl and tie. * Rw, lr of 4 ds, 3 sm p's sep by 2 ds, 4 ds, sm p, 10 ds, cl and tie. Rw, sp of ¼-inch, r of 2 ds, join to 2nd p of sr, 2 ds, 6 p's sep by 2 ds, 2 ds, cl. Sp of ¼ inch and join thread to last sm p of lr. R of 4 ds, join to last p of preceding r, 4 ds, p, 4 ds, cl and tie. Repeat from * for length desired. Tie and cut.

No. 9063 . . . . Edging

Materials: TATTING-CROCHET, *Size 70, 2 balls . . . Handkerchief.*

MOTIF (Make 4) . . . Beginning at a corner, lr of 4 ds, sm p, 10 ds, p, 4 ds, p, 6 ds, sm p, 4 ds, cl. * Sr of 4 ds, join to last sm p of preceding lr, 2 ds, 9 p's sep by 2 ds, 2 ds, cl. Rw, sp of ⅜ inch, make a center r of 8 ds, sm p, 4 ds, lp, 4 ds, sm p, 8 ds, cl. Rw, sp of ¼ inch, sr of (2 ds, p) twice, 2 ds, join to center p of preceding sr, 2 ds, 8 p's sep by 2 ds, 2 ds, cl. Rw, sp of ¼ inch, center r of 8 ds, join to last sm p of previous center r, 4 ds, join to lp of first center r, 4 ds, sm p, 8 ds, cl. Rw, sp of ⅜ inch, sr of 2 ds, 4 p's sep by 2 ds, 2 ds, join to 2nd-from-last p of last sr, 2 ds, 4 p's sep by 2 ds, 2 ds, sm p, 4 ds, cl. Lr of 4 ds, join to sm p of preceding sr, 10 ds, p, 10 ds, sm p, 4 ds, cl. Sr of 4 ds, join to sm p of preceding r, 2 ds, 9 p's sep by 2 ds, 2 ds, cl. Rw, sp of ⅜ inch, make and join another center r as before. Rw, sp of ¼ inch, r of (2 ds, p) twice, 2 ds, join to center p of last sr, 2 ds, 8 p's sep by 2 ds, 2 ds, cl. Rw, sp of ¼ inch, make and join another center r. Rw, sp of ⅜ inch, r of 2 ds, 4 p's sep by 2 ds, 2 ds, join to 2nd-from-last p of last sr,

185

2 ds, 4 p's sep by 2 ds, sm p, 4 ds, cl. R of 4 ds, join to sm p of preceding r, 6 ds, p, 4 ds, p, 10 ds, sm p, 4 ds, cl. Repeat from * once more, joining the last sm p of last center r to first sm p of first center r and joining the last sm p of last sr to the first sm p of the first lr. Tie and cut.

EDGING . . . R of 2 ds, p, 2 ds, join to 2nd free p of first lr made on a motif, 2 ds, 5 p's sep by 2 ds, 2 ds, cl. * Sp of ¼ inch, r of 2 ds, p, 2 ds, join to next-to-last p of preceding r, 2 ds, 5 p's sep by 2 ds, 2 ds, cl. Repeat from * until piece reaches corresponding position on other side of handkerchief, joining 6th p on last r of edging to the first free p of 3rd lr made on next motif. Continue thus until the 4 motifs are joined. After completing the tatting, baste the corners in place. With ruler, draw lines on handkerchief just touching the picots of the corner and fasten corners to handkerchief by buttonholing over this line, catching in the picots. Whip edging in place.

No. 9079 . . . . Edging

Materials: TATTING-CROCHET, *Size 70.*

R of 9 ds, p, 7 ds, p, 2 ds, cl. * Rw, r of 9 ds, p, 3 ds, sm p, 6 ds, cl. Rw, sp of ¼ inch, r of 2 ds, join to 2nd p of next-to-last r, 2 ds, 9 p's sep by 2 ds, 2 ds, cl. Rw, sp of ¼ inch, r of 6 ds, join to sm p of next-to-last r, 3 ds, p, 9 ds, cl. Rw, r of 2 ds, join to last p of next-to-last r, 7 ds, p, 9 ds, cl. Rw, sp of ⅛ inch, r of 6 ds, cl. Rw, sp of ⅛ inch, r of 9 ds, join to p of next-to-last r, 7 ds, p, 2 ds, cl. Repeat from * for length desired. Tie and cut.

No. 9074 . . . . Edging

Materials: TATTING-CROCHET, *Size 70.*

1st row: Tie ball and shuttle threads together. * R of 2 ds, 4 sm p's sep by 2 ds, 4 ds, p, 4 ds, cl. Rw, ch of 9 ds, p, 9 ds, join to 4th sm p of preceding r. Rw and repeat from * for desired length, ending with a joined ch. Tie and cut. **2nd row:** Fasten ball and shuttle threads to 2nd sm p of first r of 1st row. Ch of 2 ds, sm p, 7 ds, sm p, 2 ds. * Join to 2nd sm p

of next r on 1st row. Ch of 2 ds, join to sm p of preceding ch, 8 ds. Rw, r of 4 ds, (sm p, 4 ds) twice, join to 2nd sm p of next r on 1st row, (4 ds, sm p) twice, 4 ds, cl. Rw, ch of 22 ds. Rw, r of 4 ds, sm p, 4 ds, join to 3rd sm p of preceding r, 4 ds, join to same p to which preceding r is joined, (4 ds, sm p) twice, 4 ds, cl. Rw, ch of 8 ds, sm p, 2 ds, join to 2nd sm p of next r on 1st row. Ch of 2 ds, join to sm p of preceding ch, 7 ds, sm p, 2 ds. Repeat from * across. Tie and cut.

No. 9075 . . . . Edging

Materials: TATTING-CROCHET, *Size 70.*

Tie ball and shuttle threads together. R of 2 ds, 7 p's sep by 2 ds, 2 ds, cl. * Rw, ch of 6 ds, p, 6 ds. Rw, r of 2 ds, 7 p's sep by 2 ds, 2 ds, cl. Rw, ch of 6 ds, join to 6th p of next-to-last r, 5 ds, sm p, 1 ds. Rw, r of 7 ds, join to 6th p of preceding r, 3 ds, (p, 5 ds) twice, cl. Rw, r of 1 ds, join to sm p on preceding ch, 9 ds, p, 9 ds, sm p, 1 ds, cl. Rw, ch of 1 ds, join to sm p of preceding r, 14 ds. Rw, r of (2 ds, p) twice, 2 ds, join to last p of next-to-last r, 2 ds, 4 p's sep by 2 ds, 2 ds, cl. Rw, ch of 14 ds, sm p, 1 ds. Rw, r of 5 ds, join to 5th p of preceding r, 5 ds, p, 3 ds, p, 7 ds, cl. Rw, r of 1 ds, join to sm p on preceding ch, 9 ds, p, 9 ds, sm p, 1 ds, cl. Ch of 1 ds, join to sm p of preceding r, 5 ds, p, 6 ds. Rw, r of 2 ds, p, 2 ds, join to last p of next-to-last r, 2 ds, 5 p's sep by 2 ds, 2 ds, cl. Ch of 6 ds, p, 6 ds. Rw, r of 2 ds, p, 2 ds, join to p on next-to-last ch, 2 ds, 5 p's sep by 2 ds, 2 ds, cl. Repeat from * for desired length. Tie and cut.

No. 9077 . . . . Edging

Materials: TATTING-CROCHET, *Size 70.*

Tie ball and shuttle threads together. R of 3 ds, 6 p's sep by 3 ds, 3 ds, cl. Rw, ch of 1 ds, sm p, 7 ds, sm p, 2 ds. ** Rw, r of 6 ds, join to last p of preceding r, 2 ds, p, 8 ds, cl. Rw, r of 2 ds, join to sm p of preceding ch, 6 ds, p, 6 ds, sm p, 2 ds, cl. R of 2 ds, join to sm p of preceding r, 6 ds, p, 8 ds, cl and tie over closings of both r's (clover made). Rw, ch of 11 ds. R of 10 ds, p, 2 ds, sm p, 8 ds, cl. Ch of 9 ds, sm p, 3 ds. For round motif, rw, r of 7 ds, sm p, 3 ds, lp, 3 ds, sm p, 7 ds, cl. * Rw, ch of 3 ds,

4 p's sep by 3 ds, 3 ds. Rw, r of 7 ds, join to sm p of preceding r, 3 ds, join to lp of preceding r, 3 ds, sm p, 7 ds, cl. Repeat from * 2 more times. Rw, ch of 3 ds, 4 p's sep by 3 ds, 3 ds. Rw, r of 7 ds, join to sm p of preceding r, 3 ds, join to same lp, 3 ds, join to sm p of first r of round motif, 7 ds, cl. Rw, ch of 3 ds, p, 3 ds, join to free p of 3rd r of clover, (3 ds, p) twice, 3 ds. Join to base of first r of round motif, thus completing it. Ch of 3 ds, join to sm p of adjacent ch, 9 ds. R of 8 ds, join to sm p of adjacent r, 2 ds, p, 10 ds, cl. Ch of 11 ds. Rw, r of 8 ds, join to 3rd p on first ch of preceding round motif, 6 ds, sm p, 2 ds, cl. R of 2 ds, join to sm p of preceding r, 6 ds, p, 6 ds, sm p, 2 ds, cl and tie. Rw, r of 8 ds, p, 2 ds, p, 6 ds, cl (clover made). Rw, ch of 2 ds, join to sm p of next-to-last r, 7 ds, sm p, 1 ds. Rw, r of 3 ds, join to 2nd p of preceding r, 3 ds, 5 p's sep by 3 ds, 3 ds, cl. Rw, ch of 1 ds, join to sm p of preceding ch, 7 ds, sm p, 2 ds. Repeat from ** for length desired. Tie and cut.

No. 9080 . . . . Edging

Materials: TATTING-CROCHET, *Size 70.*

1st row: Sr of 2 ds, 5 sm p's sep by 2 ds, 2 ds, cl. Sp of ¼ inch, ** r of 5 ds, join to next-to-last sm p on preceding sr, 5 ds, p, 5 ds, sm p, 5 ds, cl. Sp of ½ inch, make a flower as follows: R of 2 ds, sm p, 5 ds, join to sm p of preceding r, 5 ds, sm p, 2 ds, close to within 1/16 inch (this closing will be referred to as "part cl"). * R of 2 ds, join to last sm p of preceding r, (5 ds, sm p) twice, 2 ds, part cl. Repeat from * 2 more times. R of 2 ds, join to sm p of preceding r, 5 ds, sm p, 5 ds, join to first sm p of first r of flower, 2 ds, part cl. Join to base of first r of flower. Join thread to sm p joining first and 5th r's of flower. Sp of ½ inch, r of 5 ds, join to sm p of preceding r, 5 ds, p, 5 ds, sm p, 5 ds, cl. Sp of ¼ inch, r of 2 ds, sm p, 2 ds, join to sm p of preceding r, 2 ds, 3 sm p's sep by 2 ds, 2 ds, cl. Repeat from ** for length desired, ending with a sr. Now work along edge of 1st row as follows: **2nd row:** * Sp of ⅜ inch, join thread to sp at base of next r. R of 10 ds, sm p, 6 ds, cl and tie over closing, drawing thread through between the 2 sp-threads

just preceding the r. Sp of ½ inch, r of 3 ds, join to sm p of preceding r, 7 ds, p, 7 ds, sm p, 3 ds, cl. Sp of ⅜ inch and join to base of next r of 1st row. R of 6 ds, join to sm p of preceding r, 10 ds, cl and tie. Sp of ⅜ inch and join to base of next sr. Repeat from * across. Tie and cut.

No. 9076 . . . . Edging

Materials: TATTING-CROCHET, *Size 70.*

1st row: Tie ball and shuttle threads together. ** Sr of 3 ds, 6 p's sep by 3 ds, 3 ds, cl. Rw, ch of 3 ds, 9 p's sep by 3 ds, 3 ds, sm p, 3 ds. Rw, sp of ⅛ inch, lr of 3 ds, sm p, 3 ds, 7 p's sep by 3 ds, 3 ds, sm p, 3 ds, cl. * Lr of 3 ds, join to last sm p of preceding r, 3 ds, 7 p's sep by 3 ds, 3 ds, sm p, 3 ds, cl and tie to base of preceding r. Repeat from * once more. Lr of 3 ds, join to sm p of preceding r, 3 ds, 7 p's sep by 3 ds, 3 ds, join to first sm p of first lr, 3 ds, cl and tie to base of preceding r. Tie thread over the closing of first r to complete circle and carry thread to sm p joining the first and 4th lr's and fasten (clover made). Rw, ch of 3 ds, join to sm p of preceding ch, 3 ds, 9 p's sep by 3 ds, 3 ds (scallop complete). Rw, repeat from ** for length desired, ending with a sr and allowing 1½ inches for each scallop. Rw, ch of 3 ds, 12 p's sep by 3 ds, 3 ds. Now work along edge of 1st row as follows: **2nd row:** Rw, r of 4 ds, join to next-to-last p of last sr of 1st row, 6 ds, p, 3 ds, join to 4th p of adjacent r of next clover, 7 ds, cl. Rw, ch of 3 ds, 5 p's sep by 3 ds, 3 ds, join to 4th p of next r of same clover, * 3 ds, 9 p's sep by 3 ds, 3 ds, join to 4th p of next r of same clover, 3 ds, 5 p's sep by 3 ds. Rw, r of 7 ds, join to 4th p of next r of same clover, 3 ds, p, 6 ds, join to 2nd p of next sr, 4 ds, cl. Rw, ch of 3 ds, join to last p of preceding ch, (3 ds, p) twice, 3 ds. Rw, r of 4 ds, join to next-to-last p of last sr, 6 ds, p, 3 ds, join to 4th p of adjacent r of next clover, 7 ds, cl. Rw, ch of 3 ds, join to last p of preceding ch, 3 ds, 4 p's sep by 3 ds, 3 ds, join to 4th p of next r of same clover. Repeat from * across, ending with ch of 3 ds, join to last p of preceding ch, 11 p's sep by 3 ds, 3 ds. Tie to base of first sr made and cut.

No. 9085 . . . . Edging

Materials: PEARL COTTON, *Size 5, 2 balls* . . . A *Turkish towel.*

Tie ball and shuttle threads together. R of 4 ds, p, 8 ds, sm p, 12 ds, cl. Rw, ch of 3 ds, 5 p's sep by 3 ds, 3 ds. Fasten to sm p on preceding r. * R of 12 ds, sm p, 12 ds, cl. Rw, ch of (3 ds, p) twice, 3 ds. On outside of curve of ch make r of 7 ds, p, 5 ds, lp, 2 ds, sm p, 10 ds, cl. Continue ch with (3 ds, p) twice, 3 ds. Fasten to sm p on next-to-last r. R of 12 ds, sm p, 12 ds, cl. Rw, ch of 3 ds, 5 p's sep by 3 ds, 3 ds. Fasten to sm p on preceding r. R of 12 ds, p, 2 ds, sm p, 10 ds, cl. Rw, ch of (3 ds, p) twice, 3 ds. On outside curve of ch make r of 10 ds, join to sm p on 2nd-from-last r, 2 ds, join to lp on same r, 2 ds, sm p, 10 ds, cl. Continue ch with (3 ds, p) twice, 3 ds. Rw, r of 10 ds, join to sm p on next-to-last r, 2 ds, join to p on same r, 12 ds, cl. Rw, r of 12 ds, sm p, 12 ds, cl. Rw, ch of 3 ds, 5 p's sep by 3 ds, 3 ds. Fasten to sm p of preceding r. R of 12 ds, sm p, 12 ds, cl. Rw, ch of (3 ds, p) twice, 3 ds. On outside of curve of ch make r of 10 ds, join to sm p of 3rd-from-last r, 2 ds, join to lp, 5 ds, p, 7 ds, cl. Continue ch with (3 ds, p) twice, 3 ds and fasten to sm p on next-to-last r. R of 8 ds, p, 4 ds, sm p, 12 ds, cl. Rw, ch of 3 ds, 5 p's sep by 3 ds, 3 ds. Fasten to sm p on preceding r. Rw, ch of 3 ds, p, 3 ds. R of 4 ds, p, 8 ds, sm p, 12 ds, cl. Rw, ch of 3 ds, join to last p on next-to-last ch, 3 ds, 4 p's sep by 3 ds, 3 ds and fasten to sm p on preceding r. Repeat from * for length desired. Sew to towel as illustrated.

No. 9096 . . . . Edging

Materials: PEARL COTTON, *Size 5, 1 ball each of Dusty Pink and Hunter's Green . . . A Turkish towel.*

FLOWER . . . With Pink, r of 4 ds, sm p, 8 ds, p, 8 ds, sm p, 4 ds, cl and tie. * R of 4 ds, join to last sm p of preceding r, 8 ds, p, 8 ds, sm p, 4 ds, cl and tie. Repeat from * 3 more times, joining the 5th r to the first sm p of the first r. Tie and cut. For a 16½-inch towel make 9 flowers.

LEAF . . . Tie Green ball and Green shuttle threads together. R of 3 ds, sm p, 1 ds, p, 1 ds, sm p, 3 ds, cl. Rw, ch of 6 ds, p, 1 ds, sm p, 1 ds and join to last sm p on preceding r. Ch of 1 ds, join to sm p on preceding ch, 4 ds, p, 4 ds, sm p, 1 ds and fasten to first sm p on preceding r. Ch of 1 ds, join to sm p of preceding ch, 1 ds, join to a p of a Flower, 6 ds and fasten at base of preceding r.

STEM . . . * Ch of 5 ds. Rw, r of 6 ds, p, 6 ds, cl. Rw, ch of 5 ds. Rw and make another Leaf, joining it to the p on the 2nd r of the same Flower. Rw, complete stem with ch of 10 ds, 5 p's sep by 2 ds, 10 ds. Make another Leaf just like the first, joining the 2nd ch to the p on the 2nd ch of the preceding Leaf. Repeat from * until all Flowers are joined.

No. 9102 . . . . Edging

Materials: BEST SIX CORD MERCERIZED CROCHET, *Size 30.*

CENTER MOTIF . . . **1st rnd:** R of 1 ds, 7 p's sep by 1 ds, 1 ds, cl. Leave thread ends long enough to form the 8th p, tie and cut. **2nd rnd:** Tie ball and shuttle threads together. R of 8 ds, sm p, 2 ds, join to p of center r, 2 ds, sm p, 8 ds, cl. * Rw, ch of 9 ds, p, 9 ds. Rw, r of 8 ds, join to last sm p of preceding r, 2 ds, join to next p of center r, 2 ds, sm p, 8 ds, cl. Repeat from * around, joining the 8th r to the first sm p of the first r and fastening the 8th ch at the base of the first r. Tie and cut. **3rd rnd:** R of 10 ds, join to p on ch of preceding rnd, 2 ds, sm p, 8 ds, cl. Rw, ch of 3 ds, sm p, 8 ds, p, 8 ds, sm p, 1 ds. * Rw, r of 8 ds, join to sm p of preceding r, 2 ds, join to same p on preceding rnd, 2 ds, sm p, 8 ds, cl. Rw, ch of 1 ds, join to sm p on preceding ch, 8 ds, p, 8 ds, sm p, 3 ds. Rw, r of 8 ds, join to sm p on preceding r, 2 ds, join to same p on preceding rnd, 10 ds, cl. R of 10 ds, join to p on next ch of preceding rnd, 2 ds, sm p, 8 ds, cl. Rw, ch of 3 ds, join to sm p on preceding ch, 8 ds, p, 8 ds, sm p, 1 ds. Repeat from * around, joining the last ch to the first sm p of the first ch and fastening threads at base of the first r. Tie and cut.

SIDE MOTIF . . . **1st rnd:** Work same as 1st rnd of Center Motif. **2nd rnd:** R of 6 ds, sm p, 2 ds, join to p on center r, 2 ds, sm p, 6 ds, cl. * Rw, ch of 8 ds, p, 8 ds. Rw, r of 6 ds, join to last sm p of preceding r, 2 ds, join to next p on center r, 2 ds, sm p, 6 ds, cl. Repeat from * around, joining the 8th r to the first sm p of the first r and fastening last ch at base of first r, but do not cut.

To complete, ch of 8 ds, p, 4 ds, p, 6 ds. Rw, r of 10 ds, join to p on first ch of preceding rnd, 8 ds, sm p, 2 ds, cl. R of 2 ds, join to sm p on preceding r, 8 ds, p, 10 ds, cl. Rw, ch of (7 ds, p) twice, 7 ds. Rw, r of 5 ds, join to p on a ch of Center Motif, 5 ds, p, 2 ds, sm p, 8 ds, cl. Rw, ch of 6 ds, join to p of next-to-last r, 6 ds, p, 6 ds. Rw, r of 8 ds, join to sm p of preceding r, 2 ds, join to p of same r, 2 ds, sm p, 8 ds, cl. Rw, ch of (6 ds, p) twice, 6 ds. Rw, r of 8 ds, join to sm p of preceding r, 2 ds, join to p of next-to-last r, 5 ds, join to next p on Center Motif, 5 ds, cl. Rw, ch of 9 ds, p, 9 ds. Rw, r of 10 ds, join to last p on next-to-last ch, 10 ds, cl. Rw, r of 10 ds, sm p, 10 ds, cl. Rw, ch of 10 ds, skip 1 p on Side Motif, join to next p on Side Motif, 10 ds and fasten to sm p on preceding r. Rw, ch of 8 ds, p, 8 ds. Rw, r of 10 ds, join to next p on Side Motif, 2 ds, sm p, 8 ds, cl. Rw, ch of 8 ds, p, 8 ds. Rw, r of 8 ds, join to sm p of preceding r, 2 ds, join to same p of Side Motif, 10 ds, cl. * Rw, ch of 8 ds, p, 8 ds. Rw, r of 10 ds, p, 2 ds, sm p, 8 ds, cl. Rw, ch of 8 ds, p, 8 ds. Rw, r of 8 ds, join to sm p of preceding r, 2 ds, join to p of same r, 10 ds, cl. Repeat from * for length desired. Work other side to correspond.

Place tatting on end of towel and baste firmly to material. With a pencil, draw a line on the towel, just touching the picots. Buttonhole stitch over line, catching in picots. Cut away fabric underneath.

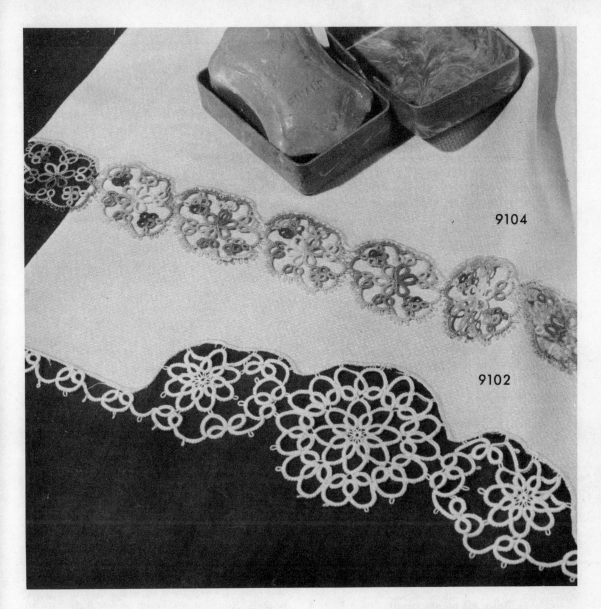

No. 9104 . . . . Edging

Materials: TATTING-CROCHET, *Size 70, 2 balls of Shaded Greens and 1 ball each of Shaded Dark Blues, Shaded Dark Pinks and Shaded Yellows . . . A linen guest towel.*

FIRST MOTIF . . . Beginning with large flower in center of Motif, with Pink, make r of 5 ds, sm p, 7 ds, sm p, 3 ds, sm p, 10 ds, sm p, 5 ds, cl. R of 5 ds, join to last sm p of preceding r, 10 ds, sm p, 3 ds, sm p, 7 ds, sm p, 5 ds, cl. R of 5 ds, join to sm p of preceding r, 10 ds, sm p, 10 ds, sm p, 5 ds, cl. R of 5 ds, join to last sm p of preceding r, 7 ds, sm p, 3 ds, sm p, 10 ds, sm p, 5 ds, cl. R of 5 ds, join to last sm p

of preceding r, 10 ds, sm p, 3 ds, sm p, 7 ds, sm p, 5 ds, cl. R of 5 ds, join to last sm p of preceding r, 10 ds, sm p, 10 ds, join to first sm p of first r, 5 ds, cl. Tie and cut. To make small flower, with Blue, make r of 4 ds, sm p, 8 ds, sm p, 4 ds, cl. R of 4 ds, join to 2nd sm p of first r, 8 ds, sm p, 4 ds, cl. R of 4 ds, join to sm p of preceding r, 4 ds, join to the single p of 3rd r of large flower, 4 ds, sm p, 4 ds, cl. R of 4 ds, join to sm p of preceding r, 8 ds, join to first sm p of first r of this flower, 4 ds, cl. Tie and cut. Make another small flower and join it in the same way to the 6th r of the large flower. Using Green for the edge of the Motif, tie ball and shuttle threads together. * R of 6 ds, join to p between first and 2nd r's of Blue

191

flower (having wrong side of work upper-most), 6 ds, cl. Rw, ch of 3 ds, 5 p's sep by 3 ds, 3 ds. Rw, r of 9 ds, join to first free p of next free r of large flower, 3 ds, sm p, 6 ds, cl. Rw, ch of 3 ds, 3 p's sep by 3 ds, 3 ds. Rw, r of 6 ds, join to sm p of preceding r, 3 ds, join to next p of same r of large flower, 9 ds, cl. Rw, ch of 3 ds, 5 p's sep by 3 ds, 3 ds. Rw, r of 9 ds, join to next p of next r of large flower, 3 ds, sm p, 6 ds, cl. Rw, ch of 3 ds, 3 p's sep by 3 ds, 3 ds. Rw, r of 6 ds, join to sm p of preceding r, 3 ds, join to next p of same r of large flower, 9 ds, cl. Rw, ch of 3 ds, 5 p's sep by 3 ds, 3 ds. Rw, r of 6 ds, join to p between the first and 4th r's of the next Blue flower, 6 ds, cl. Rw, ch of 3 ds, 5 p's sep by 3 ds, 3 ds. Repeat from * once more, joining the last ch at base of first r.

SECOND MOTIF . . . Making large flower with Yellow, instead of Pink, work exactly the same as First Motif, joining them in center of next-to-last ch as follows: Ch of (3 ds, p) twice, 3 ds, join to 3rd p of 5th ch of preceding Motif, (3 ds, p) twice, 3 ds.

Make necessary number of Motifs, alternating colors of large flowers and joining them as Second Motif was joined to First Motif. Sew to edge of towel.

No. 9068 . . . . Edging

Materials: TATTING-CROCHET, *Size 70, 2 balls of Shaded Rose . . . Handkerchief.*

Make all picots small.

Beginning work at one side of the corner motif and, working toward the outer edge, tie ball and shuttle threads together. R of 15 ds, p, 7 ds, p, 8 ds, cl. Ch of 5 ds, 6 p's sep by 5 ds, 5 ds. Rw, r of 5 ds, 5 p's sep by 5 ds, 5 ds, cl. Rw, ch of 5 ds, (p, 5 ds) twice. Rw, r of 5 ds, 3 p's sep by 5 ds, 5 ds, join to last p of first r, 5 ds, p, 5 ds, cl. R of 5 ds, join to last p of preceding r, 5 ds, join to first p of first r, 5 ds, 3 p's sep by 5 ds, 5 ds, cl. R of 5 ds, join to last p of preceding r, 5 ds, 4 p's sep by 5 ds, 5 ds, cl.

Rw, ch of 5 ds, join to last p of preceding ch, 5 ds, p, 5 ds, join to 4th p of 2nd r, 5 ds, 6 p's sep by 5 ds, 5 ds. Rw, r of 8 ds, join to first free p of preceding r, 7 ds, join to adjacent free p in next-to-last r, 15 ds, cl. Rw, ch of 5 ds, 5 p's sep by 5 ds, 5 ds. Rw, r of 5 ds, 5 p's sep by 5 ds, 5 ds, cl. R of 5 ds, join to last p of preceding r, 5 ds, 4 p's sep by 5 ds, 5 ds, cl. Rw, r of 5 ds, join to last p on preceding ch, 5 ds, 4 p's sep by 5 ds, 5 ds, cl. Ch of 5 ds, join to last p of next-to-last r, (5 ds, p) twice, 5 ds and fasten to 3rd free p of preceding r. Reverse curve of ch, ch of 5 ds, 7 p's sep by 5 ds, 5 ds, p, 1 ds. Reverse curve of ch, ch of (5 ds, p) twice, 5 ds, join to first free p of next-to-last r, 5 ds, join to next p of same r. Rw, r of 5 ds, p, 5 ds, join to p in ch immediately preceding the reversing of the curve in the last ch, 5 ds, 3 p's sep by 5 ds, 5 ds, cl. Rw, r of 5 ds, join to the remaining free p of the center r, 5 ds, 4 p's sep by 5 ds, 5 ds, cl. Rw, ch of 5 ds, join to last p of next-to-last r, 5 ds, 4 p's sep by 5 ds, 5 ds and fasten at base of first r. This completes the central portion of the corner motif.

Completing one side of the corner, rw, ch of 5 ds, join to first p of first ch, 5 ds, 4 p's sep by 5 ds, 5 ds. Rw, r of 5 ds, 5 p's sep by 5 ds, 5 ds, cl. Rw, ch of (5 ds, p) twice, 5 ds. R of (5 ds, p) twice, 5 ds, join to 3rd p of last ch on central motif, (5 ds, p) twice, 5 ds, cl. R of 5 ds, join to last p of preceding r, 5 ds, 4 p's sep by 5 ds, 5 ds, cl. Make another r just like the one just completed. Rw, ch of 5 ds, join to last p of preceding ch, 5 ds, p, 5 ds, join to 4th p of 4th-from-last r, (5 ds, p) twice, 5 ds. * Rw, r of 5 ds, 5 p's sep by 5 ds, 5 ds, cl. Ch of 5 ds, p, 5 ds. Rw, r of (5 ds, p) twice, 5 ds, join to 3rd p of next-to-last r, (5 ds, p) twice, 5 ds, cl. Make another r of 5 ds, 5 p's sep by 5 ds, 5 ds, cl. Rw, ch of 5 ds, p, 5 ds, join to 4th p of 3rd-from-last r, (5 ds, p) twice, 5 ds. Repeat from * around handkerchief, at the end finishing the other side of the corner with a group of 3 r's and a ch to correspond with first half.

Sew edging around handkerchief in usual way and, after basting corners in place, draw line on material just touching picots and buttonhole over line, catching in picots. Cut away material beneath corner motif.

No. 9067 . . . . Edging

Materials: TATTING-CROCHET, *Size 70, 3 balls.*

Tie ball and shuttle threads together. R of (7 ds, sm p) twice, 7 ds, cl. * Rw, ch of 7 ds, lr of 9 ds, p, 9 ds, sm p, 6 ds, cl. Ch of 7 ds, sm p, 1 ds. Rw, r of 7 ds, join to p of next-to-last r, 11 ds, sm p, 3 ds, cl. R of 3 ds, join to p of preceding r, 11 ds, p, 11 ds, sm p, 3 ds, cl. R of 3 ds, join to last p of preceding r, 11 ds, sm p, 7 ds, cl. Rw, ch of 1 ds, join to sm p of preceding ch, 7 ds, join to sm p of lr, 7 ds. Rw, r of 7 ds, join to p of preceding r, 7 ds, sm p, 7 ds, cl. Repeat from * for length desired. Tie and cut.

No. 9064 . . . . Edging

Materials: TATTING-CROCHET, *Size 70, 2 balls . . . Handkerchief.*

CORNER . . . First make the 5 flower motifs. R of 3 ds, sm p, 5 ds, p, 5 ds, sm p, 3 ds, cl. R of 3 ds, join to last sm p of preceding r, 5 ds, p, 5 ds, sm p, 3 ds, cl. Make 2 more r's the same way, joining the last sm p of the 4th r to the first sm p of the first r. Tie and cut—a small flower made. R of 4 ds, sm p, 6 ds, p, 6 ds, sm p, 4 ds, cl. Make 3 more r's same as this, joining them as r's of small flower were joined —a large flower made. Tie and cut. Make 3 more large flowers. Next make a scroll. Begin-

9068

9067

ning at the inner corner, tie ball and shuttle threads together. R of 7 ds, join to p of first large flower, 5 ds, p, 12 ds, cl. Rw and, curving ch away from flower, make ch of 9 ds, p, 11 ds. Rw, r of 14 ds, join to p of 2nd large flower, 6 ds, cl. Join to p of small flower. Reversing curve of ch, ch of 14 ds, join to next p of small flower, r of 6 ds, join to next p of 2nd large flower, 14 ds, cl. Rw, ch of 9 ds. Rw, r of 12 ds, p, 12 ds, cl. R of 4 ds, sm p, 6 ds, cl. Tie and cut. Make another scroll to correspond on the other side of this piece, joining to next p on the first large flower, then joining the first ch of the 2nd scroll to the p in the first ch of the first scroll. Join 3rd large flower to correspond with 2nd large flower. End by fastening the last ch of the 2nd scroll to the sm p of the last r on the first scroll. R of 12 ds, p, 12 ds, cl. Tie and cut.

SIDE SCROLL . . . R of (5 ds, p) twice, 10 ds, cl. Rw, ch of 18 ds and fasten to sm p between the 2 inner r's of the 2nd large flower. Carry thread on wrong side of work to the opposite p, fasten and make ch of 12 ds, p, 6 ds. Rw, r of 16 ds, cl. Rw, ch of 20 ds. Rw, r of 10 ds, p, 8 ds, sm p, 2 ds, cl. R of 2 ds, join to sm p of preceding r, 2 ds, (p, 4 ds) 3 times, cl. Rw, ch of 20 ds, sm p, 4 ds, sm p, 6 ds. R of 10 ds, p, 4 ds, join to 2nd p of first r of this scroll, 6 ds, cl. Tie and cut. Make another Side Scroll to correspond on other side. To complete corner, fasten ball and shuttle threads to sp at base of the r of 16 ds on the first Side Scroll. Ch of 20 ds. Rw, r of 4 ds, p, 4 ds, join to p in 2nd ch of Side Scroll, 4 ds, p, 2 ds, sm p, 2 ds, cl. R of 2 ds, join to sm p of preceding r, 8 ds, (p, 5 ds) twice, cl. Rw, ch of 20 ds. Rw, r of 4 ds, p, 4 ds, join to last p of preceding r, 4 ds, p, 2 ds, sm p, 2 ds, cl. R of 2 ds, join to sm p of preceding r, 4 ds, join to p on last r of first scroll, 4 ds, join to a p of the remaining large flower, 10 ds, cl. Rw, (ch of 20 ds, join to p in next r of same flower) twice, ch of 20 ds.

9064

Rw, r of 10 ds, join to last p on same flower, 4 ds, join to p in last r of 2nd scroll, 4 ds, sm p, 2 ds, cl. R of 2 ds, join to sm p of preceding r, 2 ds, 3 p's sep by 4 ds, 4 ds, cl. Rw, ch of 20 ds. Rw, r of 5 ds, join to 2nd p of preceding r, 5 ds, p, 8 ds, sm p, 2 ds, cl. R of 2 ds, join to sm p of preceding r, 2 ds, p, 4 ds, join to p in 2nd ch of the Side Scroll, 4 ds, p, 4 ds, cl. Rw, ch of 20 ds, fasten at base of r of 16 ds. Tie and cut.

To complete the corner and start the edging, r of (5 ds, p) twice, 10 ds, cl. Ch of 4 ds, join to 2nd sm p of last ch of Side Scroll, 4 ds, join to first sm p of same ch, 20 ds. R of 10 ds, join to 2nd p of preceding r, 8 ds, sm p, 2 ds, cl. * R of 2 ds, join to sm p of preceding r, 2 ds, (p, 4 ds) 3 times, cl. Rw, ch of 20 ds. Rw, r of 5 ds, join to 2nd p of preceding r, 5 ds, p, 8 ds, sm p, 2 ds, cl. For edge, repeat from * for re-

quired length. Finish with a ch of 20 ds, join to sm p of Side Scroll, 4 ds, join to next sm p, 4 ds. R of 10 ds, join to p of preceding r, 5 ds, p, 5 ds, cl.

Baste corner to handkerchief, mark material with a pencil just touching picots and work buttonhole stitch over this line, catching in corresponding picots. Cut away material from under corner.

No. 9105 . . . . . Guest Towel

Materials: TATTING-CROCHET, *Size 70, 1 ball each of Shaded Yellows, Shaded Turquoise, Shaded Fuchsia and Shaded Greens . . . A linen guest towel.*

Leave all thread-ends long enough to be threaded into a needle and, after motif has been basted to towel, pull the thread ends through to the wrong side and fasten securely.

SPRAY . . . Begin design with Large Flower at center. Using Yellow, tie ball and shuttle threads together. R of 4 ds, sm p, 2 ds, 6 lp's sep by 2 ds, 2 ds, sm p, 2 ds, 6 lp's sep by 2 ds, 2 ds, sm p, 4 ds, cl. Rw, ch of 5 ds, join by shuttle thread to last sm p of r, 5 ds, sm p, * 5 ds, 3 p's sep by 5 ds, 5 ds, join to center sm p of r, 5 ds, 3 p's sep by 5 ds, 5 ds, sm p, 5 ds, join by shuttle thread to first sm p of r, 5 ds and fasten at base of r. This completes the first petal. Rw, make another r. Rw, ch of 5 ds, join by shuttle thread to last sm p of preceding r, 5 ds, join to sm p of preceding ch. Repeat from * once more. Complete the 3rd petal in the same manner as the 2nd petal and make the 4th petal like the others, joining it by the last p in the ch to the first petal. Tie and cut.

MEDIUM FLOWER . . . With Fuchsia, make r of 4 ds, sm p, 8 ds, p, 8 ds, sm p, 4 ds, cl. R of 4 ds, join to last sm p of preceding r, 8 ds, p, 8 ds, sm p, 4 ds, cl. Make 3 more r's same as last r. R of 4 ds, join to sm p of preceding r, 8 ds, join to p at left center of ch on Large Flower, 8 ds, join to first sm p of first r, 4 ds, cl, tie and cut. Make another Medium Flower with Fuchsia and join in the same way to center p on left part of ch on Large Flower, having a whole petal of Large Flower free between Medium Flowers. Make another Medium Flower with Turquoise and join it to the center p on the right part of ch of next petal on Large Flower.

SMALL FLOWER . . . With Fuchsia, r of 4 ds, sm p, 8 ds, sm p, 4 ds, cl. R of 4 ds, join to last p of preceding r, 8 ds, sm p, 4 ds, cl. Make another r same as last r. R of 4 ds, join to last p of preceding r, 8 ds, join to first p of first r, 4 ds, cl. Tie and cut. Make another flower same as this, using Turquoise.

STEMS AND LEAVES . . . First make the stem and leaf at the top of the Large Flower. Use Green ball and shuttle threads fastened together and to the p between the 4th and first petals of the Large Flower. Ch of 5 ds, r of 15 ds, p, 15 ds, cl. Tie and cut. Next, fasten ball and shuttle threads to center p of next ch to the right of stem and leaf just made, ch of 3 ds, fasten to p joining adjacent r's of the

Medium Fuchsia Flower. Carry threads on wrong side of work to p joining the 3rd and 4th r's of the same flower, ch of 6 ds. R of 14 ds, p, 14 ds, cl. Tie and cut. Now fasten ball and shuttle threads to p between next 2 r's of same flower, ch of 5 ds. R of 14 ds, p, 14 ds, cl. Rw and make another r in the same way. Ch of 9 ds, join to p between r's of Small Turquoise Flower, carry threads on wrong side of work to p between opposite 2 r's of same flower. Ch of 5 ds. R of 14 ds, p, 14 ds, cl. Tie and cut. For the lower spray, begin with the stem and leaf to the left of the long spray. Using Green as before, tie ball and shuttle threads together and fasten to first p of ch in 3rd petal of Large Flower, ch of 10 ds, fasten to first free p of Fuchsia Medium Flower, r of 14 ds, p, 14 ds, cl. Tie and cut. For the long spray, fasten ball and shuttle threads to p joining the next 2 petals of the Large Flower. Curving chain to left, ch of 9 ds, join to first free p of Turquoise Medium Flower. Reverse curve and make a ch of 18 ds. R of 14 ds, p, 14 ds, cl. Make another r the same way. Reverse curve and make another ch of 10 ds. Make another pair of r's like those just made. Reverse curve, make a ch of 10 ds, join to p between the 2 r's of the Fuchsia Small Flower. Carry thread to p between opposite 2 r's, fasten. Ch of 5 ds. R of 14 ds, p, 14 ds, cl. Tie and cut. For the 3rd spray, fasten ball and shuttle threads to last p of ch of 2nd petal of Large Flower, ch of 5 ds, join to p between adjacent r's of the Turquoise Medium Flower. Carry thread to p between opposite 2 r's of same flower, fasten. Ch of 5 ds, r of 14 ds, p, 14 ds, cl. Tie and cut. Pin spray in desired position on towel. Tack all picots to towel.

No. 9112 . . . . . **Guest Towel**

Materials: TATTING-CROCHET, *Size 70, 1 ball each of Green, Shaded Lavenders, Shaded Pinks and Shaded Yellows . . . A fingertip towel.*

LARGE FLOWER . . . Tie ball and shuttle threads together. With Lavender, make r of 3 ds, (sm p, 9 ds) twice, sm p, 3 ds, cl. Ch of 3 ds, join by shuttle thread to last p of r, 1 ds, (sm p, 6 ds) twice, p, 6 ds, join by shuttle thread to next p on r, 12 ds, sm p, 6 ds, sm p,

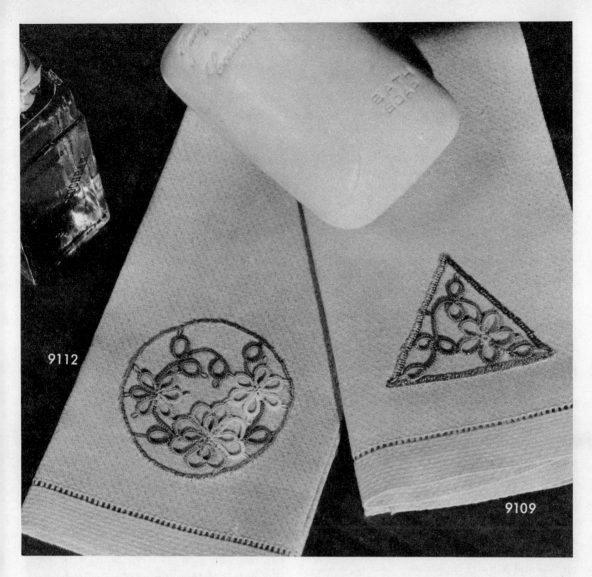

9112

9109

1 ds, join by shuttle thread to first p of r, 3 ds, fasten at base of r (petal made). * R of 3 ds, (sm p, 9 ds) twice, sm p, 3 ds, cl. Ch of 3 ds, join by shuttle thread to last p of last r, 1 ds, join by ball thread to last sm p of preceding ch, 6 ds, join by ball thread to next p of same ch, 12 ds, join by shuttle thread to next p of last r, 6 ds, p, (6 ds, sm p) twice, 1 ds, join by shuttle thread to next p of same r, 3 ds, fasten at base of r. Repeat from * 2 more times, joining last p's of last ch to free p's of first ch. Tie and cut, leaving a length of thread for sewing.

SMALL FLOWER . . . With Pink, make r of 3 ds, sm p, 9 ds, join to a free p on Large Flower, 9 ds, sm p, 3 ds, cl. * R of 3 ds, join to last p of last r, 9 ds, p, 9 ds, sm p, 3 ds, cl and

tie. Repeat from * 4 more times, joining last p of last r to first p of first r. Tie and cut, leaving a length of thread for sewing. Make another Small Flower, using Yellow and joining it to next free p on Large Flower (to the right of Pink Flower).

LEAVES AND STEMS . . . Attach ball and shuttle (or 2 shuttles) of Green to center top of a petal on Large Flower (following p where Pink Flower is joined), make r of 14 ds, p, 12 ds, sm p, 2 ds, cl and tie. Rw, ch of 2 ds, join to last p of last r, 12 ds. Join between the 2 petals, following joining of Pink and Lavender flowers. This completes first unit. For 2nd unit carry thread across back and fasten between 2 petals directly opposite. Ch of 12 ds. Rw, r of 4 ds, join to adjacent p of Pink

197

flower, 10 ds, p, 14 ds, cl. Rw, r of 14 ds, p, 10 ds, sm p, 4 ds, cl. Rw, ch of 4 ds, join to last p of last r, 14 ds. R of 9 ds, join to p on Yellow flower preceding joining of Yellow and Lavender flowers, 5 ds, p, 14 ds, cl. Tie and cut, leaving a length of thread for sewing. Attach Green to center top of petal directly opposite start of first unit of stems and leaves and work 3rd unit to correspond with first unit. For 4th unit, carry thread across back and fasten between 2 petals directly opposite. Ch of 10 ds, r of 12 ds, p, 12 ds, cl. Tie and cut. Outline a 2-inch circle in center of one end of towel. Arrange piece inside this circle, tacking with threads left for this purpose. With Green work buttonhole stitch over circle, catching those picots which touch circle.

No. 9109 . . . . . Guest Towel

Materials: Tatting-Crochet, *Size 70, 1 ball each of Shaded Pinks and Shaded Greens and a few yards of Yellow . . . Fingertip towel.*

FLOWER CENTER . . . With Yellow, r of 1 ds, 5 sm p's sep by 2 ds, 1 ds, cl. Tie and cut.

FLOWER PETALS . . . Attach Pink ball and shuttle to a p of Flower Center, ch of 3 ds, sm p, 8 ds, p, 8 ds, sm p, 3 ds. * Draw shuttle thread tight to form loop and fasten to next p of Flower Center. Ch of 3 ds, join to last p of preceding ch, 8 ds, p, 8 ds, sm p, 3 ds. Repeat from * around, joining last ch to first p on first ch. Tie and cut.

SMALL STEM AND LEAF . . . Attach Green ball and shuttle to joining p between petals of flower, make a ch of 4 ds. R of 12 ds, p, 12 ds, cl. Tie and cut.

LARGE STEM AND LEAVES . . . Attach Green ball and shuttle to 2nd joining p to the left of Small Stem and Leaf, make a ch of 14 ds. R of 12 ds, join to p of next petal, 12 ds, cl. Rw, r of 12 ds, p, 12 ds, cl. Rw, ch of 15 ds, p, 12 ds. R of 12 ds, join to p of next petal, 12 ds, cl. Rw, r of 12 ds, p, 12 ds, cl. Rw, ch of 12 ds, r of 12 ds, p, 12 ds, cl. Tie and cut.

Draw a 2-inch triangle on fingertip towel, arrange and sew flower and leaves as in illustration so that picots touch the lines of the triangle. Finish by working buttonhole stitch over line, catching in the picots.

No. 9106 . . . . . Glass Doily

Materials: Best Six Cord Mercerized Crochet, *Small Ball, Size 50, 3 balls of White only . . . A piece of linen 3½ inches square.*

Doily measures 4½ inches square

CORNER MOTIF . . . Tie ball and shuttle threads together. R of 10 ds, sm p, 5 ds, p, 5 ds, sm p, 10 ds, cl. Rw, ch of 4 ds, 5 p's sep by 4 ds, 4 ds. Rw, lr of 17 ds, p, 17 ds, cl. Rw, ch of 4 ds, 5 p's sep by 4 ds, 4 ds. Rw, r of 7 ds, join to p of lr, 3 ds, join to 3rd p of r, 5 ds, join to center p of same r, 5 ds, sm p, 10 ds, cl. Rw, ch of 4 ds, 3 p's sep by 4 ds, 4 ds. Rw, r of 10 ds, join to sm p of preceding r, 5 ds, join to center p, 5 ds, sm p, 10 ds, cl. Rw, ch of 4 ds, 5 p's sep by 4 ds, 4 ds. Rw, r of 10 ds, join to p of preceding r, 5 ds, join to center p, 5 ds, sm p, 10 ds, cl. Rw, ch of 4 ds, 3 p's sep by 4 ds, 4 ds. Rw, r of 10 ds, join to sm p of preceding r, 5 ds, join to center p, 5 ds, sm p, 3 ds, p, 7 ds, cl. Rw, ch of 4 ds, 5 p's sep by 4 ds, 4 ds. Rw, r of 17 ds, join to last p of preceding r, 17 ds, cl. Rw, ch of 4 ds, 5 p's sep by 4 ds, 4 ds. Join to base of first r. Tie and cut.

SIDE MOTIF . . . R of 15 ds, sm p, 10 ds, sm p, 5 ds, cl. R of 5 ds, join to 2nd sm p of preceding r, 10 ds, sm p, 15 ds, cl. Rw, ch of 4 ds, 4 p's sep by 4 ds, 4 ds. Rw, r of 15 ds, join to p of preceding r, 10 ds, sm p, 5 ds, cl. R of 5 ds, join to p of preceding r, 10 ds, sm p, 15 ds, cl. Rw, ch of 4 ds, 5 p's sep by 4 ds, 4 ds, join to free p of preceding r. Ch of 4 ds, 4 p's sep by 4 ds, 4 ds, join to p between 2nd and 3rd r's. Ch of 4 ds, 4 p's sep by 4 ds, 4 ds, join to free p of first r. Ch of 4 ds, p, 4 ds, join to first p of 2nd ch on Corner Motif, 4 ds, 3 p's sep by 4 ds, 4 ds. Join to base of first r. Tie and cut.

Work Corner and Side Motifs alternately joining them to correspond with first joinings until 4 Corner and 4 Side Motifs are made and joined to form a hollow square. Place lace on linen; draw a line lightly along inner edge of lace, having the line touch the picots. Embroider with buttonhole stitch along the outline, catching the touching picots. Cut away excess linen.

9106

No. 9111 . . . . . . Tray Mat

Materials: BEST SIX CORD MERCERIZED CRO-
CHET, *Size 30, 1 ball each of White and Blue
. . . A piece of white organdie, 13½ x 14½
inches . . . 2 pieces of colored organdie, each
5 x 13½ inches.*

Tray Mat measures about 13 x 20 inches
Make a narrow hem all around white organdie.
Fold each piece of colored organdie in half
lengthwise and machine stitch around raw
edges, leaving a large enough space to allow
for turning piece inside out. Turn and press,
then turn under remaining raw edges and sew
neatly. Use Blue on shuttle and White on ball.
Tie ball and shuttle threads together. * R of
6 ds, p, 6 ds, cl. Rw, ch of 4 ds, 3 p's sep by
4 ds, 4 ds. Rw, r of 6 ds, join to p of last r,
6 ds, cl. Rw, ch of 4 ds. Repeat from * until
piece is 13 inches long, omitting the ch of 4 ds

on last repeat. Continue along other side as
follows: Ch of 4 ds, p, 4 ds. Rw, ** r of 6 ds,
join to same p as opposite r's, 6 ds, cl. Rw, ch
of 4 ds, 3 p's sep by 4 ds, 4 ds. Rw, r of 6 ds,
join to same p as preceding r, 6 ds, cl. Rw,
ch of 4 ds. Repeat from ** across, ending with
ch of 4 ds, p, 4 ds. Tie at base of first r and cut.
Make another piece like this. Sew tatting between white and colored organdie pieces by
catching the center picot of each chain.

No. 9086 . . . . . Tablecloth

Materials: BEST SIX CORD MERCERIZED CROCHET, *Big Ball, Size 30, 77 balls of White or Ecru.*

Tablecloth measures 72 x 108 inches

GAUGE: Each motif measures about 1¼ inches.

FIRST MOTIF . . . 1st rnd: R of 1 ds, 8 p's sep by 1 ds, 1 ds, cl. Tie and cut. Tie ball and shuttle threads together. **2nd rnd:** R of 3 ds, p, 3 ds, join to a p on 1st rnd, 3 ds, p, 3 ds, cl. * Rw, ch of 4 ds, p, 4 ds. Rw, r of 3 ds, join to p of adjacent r, 3 ds, join to next p on 1st rnd, 3 ds, p, 3 ds, cl. Repeat from * around, joining last part of last r to first p made and joining last ch to base of first r made. Tie and cut.

SECOND MOTIF . . . 1st rnd: Work same as 1st rnd of First Motif. **2nd rnd:** R of 3 ds, p, 3 ds, join to a p on 1st rnd, 3 ds, p, 3 ds, cl. * Rw, ch of 4 ds, join to p on ch on First Motif, 4 ds. Rw, r of 3 ds, join to p of adjacent r, 3 ds, join to next p on 1st rnd, 3 ds, p, 3 ds, cl. Repeat from * once more. Complete 2nd rnd same as 2nd rnd of First Motif (no more joinings).

Make 58 x 87 motifs, joining them as Second Motif was joined to First Motif.

9086

No. 9093 . . . . . Tray Doily

Materials: BEST SIX CORD MERCERIZED CROCHET, *Size 30, 3 balls of Pastels.*

Doily measures about 8 inches in diameter

STAR . . . Tie ball and shuttle threads together. R or 4 ds, lp, 4 ds, cl. * Rw, ch of 2 ds, p, 3 ds, p, 2 ds. Rw, r of 4 ds, join to lp of first r, 4 ds, cl. Repeat from * 3 more times. Rw, ch of 2 ds, p, 3 ds, p, 2 ds. Join to base of first r. Tie and cut. **1st rnd:** R of 4 ds, join to any p of Star, 4 ds, cl. * Rw, ch of 2 ds, lp, 3 ds, lp, 2 ds. Rw, r of 4 ds, join to next p on Star, 4 ds, cl. Repeat from * around, joining last ch to base of first r. Tie and cut. **2nd rnd:** R of 4 ds, join to any p on 1st rnd, 4 ds, cl: * Rw, ch of 4 ds, p, 4 ds. Rw, r of 4 ds, join to next p on previous rnd, 4 ds, cl. Repeat from * around, joining last ch to base of first r. Tie and cut.

3rd rnd: R of 4 ds, join to any p on 2nd rnd, 4 ds, cl. * Rw, ch of (2 ds, p) twice, 2 ds. Rw, r of 4 ds, join to next p on previous rnd, 4 ds, cl. Repeat from * around, joining last ch to base of first r. Tie and cut. **4th rnd:** R of 4 ds, join to any p on 3rd rnd, 4 ds, cl. ** Rw, ch of (2 ds, p) 3 times, 2 ds. * Rw, r of 4 ds, join to next p on 3rd rnd, 4 ds, cl. Rw, ch of (2 ds, p) twice, 2 ds. Repeat from * 4 more times. Repeat from ** around. Fasten to base of first r. Tie and cut. **5th rnd:** R of 2 ds, join to any p on previous rnd, 2 ds, cl. * Sp of ¾ inch, r of 2 ds, join to next p on previous rnd, 2 ds, cl. Repeat from * around. Hereafter mark the end of each rnd. **6th rnd:** * Sp of ¾ inch, r of 2 ds, join to thread between next 2 r's on previous rnd, 2 ds, cl. Repeat from * around. **7th to 10th rnds incl:** Work same as 6th rnd, only making the sp between r's ¼ inch longer on each successive rnd. Tie and cut at end of 10th rnd. Starch and press.

9093

9089

No. 9089 . . Napkin—Place Mat

Materials: BEST SIX CORD MERCERIZED CRO-
CHET, *Size 30, 3 balls . . . Linen.*

MOTIF . . . 1st rnd: R of (4 ds, sm p) twice;
4 ds, p, (4 ds, sm p) twice, 4 ds, cl and tie.
* R of 4 ds, join to last sm p of preceding r,
4 ds, sm p, 4 ds, p, (4 ds, sm p) twice, 4 ds, cl,
tie. Repeat from * 2 more times, joining the
last sm p of the 4th r to the first sm p of the
first r. Tie and cut. **2nd rnd:** Fasten ball and
shuttle threads to 2nd sm p of first r of preceding rnd. * Ch of 5 ds, 3 sm p's sep by 5 ds,
5 ds and fasten to 3rd sm p of same r. Ch of
4 ds, p, 4 ds and fasten to 2nd sm p of next r
of preceding rnd. Repeat from * around, fastening last ch to same sm p from which first ch

started. Tie and cut. (For napkin, use only the
1st and 2nd rnds, making p's in 1st rnd instead
of sm p's.) **3rd rnd:** Tie ball and shuttle
threads together. * R of 10 ds, join to 1st sm p
of ch on preceding rnd, 10 ds, cl. Rw, ch of
3 ds, 8 p's sep by 3 ds, 3 ds. Rw, r of 10 ds, join
to 2nd sm p of same ch on preceding rnd,
10 ds, cl. Rw, make another ch like the preceding one. Rw, r of 10 ds, join to 3rd sm p on
same ch of preceding rnd, 10 ds, cl. Skip p in
short chain and repeat from * around, fastening the 12th r at the base of the first r. Tie and
cut. **4th rnd:** Tie ball and shuttle threads together. With wrong side of work toward you,
r of 9 ds, join to 3rd p in first ch of preceding
rnd, * 7 ds, sm p, 2 ds, cl. R of 2 ds, join to
sm p of preceding r, 7 ds, p, 9 ds, cl. Carry
threads to sm p joining these 2 r's, fasten and

203

make a ch of 9 ds, join to 6th p in same ch of preceding rnd, 4 ds. R of 6 ds, sm p, 3 ds, p, 9 ds, cl. Reversing curve of chain, ch of 3 ds, 15 p's sep by 3 ds, 3 ds. Rw, r of 9 ds, p, 3 ds, join to sm p of preceding r, 6 ds, cl. Reversing curve of ch, make a ch of 4 ds, join to 3rd p of next ch on preceding rnd, 9 ds. Sp of 1/16 inch, rw, r of 2 ds, sm p, 7 ds, join to 6th p of same ch of preceding rnd, 9 ds, cl. Rw, r of 2 ds, join to sm p of preceding r, 7 ds, p, 9 ds, cl. Ch of 3 ds, 4 p's sep by 3 ds, 3 ds. R of 9 ds, join to 3rd p of next ch of preceding rnd. Repeat from * around, fastening the last ch at the base of the first 2 r's. Tie and cut.

The motifs are 3⅛ inches square. For each place mat, cut linen 13½ by 18½ inches; for each napkin, cut linen 12½ inches square. Hemstitch, making 1 inch hems. For place mat, with a sharp pencil draw 3¼ inch lines ¼ inch inside the hemstitching and parallel to each corner. Using these lines as guides, complete 3¼ inch squares in each corner and baste the motifs in place. Buttonhole stitch over the lines catching in the picots. Cut away the material from under the tatting. Finish napkins same as place mat on smaller scale required.

No. 9103 . . . . Doily

Materials: BEST SIX CORD MERCERIZED CROCHET, *Size 20, 3 balls of White or Ecru . . . A hemmed linen circle, 7 inches in diameter.*

Doily measures about 10 inches in diameter

1st rnd: Tie ball and shuttle threads together. * R of 3 ds, 3 p's sep by 3 ds, 3 ds, cl. Rw, ch of 4 ds, 3 p's sep by 4 ds, 4 ds, rw. Repeat from * until there are 40 r's and 40 ch's. Join last ch to base of first r. Tie and cut. **2nd rnd:** R of 3 ds, 3 p's sep by 3 ds, 3 ds, cl. * Close to this, make r of 3 ds, 3 p's sep by 3 ds, 3 ds, cl. Rw, ch of 4 ds, p, 4 ds, join to center p of ch on 1st rnd, 4 ds, p, 4 ds, p, 6 ds. Rw, r of 3 ds, p, 3 ds, join to center p of adjacent r, 3 ds, p, 3 ds, cl. Rw, ch of 6 ds. Rw, r of 3 ds, 3 p's sep by 3 ds, 3 ds, cl. Rw, ch of 6 ds. Rw, r of 3 ds, 3 p's sep by 3 ds, 3 ds, cl. Rw, ch of 6 ds, join to last p of opposite ch, 4 ds, p, 4 ds, join to center p of next ch on 1st rnd, 4 ds, p, 4 ds. Rw, r of 3 ds, p, 3 ds, join to center p of adjacent r, 3 ds, p, 3 ds, cl. Repeat from * around, joining last ch to base of first r. Tie and cut. Sew to linen circle.

9103

CHAPTER VI

RUGS . . . *handsome foundation for your decorative schemes*

*H*OW IS THE FLOOR SHOW at your house? Shall we start with the living room? Want to give it a modern uncluttered feeling—a lap-of-luxury-look? Try Shaggy (made in 12 inch squares) and choose a color that is becoming to your room and you. We like two shades of dusty beige or caramel or grey but you may have other ideas. You can make it from wall-to-wall size or large enough to place in front of the sofa. If your room is in maple and your lamps are brass, accent it with Daisies, white on a rich, red background. For a colonial bedroom or sewing room there is—you guessed it!—Colonial, a charming circular design. For the younger generation there are little coal black scotties romping on a pale blue with cream background.

There is another gem of a round rug, Circular, for your guest room. For the well-groomed bathroom choose Mosaic or Checkers; for the fireside Crisscross or Stripes. Whether you choose to make a rug of yarn or rags, by following these easy-to-follow directions, you will soon be in a splendid rug-ged shape.

10-21

No. 10-21 . . . . Rug

39 x 58 Inches (including fringe)

Materials: RUG COTTON, *60 balls of Tulip Yellow . . . Steel Crochet Hook Size G.*

Use 2 strands throughout

Starting at center, make a chain 18 inches long (3 ch sts to 1 inch). **1st row:** Sc in 2nd ch from hook and in each ch across, 3 sc in last ch; now, working along opposite side of starting chain, make sc in each ch across, 2 sc in same ch as first sc was made. **Hereafter work over 10 strands of Rug Cotton. 2nd row:** 2 sc in next sc (1 sc increased), sc in each sc to within the 3-sc group, 2 sc in each of next 3 sc (3 more sc increased), sc in each sc, 2 sc in last 2 sc (2 more sc increased)—6 sc increased in all. Working over 10 strands as before, make sc in each sc around, increasing as necessary at ends of oval to keep work flat until piece measures 33 x 52 inches. Break off.

FRINGE . . . Cut 6 strands, each 8 inches long. Double these strands to form a loop. Insert hook through an sc and draw loop through. Draw loose ends through loop and pull up tightly. Make fringe in this manner in each sc around. Trim ends evenly.

9461

No. 9461 . . . . Mosaic

24 x 36 Inches

Materials: COTTON RUG YARN, *13 balls of Green and 11 balls of White* . . . *Rug Hook, Size G.*

Starting at narrow end with Green, make a chain 30 inches long (3 ch sts to 1 inch). **1st row:** Sc in 2nd ch from hook and in each ch across until there are 61 sc on row. Cut off remaining chain. Drop Green. Attach White. **2nd row:** Sc in each sc across. Ch 1, turn. **3rd row:** Sc in each sc across. Drop White. **4th row:** Pick up Green, sc in next 5 sc, * insert hook at base of next st 3 rows down and draw loop through to height of row in work, (yarn over hook, insert hook in same place and draw loop through to same height as last loop) 3 times; yarn over and draw through all loops on hook (group st made), skip the sc under group st, sc in next 9 sc. Repeat from * across, ending with sc in last 5 sc. Ch 1, turn. **5th row:** Sc in each st across (61 sts). Drop Green. **6th row:** Pick up White, sc in next 4 sc, * make a group st over next st 3 rows down, skip the sc under group st, sc in next sc, make a group st over next st 3 rows down, skip the sc under group st, sc in next 7 sc. Repeat from * across, ending with 4 sc. Ch 1, turn. **7th row:** Sc in each st across. Drop White. **8th row:** Pick up Green, sc in next 3 sc, * make a group st over next st 3 rows down, skip the sc under group st, (sc in next sc, group st over next st 3 rows down, skip the sc under group st) twice; sc in next 5 sc. Repeat from * across, ending with 3 sc. Ch 1, turn. **9th row:** Sc in each st across. Drop Green.

NOTE: Work 2 rows of each color throughout.

10th row: Sc in next 2 sc, * group st over next sc 3 rows down, skip the sc under the group st, (sc in next sc, group st over next sc 3 rows down, skip the sc under the group st) 3 times; sc in next 3 sc. Repeat from * across, ending with 2 sc. Ch 1, turn. **11th and all odd rows:** Sc in each st across. Ch 1, turn. **12th row:** * Sc in next sc, group st over next sc 3 rows down, skip the sc under the group st. Repeat from * across, ending with an sc. Ch 1, turn. **14th row:** * Make a group st over next sc 3 rows down, skip the sc under the group st, sc in next sc. Repeat from * across. Ch 1, turn. **16th to 24th rows incl:** Repeat back 12th to 4th rows incl. Repeat 5th to 24th rows incl until piece measures 36 inches, ending to correspond with beginning. Break off.

FRINGE . . . Cut 10 strands of Green, each 10 inches long. Double these strands to form a loop. Draw this loop through first sc on one short side, draw loose ends through and pull up tightly. Make a fringe in every 3rd sc on each short side.

No. 9453 . Simplicity in Stripes

24 x 36 Inches

Materials: COTTON RUG YARN, *9 balls each of Deep Rose and Beauty Rose* . . . *Rug Hook, Size G.*

With Deep Rose, make a chain 40 inches long. Lay this chain aside. From another ball of the same color cut 10 strands, each 45 inches long. Knot strands together 3 inches in from each end. **1st row:** Starting after the first knot, hold the strands at top of chain and, working over them, make sc in 2nd ch from hook and in each ch across, until other knot is reached. Break off, leaving a 4-inch length. Draw this length through knot. Cut off remaining chain. **2nd row:** Attach Beauty Rose to first sc of previous row. Cut and knot 10 strands of the same color, each 45 inches long. Starting after the first knot, hold the strands at top of previous row and, working over them, make sc in each sc across. Break off, leaving a 4-inch length. Draw this length through knot. Repeat 2nd row, alternating colors, until Rug measures 24 inches, ending with Deep Rose. Trim ends evenly.

9453

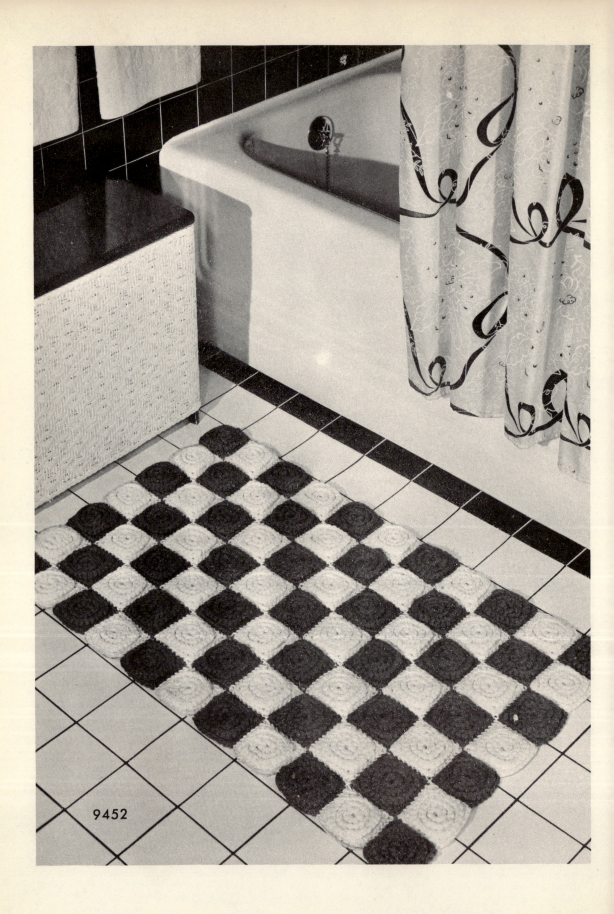

9452

No. 9452 . . . . Checkers
24 x 36 Inches

Materials: COTTON RUG YARN, 9 *balls each of Royal Blue and White. Rug Hook, Size G.*

SQUARE . . . Starting at center, ch 2. **1st rnd:** 8 sc in 2nd ch from hook, sl st in first sc. **Hereafter pick up only the back loop of each sc. 2nd rnd:** 2 sc in first sc, * sc in next sc, 3 sc in next sc. Repeat from * around, ending with sc where first 2 sc were made. Sl st in first sc. **3rd and 4th rnds:** 2 sc in first sc, * sc in each sc to center sc of next 3-sc group, 3 sc in center sc. Repeat from * around, ending as before. Join. Break off at end of 4th rnd. Starting at center, attach 2 strands to first free loop of first rnd and make sc in each free loop around. Join and break off (a round ridge made). Make another ridge on top of next 2 rnds.

Make 39 Royal Blue and 38 White Squares. Make 7 rows of 11 squares, alternating colors and having a Blue Square at each corner. Sew neatly together on wrong side.

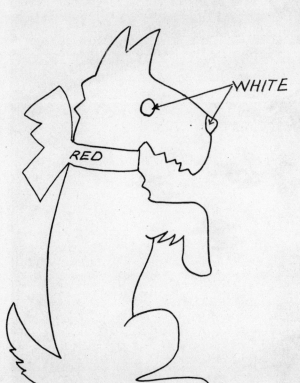

No. 9456 . . . . Scotty
30 x 40 Inches

Materials: COTTON RUG YARN, *23 balls each of Cream and Blue . . . Rug Hook, Size G . . . ¼ yard each of red and black felt.*

Starting at one side, with double strand of Cream make a chain 30 inches long. **1st row:** Sc in 2nd ch from hook and in each ch across, until row measures 24 inches. Cut off remaining chain. Ch 1, turn. **2nd row:** Sc in each sc across. Ch 1, turn. Repeat 2nd row until piece measures 34 inches. Break off.

BORDER . . . **1st rnd:** With single strand of Blue, work a row of sc all around outer edges, making 3 sc in each corner. **Hereafter pick up only the back loop of each sc throughout. 2nd rnd:** Sc in each sc around, making 3 sc in center sc of each 3-sc group at corners. Repeat 2nd rnd 8 more times. Sl st in next st. Break off.

LOOPS . . . With a single strand of Blue, attach yarn to first free loop of first rnd of Border, * ch 5, sc in same loop, ch 5, sc in next loop. Repeat from * around, until Border is completely covered with loops. Line Border on wrong side with unbleached cotton to keep it flat.

Cut 8 animals according to diagram and sew in place as in illustration. Cut 4 strips of red, ⅜ inch wide, for leashes in varying length, and sew to 4 animals (see illustration). Sew on a small white button for each eye.

9456

9450

No. 9450 . . . . Shaggy
A Rug to accommodate any room, made in 12-inch squares

Materials: COTTON RUG YARN, *4 balls of Dusty Pink will make 1 square . . . Rug Hook, Size G.*

SQUARE . . . Ch 39 to measure 12½ inches. **1st row:** Sc in 2nd ch from hook and in each ch across. Ch 1, turn. **2nd row:** Sc in back loop of each sc across. Ch 1, turn. **3rd row:** Sc in front loop of each sc across. Ch 1, turn. Repeat 2nd and 3rd rows alternately until piece is square. Break off. The side with the ridges is the side on which the loops are made.

LOOPS . . . Attach yarn to first st of first ridge, sc in same st, draw loop on hook out to measure 1 inch, insert hook in same place as last st and draw a loop through, thread over and draw through one loop, making a ch st of it; draw last loop on hook out to same height as previous loop (2 loop sts made in 1 st). Make 2 loop sts in each st across. Break off. Work a row of loops on each ridge. Break off.

Make the necessary number of squares for the size of rug you wish to make. Sew them together neatly on wrong side. For variation in texture, cut the loops of every other square.

9460

No. 9460 . . . . . Criss-Cross

24 x 36 Inches

Illustrated in Color on page 206

Materials: COTTON RUG YARN, *14 balls of Dark Green and 5 balls each of Red and White* . . . *Rug Hook, Size G.*

Starting at one short end with Green, make a chain 30 inches long. **1st row:** Sc in 2nd ch from hook and in each ch across until row measures 24 inches and has an odd number of sts. Cut off remaining chain. Ch 1, turn. **2nd row:** Sc in each sc across. Ch 1, turn. **3rd row:** * Sc in next sc, insert hook at base of next st 2 rows down and draw loop through to height of row in work, complete as for an sc (long sc made). Repeat from * across, ending with sc. **This row will be referred to as pattern row. 4th, 5th and 6th rows:** Sc in each st across. Ch 1, turn. The last 4 rows constitute pattern. Work in pattern until piece

216

measures 36 inches, ending with the 3rd row and having an even number of pattern rows. Break off.

WOVEN STRIPES (Woven across width) . . . Cut 5 strands of Red, each 2 yards long, and draw strands through first long sc of first pattern row. * Skip 1 long sc on second pattern row and draw strand through next long sc; skip 1 long sc on first pattern row and draw strands through next long sc. Repeat from * across, turn. Work back in the same manner, drawing strands through the long sc skipped on both pattern rows. Fasten ends securely on wrong side. Cut 5 strands of White, each 2 yards long, and weave a White stripe through long sc of second and third pattern rows as before. Weave stripes in this manner, alternating colors and ending with a Red stripe.

Attach Green to one corner and, working along one short side, make sc in first st, * ch 2, skip 1 st, sc in next st. Repeat from * across. Then work sc closely together along next long side, keeping work flat. Work other two sides to correspond. Join and break off.

FRINGE . . . Cut 10 strands of Green, each 10 inches long. Double these strands to form a loop. Insert hook in ch-2 loop and draw loop through. Draw loose ends through loop and pull up tightly. Make a fringe in each ch-2 loop across each short side. Trim ends evenly.

9459

No. 9459 . . . . Daisies
24 x 36 Inches

Materials: COTTON RUG YARN, *12 balls each of Red and White . . . Rug Hook, Size G.*

Use 2 strands throughout

MOTIF . . . Starting at center with Red, ch 5. Join with sl st to form ring. **1st rnd:** 12 sc in ring. Drop Red, insert hook in first sc and, with White, make a sl st. **2nd rnd:** With White, ch 2, (yarn over hook, insert hook in same place as sl st and draw loop through to height of ch-2) 3 times; yarn over and draw through all loops on hook (cluster made), * ch 1, cluster in next sc. Repeat from * around, ending with ch 1. Drop White, insert hook in tip of first cluster and, with Red, make a sl st. **3rd rnd:** In same place as sl st (with Red) make half dc, dc and half dc (corner), * (sc between clusters, sc in next cluster) twice; sc between clusters, in next cluster make half dc, dc and half dc. Repeat from * around. Join and break off. Make 7 rows of 10 motifs and sew neatly together on wrong side.

9462

No. 9462 . . . . Basket Weave
24 x 36 Inches

Materials: COTTON RUG YARN, *24 balls of Indian Pink . . . Rug Hook, Size G.*

Starting at one short end with 2 strands of yarn, make a chain 30 inches long. **1st row:** Sc in 2nd ch from hook and in each ch across until row measures 24 inches, being sure to have an even number of sc. Cut off remaining chain. Ch 1, turn. **2nd row:** * Sc in next st, sc at base of next st (long sc made). Repeat from * across, ending with long sc. Ch 1, turn. Repeat 2nd row until piece measures 36 inches. **Next row:** Sc in first st, * ch 2, skip 1 st, sc in next st. Repeat from * across. Break off.

FRINGE . . . Cut 10 strands, each 10 inches long. Double these strands to make a loop. Insert hook in ch-2 loop and draw loop through. Draw loose ends through loop. Make a fringe in each ch-2 loop across. Trim ends evenly. Complete opposite end to correspond.

No. 10-20 . . . . Rug
30 x 46 Inches

Materials: RUG COTTON, *24 balls of Light Green, 5 balls of Powder Green, and 5 balls of Dusty Jade . . . Steel Crochet Hook, Size G.*

Use 2 strands throughout

Center Section . . . Starting at one narrow end with Light Green, make a chain 25 inches long. **1st row:** Sc in 2nd ch from hook, sc in next 2 ch, * tr in next ch, sc in next 3 ch. Repeat from * across until row measures 18 inches, ending with tr and 3 sc. Cut off remaining chain. Ch 1, turn. **2nd and all even rows:** Sc in each st across. Ch 1, turn. **3rd row:** Sc in next sc, tr under loop of next tr below, skip the sc behind the tr just made, * sc in next 3 sc, holding back on hook the last loop of each tr make tr in same place as last tr was made and tr in next tr below, thread over and draw through all loops on hook (joint tr made), skip the sc behind the joint tr just made. Repeat from * across, ending with tr in last tr below, sc in last sc. Ch 1, turn. **5th row:** * Sc in next 3 sc, make a joint tr as before, having 1 tr under the first tr below and the 2nd tr under next joint tr, skip the sc behind the joint tr just made. Repeat from * across, ending with 3 sc. Ch 1, turn. **7th row:** Sc in next sc, tr under next joint tr as before, skip the sc behind the tr just made, * sc in next 3 sc, make a joint tr, having 1 tr under the same joint tr below where last tr was made and the 2nd tr under next joint tr, skip the sc behind the joint tr just made. Repeat from * across, ending with sc in last sc. Ch 1, turn. **8th row:** Repeat 2nd row. Now repeat 5th to 8th rows incl until piece measures 34 inches, ending with the 7th row. Break off.

BORDER . . . Attach Powder Green and work 7 rnds of sc, making 3 sc in each corner st and joining each rnd. Attach Dusty Jade and work 7 more rnds of sc, working over corners and joining rnds as before. Break off.

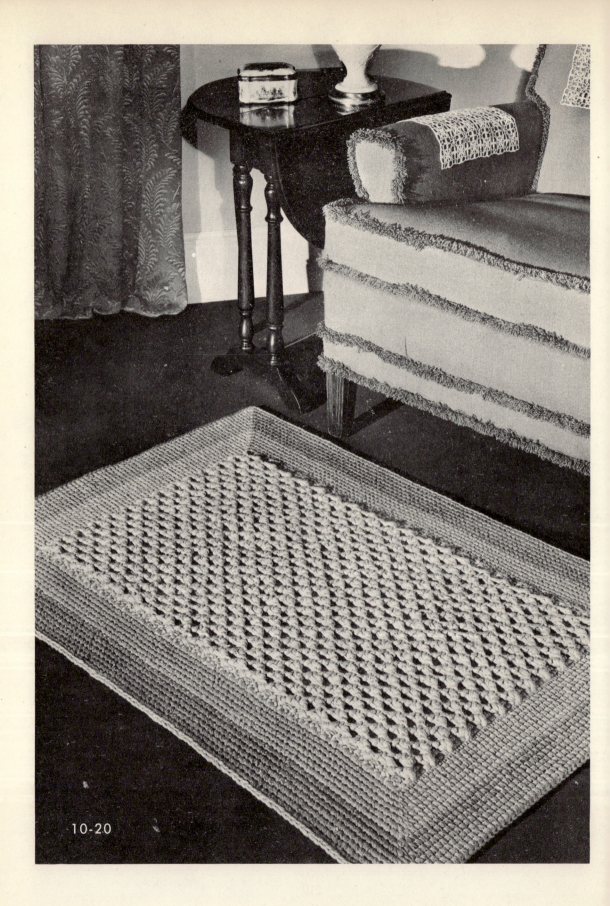

10-20

9463

No. 9463 · · · · · · · Circular

31 Inches in diameter

Materials: COTTON RUG YARN, *22 balls of Steel Blue . . . Rug Hook, Size G.*

Use 2 strands throughout

Starting at center, ch 2 loosely. **1st rnd:** 14 sc in 2nd ch from hook. Join with sl st. **2nd rnd:** Ch 2, (insert hook in same place as sl st and draw loop through to height of ch-2, yarn over hook) 4 times; draw through all loops on hook (cluster made). Make a cluster in each sc around. Join with sl st. **3rd rnd:** 2 sc in back loop of each cluster (28 sc). Join. **4th rnd:** Repeat 2nd rnd. **5th rnd:** Sc in back loop of each cluster, increasing 14 sc evenly around—*to inc 1 sc, make 2 sc in 1 cluster.* Repeat 4th and 5th rnds alternately until Rug measures 31 inches in diameter, ending with an sc rnd. Break off.

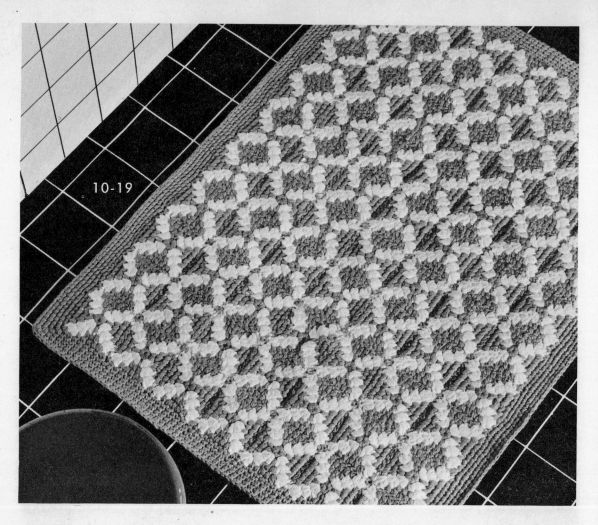

No. 10-19 . . . . Rug

32 x 44 Inches

Materials: RUG COTTON, *26 balls of Tropic Blue and 16 balls of White . . . Steel Crochet Hook, Size G.*

Use 2 strands throughout

GAUGE: Each motif measures 4 inches square.

MOTIF . . . Starting at center with Blue, ch 2. **1st rnd:** 8 sc in 2nd ch from hook. Join with sl st to first sc. **2nd rnd:** Ch 1, insert hook in same place as sl st and draw loop through, drop Blue, draw a loop of White through the 2 loops on hook, thus changing color, * with White make 3 dc in next sc, drawing Blue through the last 2 loops of the last dc (thus changing color again)—**always change color in this manner.** With Blue make sc in next sc,

drawing White through last 2 loops on hook to change color. Repeat from * around. Join. **3rd rnd:** With Blue, ch 1, sc in same place as sl st, sc in next dc, changing to White as before, * with White make 3 dc in next dc as before, drawing Blue through last 2 loops of last dc; with Blue make sc in next 3 sts, changing to White as before. Repeat from * around. Join. **4th rnd:** With Blue ch 1, make sc in same place as sl st, sc in next sc and in next dc, drawing White through last 2 loops of last sc; * in next dc make dc, tr and dc, drawing Blue through last 2 loops of last dc; sc in next 5 sts, drawing White through last 2 loops of last sc. Repeat from * around. Join and break off.

Make 7 rows of 10 motifs in all, sewing adjacent sides with neat over-and-over sts on wrong side.

BORDER . . . With Blue, make 5 rnds of sc, having 3 sc at each corner. Join and break off.

No. 10-24 . . . . Rug
28 x 40 Inches

Materials: RUG COTTON, *40 balls of Empire Blue* . . . *Steel Crochet Hook, Size G.*

GAUGE: 3 ch sts make 1 inch.

Starting at one narrow end, make a chain 24 inches long. **1st row:** Sc in 2nd ch from hook and in each ch across. Ch 1, turn. **2nd row:** Sc in back loop of each sc across. Ch 1, turn.

3rd row: Sc in front loop of each sc across. Ch 1, turn. Repeat 2nd and 3rd rows alternately until piece measures 36 inches. Break off. Now work chain loops as follows: Attach thread in free loop of first sc on 1st row, * ch 5, sc in free loop of next sc. Repeat from * across. Break off. Work loops in this manner over all ridges.

BORDER . . . Work 6 rnds of sc, making 3 sc in each corner st.

10-24

9448

No. 9448 . . . . Colonial

58 Inches in diameter

Materials: Cotton Rug Yarn, *12 balls each of Red and Yellow; 18 balls of Green.*

Knot 5 strands of each color together (15 strands in all). Place a weight on the knot. Then separate the three colors into separate groups (3 groups in all) and make a braid 4 yards long. Go back to the beginning and, starting at center of Rug, sew braid in rounds to form a circle, being careful to keep work flat. Continue in this manner until Rug measures 48 inches in diameter. Break off Red and Yellow and add 10 more strands of Green. Make a braid of Green only and sew around as before until Rug measures 58 inches in diameter. Fasten ends securely and break off.

PH 4789

No. P. H. 4789 . . . . Rag Rug

49 x 74 Inches

Materials: J. & P. Coats Heavy Duty Mercerized Sewing Thread, *6 spools of Black . . . 20 pounds of rags of a heavy cotton fabric— half of this amount to consist of 3 dark shades (Green, Black and Brown) to be braided together to form the dark braid; and the other half in an assortment of mixed bright colors to be braided together to form the light braid.*

It is important that the material used be of a similar weight and texture to assure uniformity of braid throughout.

Cut material into strips, each 2½ inches wide (see diagram). Join ends of pieces to form a long continuous strip by piecing the ends on the bias. Roll strips into balls, keeping colors separately. These strips are then folded twice as shown in Fig. A and braided as in Fig. B. Braid 3 strips of the darker shades (Green, Black and Brown) together (1 strand of each color) to form dark braid. Braid 3 strips of bright colors to form light braid.

To make rug, measure off 25 inches of light braid and, using this as a straight center, coil light braid around this center, sewing each rnd in place until piece measures 17 x 42 inches. Cut off light braid. Coil dark braid around this section, sewing each rnd in place as before, until piece measures 26 x 51 inches. Cut off dark braid. Using light braid, work as before until piece measures 40 x 65 inches. Cut off light braid. With dark braid, work as before until piece measures 49 x 74 inches.

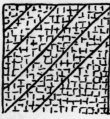

How To Cut Bias Strips

Fig. A

Fig. B

CHAPTER VII

AFGHANS . . . *fair and warm for cozy moments*

*H*OSPITALITY—the generous gesture, the understanding heart, the friendly atmosphere—these are what give a house its welcoming warmth.

We, of course, have a specially warm place in our hearts for afghans, and they have always reciprocated our affections, kept us comfortable and cozy through innumerable "forty winks" down the years. Their soft, luxurious texture, their glowing colors, their lovely patterns have always given them first place in our home. We take pride in presenting you with some of our favorite afghan patterns—may they keep your fingers busy and your toes warm!

How to Make Afghan Stitch

Make a chain of 45 stitches. **1st row:** Insert hook in 2nd ch from hook and draw up a loop; retaining all loops on hook draw up a loop in each ch across (Fig. 1). There are 45 loops on hook. Yarn over and draw through 1 loop, * yarn over and draw through 2 loops. Repeat from * across (Fig. 2). **The loop which remains on hook always counts as the first st of next row (Fig. 3). 2nd row:** Insert hook under 2nd vertical bar and draw loop through; retaining all loops on hook draw up a loop in each vertical bar across to within last vertical bar (Fig. 4). **Insert hook through the last vertical bar and the stitch directly behind it and draw a loop through—this gives a firm edge to this side (45 loops on hook),** complete last half of row to correspond with first

row. Repeat 2nd row as specified in directions. Then make a sl st in each vertical bar across. Break off.

How to Increase in Afghan Stitch: *To inc 1 vertical bar at beginning of row, insert hook under vertical bar directly below loop on hook (Fig. 5) and draw loop through.* Retaining all loops on hook work across row as before to last vertical bar—*to inc 1 vertical bar at end of row, insert hook under last vertical bar and draw up a loop, insert hook under stitch directly behind last vertical bar (Fig. 5) and draw loop through* (1 st increased at both ends).

How to Decrease in Afghan Stitch: *To dec 1 st at both ends of row, insert hook under 2 vertical bars at one time (Fig. 6) and draw loop through.*

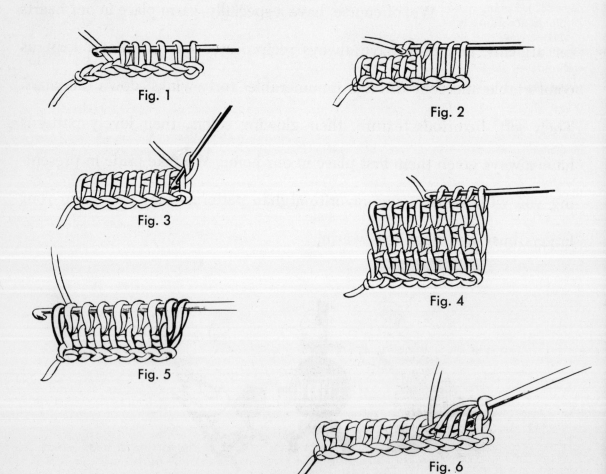

Fig. 1

Fig. 2

Fig. 3

Fig. 4

Fig. 5

Fig. 6

No. 6142 . . . . Afghan
Illustrated in Color on page 171
Approximately 49 x 68 Inches

Materials: KNITTING WORSTED, *60 balls (1 oz. balls) of Light Yellow; 8 balls of Wood Brown for Border and Embroidery . . . Bone Afghan Hook No. 6 (4¼ mm. size).*

GAUGE: 5 sts make 1 inch; 4 rows make 1 inch.

BLOCK (Make 35) . . . With Yellow, ch 45 to measure 9¼ inches and work in afghan stitch (see page 228) until piece is square (36 rows). Break off. Attach Brown to corner st, make 3 sc in corner, * ch 1, skip 1 st, sc in next st. Repeat from * around, making 3 sc in each corner. Join and break off.

EMBROIDERY . . . Examine the diagram for making cross stitches over afghan stitch (see page 233). Placing design at center, embroider 18 blocks according to chart below.

Make 5 rows of 7 blocks. Sew blocks neatly together on wrong side, alternating plain and embroidered blocks.

BORDER . . . **1st rnd:** Attach Brown to corner, 3 sc in corner, sc in each st and in each ch-1 sp around, making 3 sc in each corner. Join. **2nd rnd:** Sc in each sc around, making 3 sc in center sc of each corner. Join. **3rd rnd:** Ch 3, sc in joining, sc in next sc, 3 sc in next sc, sc in next sc, * ch 3, sc in last sc, sc in next 5 sc. Repeat from * around, making 3 sc in each corner. Join and break off.

Chart for 6142

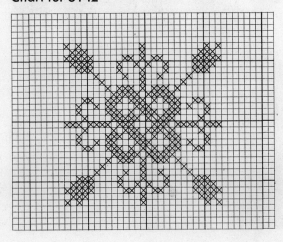

No. 6146 . . . . Afghan
Approximately 51 x 72 Inches

Materials: KNITTING WORSTED, *40 balls (1 oz. balls) of Wood Brown and 35 balls of assorted, Self-shading or Variegated colors, or use left-over yarns of the same type . . . Plastic Crochet Hook No. 7.*

GAUGE: Each block measures 5¼ inches.

BLOCK . . . Starting at center with first color, ch 6. Join with sl st to form ring. **1st rnd:** Ch 3, 2 dc in ring, (ch 3, 3 dc in ring) 3 times; ch 1, thread over, insert hook in 3rd ch of starting chain, drop first color, pick up second color and draw through all loops on hook. **Always change color in this manner. 2nd rnd:** Ch 3, 2 dc in same sp, (ch 1, in next sp make 3 dc, ch 3 and 3 dc) 3 times; ch 1, 3 dc in same sp as first 2 dc were made, ch 1. Join, changing to third color as before. **3rd rnd:** Ch 3, 2 dc in same sp, (ch 1, 3 dc in next sp, ch 1, in next sp make 3 dc, ch 3 and 3 dc) 3 times; ch 1, 3 dc in next sp, ch 1, 3 dc in first sp, ch 1. Join, changing to fourth color as before. **4th rnd:** Ch 3, 2 dc in sp, * (ch 1, 3 dc in next sp) twice; ch 1,

6146

in next corner sp make 3 dc, ch 3 and 3 dc. Repeat from * around. Join, changing to Wood Brown as before. **5th rnd:** (This rnd is always worked in Wood Brown.) Ch 3, 2 dc in same sp, * (ch 1, 3 dc in next sp) 3 times; ch 1, in next corner sp make 3 dc, ch 3 and 3 dc. Repeat from * around, ending with ch 1, 3 dc in first sp, ch 3, sl st in 3rd ch of starting chain. Break off.

Make 9 rows of 13 blocks, using colors as desired. Sew blocks neatly together on wrong side, picking up the back loop only.

BORDER . . . 1st rnd: Attach Wood Brown, ch 3 and work a rnd of dc closely together around all sides, making 3 dc in each corner. Join. **2nd rnd:** Ch 3, dc in each dc around, making 3 dc in center dc of each corner. Join and break off.

No. 6144 . . . . Afghan
Approximately 45 x 63 Inches

Materials: KNITTING WORSTED, 56 balls (1 oz. balls) of Blue; 6 balls of White for Embroidery . . . Bone Afghan Hook No. 6 (4¼ mm. size).

GAUGE: 5 sts make 1 inch; 4 rows make 1 inch.

STRIP (Make 5) . . . Starting at narrow end with Blue, ch 45 to measure 9¼ inches. Work in afghan stitch (see page 228)—45 loops on hook—until piece measures 62 inches. Sew Strips neatly together on wrong side.

EDGING . . . 1st rnd: Attach Blue and work sc closely together around all sides, making 3 sc in each corner and keeping work flat. Join.

CENTER STITCH

CENTER ROW

Charts for 6144

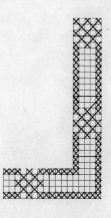

6144

Drop Blue. **2nd rnd:** Attach White and make sc in back loop of each sc around, making 3 sc in center sc of each corner. Join and break off. **3rd rnd:** Pick up Blue, sc in each sc around, making 3 sc in corner sc.

EMBROIDERY—Center . . . Examine the diagram for making cross stitches over afghan stitch (see below). The large chart on page 231 shows only one quarter of design. Determine the center of afghan and mark with a colored thread. Starting at center stitch, embroider according to chart. Omit the center row and work left half to correspond. Then omit top row and work other half to complete design.

BORDER . . . The outside row of Border is worked on the fourth row of afghan stitch. Work Border according to small chart on page 231.

No. 6137 . . . . Afghan
Approximately 50 x 70 Inches
(including fringe)

Materials: KNITTING WORSTED, *41 balls (1 oz. balls) of French Gold; 21 balls of Leaf Green; 4 balls each of Florida Blue and Deep Rose; 3 balls of Mid Rose; 2 balls each of Wild Rose, Blue Jewel and Oak Green . . . Bone Afghan Hook No. 6 (4¼ mm. size).*

WIDE STRIP (Make 5) . . . Starting at narrow end with Gold, ch 40 to measure 8¼ inches. Work in afghan stitch (see page 228)—

**Diagram for Making
Cross Stitches over Afghan Stitch**

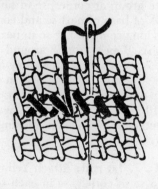

Chart for 6137

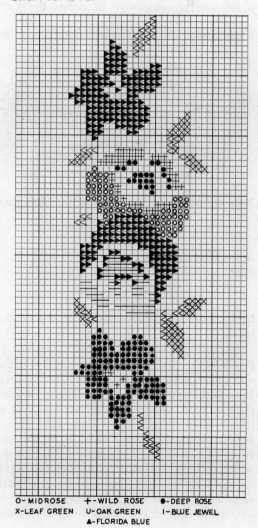

O—MID ROSE   +—WILD ROSE   ●—DEEP ROSE
X—LEAF GREEN   U—OAK GREEN   I—BLUE JEWEL
▲—FLORIDA BLUE

40 loops on hook—until piece measures 62 inches. Break off.

NARROW STRIP (Make 6) . . . With Leaf Green, ch 9 and work 3 rows of afghan stitch. **4th row:** Work in afghan stitch until there are 4 loops on hook; yarn over hook 3 times, insert hook in 2nd vertical bar 3 rows down and draw a loop through, (yarn over and draw through 2 loops) 3 times; yarn over hook 3 times, skip 5 bars 3 rows down and draw a loop through the next vertical bar, (yarn over and draw through 2 loops) 4 times—a herringbone stitch made—skip the st directly behind the herringbone st and draw a loop in each of next 4 vertical bars (9 loops on hook). Complete as for afghan stitch row. **5th row:** Work in afghan stitch. Repeat 4th and 5th rows alternately until strip measures 62 inches. Break off.

EMBROIDERY . . . Examine the diagram for making cross stitches over afghan stitch (see page 233). Embroider two complete designs according to chart on page 233 on a Wide Strip, spacing them evenly apart. Embroider 2 more Wide Strips in the same way.

Sew strips neatly together, alternating Narrow and Wide Strips, having an embroidered strip at each side and in center. Starting at one corner with Leaf Green, make a row of slip stitches around all sides. Join. Now work along short side as follows: Sc in next 2 sl sts, * ch 2, skip 2 sts, sc in next 2 sts. Repeat from * across narrow end only. Break off. Work other end to correspond.

FRINGE . . . Cut 6 strands of Leaf Green, each 12 inches long. Double these strands to form a loop, insert hook in ch-2 sp and draw loop through, draw loose ends through loop and pull up tightly. Make a fringe in each ch-2 sp across each short side. Trim evenly.

No. 6143 . . . . Afghan

Approximately 45 x 67 Inches

Materials: KNITTING WORSTED, *40 balls (1 oz. balls) of Yellow and 30 balls of Wood Brown . . . Plastic Crochet Hook No. 6.*

GAUGE: Each block measures 4¼ inches square.

BLOCK . . . Starting at center with Yellow, ch 6. Join with sl st. **1st rnd:** 12 sc in ring. Join. **2nd rnd:** Ch 3, dc in back loop of sl st, 2 dc in back loop of each sc around. Sl st in top of ch-3. Drop Yellow. **3rd rnd:** Attach Brown, sc in same place as sl st, tr in front loop of sc below (on first rnd), * sc in next dc, tr in front loop of next sc below (on first rnd). Repeat from * around. Join and break off. **4th rnd:** Pick up Yellow, sc in first sc, * (sc in next tr, sc in next sc) twice; in next tr make 2 dc, ch 1 and 2 dc; sc in next sc. Repeat from * around. Join. **5th rnd:** Sc in each st around, making 3 sc in each corner sp. Join. Drop Yellow. **6th rnd:** Attach Brown to first sc of any 3-sc group at corner, sc in same place, insert hook at base of next sc and complete as for an sc (long sc made), * sc in next sc, long sc in next sc. Repeat from * around. Join and break off. **7th rnd:** Pick up Yellow and make sc in each st around, making 3 sc in each corner st. Join and break off.

Make 10 rows of 15 blocks. Sew blocks neatly together on wrong side, picking up back loops only.

BORDER . . . 1st rnd: Attach Yellow to corner sc, * 3 sc in corner, sc in each sc to next corner. Repeat from * around. Join. **2nd to 6th rnds incl:** Sc in each sc around, making 3 sc in each corner. Join. Break off at end of 6th rnd. With double strand of Brown whip all outer edges.

6137

6143

No. 6138 . . . . Afghan

Approximately 52 x 75 Inches

Materials: KNITTING WORSTED, *12 balls (1 oz. balls) each of Light Rose, Wild Rose, Mid Rose, Deep Rose and Wine Rose . . . Plastic Crochet Hook No. 6.*

STRIP (Make 11) . . . Starting at narrow end with Light Rose, ch 22. **1st row:** Sc in 2nd ch from hook, sc in next 9 ch, 3 sc in next ch, sc in next 10 ch. Ch 1, turn. **2nd row:** Skip 1 sc, sc in back loop of each sc to center sc of 3-sc group, 3 sc in back loop of center sc, sc in back loop of each sc to last 2 sc, skip 1 sc, sc in back loop of last sc. Break off Light Rose. Attach Wild Rose. Ch 1, turn. Repeat 2nd row, working 2 rows of Wild Rose, 2 of Mid Rose, 2 of Deep Rose and 2 of Wine Rose. These 10 rows constitute stripe pattern. Work in pattern until piece measures 75 inches, completing pattern stripe. Break off. Sew strips together neatly on wrong side, matching colors.

6138

No. 6140 . . . . Afghan
Approximately 46 x 66 Inches

Materials: KNITTING WORSTED, *30 balls (1 oz. balls) each of Pearl Grey and Wine Rose . . . Plastic Crochet Hook No. 5.*

GAUGE: Each block measures 4 inches square.

BLOCK . . . Starting at center with Grey, ch 6. Join with sl st to form ring. **1st rnd:** Ch 3, 2 dc in ring, (ch 1, 3 dc in ring) 3 times; ch 1, insert hook in 3rd ch of ch-3, drop Grey, attach Wine and make a sl st. **2nd rnd:** With Wine make sc in same place as sl st, sc in next 2 dc, (5 sc in next sp—corner—sc in next 3 dc) 3 times; 5 sc in last sp. Join and break off. **3rd rnd:** Attach Grey, ch 3, * dc in each sc to center sc of corner, leaving the last 2 loops of last dc on hook, drop Grey, attach Wine and draw through 2 loops on hook, 5 Wine dc in corner sc, leaving last 2 loops of last dc on hook, change to Grey. Repeat from * around, ending with 2 Grey dc. Join. **4th rnd:** Ch 3, * dc in each Grey dc, change to Wine as before and make dc in next 3 dc, change to Grey and make 3 dc in same place as last dc, change to Wine and make another dc in same place as last dc, dc in next 2 dc, change to Grey. Repeat from * around. Join and break off.

Make 11 rows of 16 blocks and sew them neatly together on wrong side.

BORDER . . . 1st rnd: Attach Wine to one corner, * 3 sc in corner, sc in each dc to next corner. Repeat from * around. Join. **2nd to 5th rnds incl:** Sc in each sc, making 3 sc in center sc of each corner and working 4th rnd with Grey. Join. Break off at end of 5th rnd.

6140 –

CHAPTER VIII

PINEAPPLES ... *for taste-ful decoration in your home*

DECORATIVE as well as delightful, the pineapple is the all-American favorite design, and we have assembled here for your delectation a very exciting collection. Here is a tablecloth that will make a memorable setting for important dinner occasions, a choice of luncheon cloths to provide table talk for your guests, a variety of centerpieces and doilies to set off a favorite bowl of flowers, a rare lamp, a gleaming tea service . . . there is an unusually handsome chair set, several runners and — to round out the collection — two vanity sets for your bedroom. It is going to be difficult to make a choice among all these pineapple designs.

7768-A

No. 7768-A . . . . Doily

Materials: Best Six Cord Mercerized Crochet, *Size 30, 3 balls . . . Steel Crochet Hook
No. 10.*

Doily measures 8½ inches in diameter.

Starting at center, ch 10. Join with sl st to
form ring. **1st rnd:** Ch 3, 23 dc in ring. Join.
2nd rnd: Ch 4, * dc in next dc, ch 1. Repeat
from * around. Join last ch-1 to 3rd ch of ch-4.
3rd rnd: Ch 5, * dc in next dc, ch 2. Repeat
from * around. Join last ch-2 to 3rd ch of ch-5.
4th rnd: Sc in sp, * ch 5, sc in next sp. Repeat
from * around, ending with ch 2, dc in first sc.

5th, 6th and 7th rnds: * Ch 5, sc in next loop.
Repeat from * around, ending with ch 2, dc in
dc. **8th rnd:** Ch 3, in last loop make dc, ch 2
and 2 dc (shell made), in each loop around
make 2 dc, ch 2 and 2 dc (24 shells). Join. **9th
rnd:** Sl st in next dc and in sp, ch 3, in same
sp make dc, ch 2 and 2 dc (shell made over
shell), * ch 1, in sp of next shell make 2 dc,
ch 5 and 2 dc; ch 1, shell in sp of next shell,
ch 3, sc in sp of next shell, ch 3, shell over
shell. Repeat from * around. Join. **10th rnd:**
Sl st in next dc and in sp, ch 3 and complete a
shell as before, * 15 tr in ch-5 sp, shell over
shell, ch 3, sc in next 2 sps, ch 3, shell over

242

shell. Repeat from * around. Join. **11th rnd:** * Shell over shell, (tr in next tr, ch 1) 14 times; tr in next tr, shell over shell, ch 1. Repeat from * around. Join. **12th rnd:** * Shell over shell, ch 2, sc in next ch-1 sp, (ch 3, sc in next sp) 13 times; ch 2, shell over shell. Repeat from * around. Join. **13th rnd:** * Shell over shell, ch 4, sc in next ch-3 loop, (ch 3, sc in next loop) 12 times; ch 4, shell over shell. Repeat from * around. Join. **14th rnd:** * Shell over shell, ch 4, sc in next ch-3 loop, (ch 3, sc in next loop) 11 times; ch 4, shell over shell. Repeat from * around. Join.

FIRST PINEAPPLE . . . 1st row: Shell over shell, ch 4, sc in next ch-3 loop, (ch 3, sc in next loop) 10 times; ch 4, shell over shell.

Ch 5, turn. **2nd row:** Shell over shell, ch 4, sc in next ch-3 loop, (ch 3, sc in next loop) 9 times; ch 4, shell over shell. Ch 5, turn.

Repeat the 2nd row, having 1 loop less on each row until 1 loop remains. Ch 5, turn. **Next row:** Shell over shell, ch 4, sc in ch-3 loop, ch 4, 2 dc in sp of next shell, ch 1, sl st in sp of last shell, ch 1, 2 dc in same place as last 2 dc were made, ch 5, turn, sl st in joining of shells. Break off.

SECOND PINEAPPLE . . . Attach thread in sp of next shell, ch 3, shell over shell, ch 4, sc in next ch-3 loop, (ch 3, sc in next loop) 10 times; ch 4, shell over shell. Ch 5, turn. Complete as for First Pineapple. Work other pineapples to correspond.

7768-B

No. 7768-B . . . . . Centerpiece

Materials: BEST SIX CORD MERCERIZED CRO-CHET, *Size 30*, **Small Ball:** *10 balls of White or Ecru, or 12 balls of any color . . . Steel Crochet Hook No. 10.*

Centerpiece measures 23 inches in diameter

DOILY (Make 7) . . . Work exactly as for Doily No. 7768-A, page 242. Join doilies to form centerpiece by sewing together the 2 corresponding loops of adjacent doilies at tip of each pineapple (there should be 5 free loops on each side of each pineapple beyond joining and 6 loops on each side of each free pineapple).

FILL-IN-MOTIF . . . Starting at center, ch 10. Join with sl st to form ring. **1st rnd:** Ch 3, 23 dc in ring. Sl st in top of ch-3. **2nd rnd:** Sc in same place as sl st, * ch 5, skip 1 dc, sc in next dc. Repeat from * around, ending with ch 2, dc in first sc. **3rd rnd:** Ch 5, sc in 2nd free loop from base of pineapple, * ch 5, sc in next ch-5 loop of Fill-in-Motif, ch 3, sc in next free loop of same pineapple, ch 3, sc in next loop on Fill-in-Motif, ch 5, sc in next free loop of same pineapple, ch 5, sc in next loop on Fill-in-Motif, ch 13, sc in next free loop of same pineapple, sc in next free loop of next pineapple, ch 13, sc in same loop on Fill-in-Motif as last sc was made, ch 5, sc in next free loop of same pineapple, ch 5, sc in next loop on Fill-in-Motif, ch 3, sc in next free loop of same pineapple, ch 3, sc in next loop on Fill-in-Motif, ch 5, sc in next free loop of same pineapple, ch 5, sc in next loop on Fill-in-Motif, ch 9, sc in next free loop of same pineapple, sc in next free loop of next pineapple, ch 9, sc in same loop on Fill-in-Motif as last sc was made, ch 5, sc in next loop of same pineapple. Repeat from * around, ending with ch 9, sl st at base of first ch-5. Break off. Fill in all spaces between joinings like this.

No. 7768-C . . . . . Tablecloth
(Not Illustrated)

Materials: BEST SIX CORD MERCERIZED CRO-CHET, *Size 30 . . . Steel Crochet Hook No. 10.*

Make a centerpiece exactly as for No. 7768-B. Then continue to make individual doilies, joining to previous rnd of doilies as second rnd was joined to center doily, until tablecloth is size desired—see diagram for joinings.

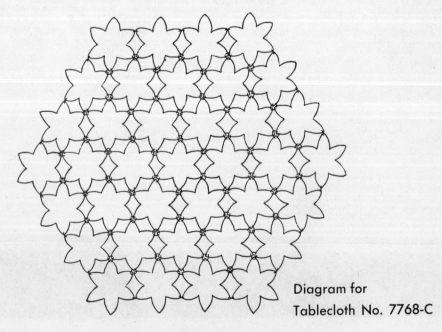

Diagram for
Tablecloth No. 7768-C

7771

No. 7771 . . . . . Centerpiece

Materials: BEST SIX CORD MERCERIZED CRO-
CHET, *Size 30,* **Small Ball:** *7 balls of White or
Ecru, or 10 balls of any color . . . Steel Crochet
Hook No. 10.*

Centerpiece measures 20 inches in diameter

Starting at center, ch 10. Join with sl st to

form ring. **1st rnd:** Ch 3, 21 dc in ring. Sl st
to top of ch-3. **2nd rnd:** Ch 5, * dc in next dc,
ch 2. Repeat from * around. Sl st in 3rd ch of
ch-5 (22 sps). **3rd rnd:** Sc in next sp, * draw
loop on hook out to measure ⅜ inch, thread
over and draw loop through, insert hook between single and double loops and draw a
loop through, thread over and draw through
2 loops on hook (knot st made), make another

knot st, sc in next sp. Repeat from * around, ending with 2 knot sts, sl st in first sc. **4th to 7th rnds incl:** * Make 2 knot sts, sc under double loop of next knot st (to the right of the knot), sc under double loop of next knot st (to the left of the same knot). Repeat from * around (22 loops). Make 1 knot st after the 7th rnd is completed. **8th rnd:** * Sc under double loop of next knot st (to the right of next knot), ch 3, sc to left of same knot, ch 6. Repeat from * around. Join last ch-6 to first sc (22 ch-3 loops). **9th rnd:** Sl st in next loop, ch 3, in same loop make dc, ch 2 and 2 dc (shell made), * ch 6, in next ch-3 loop make 2 dc, ch 2 and 2 dc (another shell made). Repeat from * around. Join to top of ch-3. **10th rnd:** Sl st in next dc and in next sp, ch 3, in same sp make dc, ch 5 and 2 dc; * ch 6, in next ch-2 sp make 2 dc, ch 2 and 2 dc; ch 6, in next ch-2 sp make 2 dc, ch 5 and 2 dc. Repeat from * around. Join.

11th rnd: Sl st in next dc and in next sp, ch 4, 12 tr in same sp, * ch 5, in next ch-2 make 2 dc, ch 2 and 2 dc; ch 5, 13 tr in next ch-5. Repeat from * around, ending with ch 5. Join. **12th rnd:** Ch 5, tr in next tr, (ch 1, tr in next tr) 11 times; * ch 3, shell in sp of next shell, ch 3, tr in next tr, (ch 1, tr in next tr) 12 times. Repeat from * around. Join to 4th st of ch-5. **13th rnd:** Sl st in first ch-1 sp, sc in same sp, * (ch 3, sc in next ch-1 sp) 11 times; ch 3, shell over shell, ch 3, sc in next ch-1 sp. Repeat from * around, ending with ch 3, sc in first ch-3 loop. **14th rnd:** (Ch 3, sc in next loop) 10 times; * ch 3, shell over shell, (ch 3, sc in next ch-3 loop) 11 times. Repeat from * around, ending as in 13th rnd. **15th rnd:** (Ch 3, sc in next loop) 9 times; * ch 3, in ch-2 of next shell make (2 dc, ch 2) twice and 2 dc; (ch 3, sc in next loop) 10 times. Repeat from * around, ending as before. **16th rnd:** (Ch 3, sc in next loop) 8 times; * ch 3, shell in next ch-2, ch 2, shell in next ch-2, (ch 3, sc in next loop) 9 times. Repeat from * around, ending as before. **17th rnd:** (Ch 3, sc in next loop) 7 times; * ch 3, shell over next shell, ch 1, shell in next ch-2 sp, ch 1, shell over next shell, (ch 3, sc in next loop) 8 times. Repeat from * around, ending as before. **18th rnd:** (Ch 3, sc in next loop) 6 times; * (ch 3, shell over next shell) 3 times; (ch 3, sc in next loop) 7 times. Repeat from * around, ending as before. **19th rnd:** (Ch 3, sc in next loop) 5 times; * ch 3,

shell over next shell, (ch 4, shell over next shell) twice; (ch 3, sc in next loop) 6 times. Repeat from * around. **20th rnd:** (Ch 3, sc in next loop) 4 times; * ch 3, shell over next shell, ch 5, in next shell make 2 dc, ch 5 and 2 dc; ch 5, shell over next shell, (ch 3, sc in next loop) 5 times. Repeat from * around. **21st rnd:** (Ch 3, sc in next loop) 3 times; * ch 3, shell over next shell, ch 3, 14 tr in next shell, ch 3, shell over next shell, (ch 3, sc in next loop) 4 times. Repeat from * around. **22nd rnd:** (Ch 3, sc in next loop) twice; * ch 3, shell over next shell, ch 3, tr in next tr, (ch 1, tr in next tr) 13 times; ch 3, shell over shell, (ch 3, sc in next loop) 3 times. Repeat from * around. **23rd rnd:** Ch 3, sc in next loop, * ch 3, shell over shell, (ch 3, sc in next ch-1 sp) 13 times; ch 3, shell over shell, (ch 3, sc in next loop) twice. Repeat from * around. **24th rnd:** * Ch 4, shell over shell, (ch 3, sc in next loop) 12 times; ch 3, shell over shell, ch 4, sc in next loop. Repeat from * around, ending with ch 4, sl st in sc. **25th rnd:** Sl st to sp of shell, ch 3, in same sp make dc, ch 2 and 2 dc; * (ch 3, sc in next loop) 11 times; (ch 3, shell over shell) twice. Repeat from * around, ending with ch 3. Join. **26th rnd:** Sl st to sp of shell, ch 3, in same sp make dc, ch 2 and 2 dc; * (ch 3, sc in next loop) 10 times; ch 3, shell over shell, ch 1, shell in next sp, ch 1, shell over shell. Repeat from * around. Join. **27th rnd:** Shell over shell, * (ch 3, sc in next loop) 9 times; (ch 3, shell over shell) 3 times. Repeat from * around. Join. **28th rnd:** Shell over shell, * (ch 3, sc in next loop) 8 times; ch 3, shell over shell, (ch 4, shell over next shell) twice. Repeat from * around. Join.

29th rnd: Shell over shell, * (ch 3, sc in next loop) 7 times; ch 3, shell over shell, ch 5, in next shell make 2 dc, ch 6 and 2 dc; ch 5, shell over shell. Repeat from * around. **30th rnd:** Shell over shell, * (ch 3, sc in next loop) 6 times; ch 3, shell over shell, ch 3, 16 tr in ch-6 loop, ch 3, shell over shell. Repeat from * around (3rd rnd of pineapples started). Continue to work around until only 1 loop remains at top of 2nd rnd of pineapples. **Next rnd:** Shell over shell, * ch 4, sc in next loop, ch 4, shell over shell, ch 4, sc in next loop, (ch 3, sc in next loop) 11 times; ch 4, shell over shell. Repeat from * around. Join. Now work as follows: **1st rnd:** * Shell over shell, 2 knot sts, shell over shell, ch 4, sc in next ch-3 loop, (ch 3, sc in next loop) 10 times; ch 4. Repeat from * around. Join. **2nd rnd:** * Shell over shell, 2 knot sts, sc under double loop of next knot st (to right of knot), sc under double loop of next knot st (to left of same knot), 2 knot sts, shell over shell, ch 4, sc in next ch-3 loop, (ch 3, sc in next loop) 9 times; ch 4. Repeat from * around. Join. **3rd rnd:** * Shell over shell, (2 knot sts, sc in next 2 double loops—on each side of next knot) twice; 2 knot sts, shell over shell, ch 4, sc in next ch-3 loop, (ch 3, sc in next loop) 8 times; ch 4. Repeat from * around. Join. Continue in this manner, having 1 ch-3 loop less on each row on each pineapple and 2 more knot sts on each knot st section until one ch-3 loop remains on each pineapple (there should be 20 knot sts on each knot st section).

Next rnd: Shell over shell, * ch 5, in next knot make (sc, ch 5) 3 times and sc. Repeat from * across knot st section, ch 5, shell over shell, ch 4, sc in next ch-3 loop, ch 4, 2 dc in next shell, ch 1, sl st in sp of last shell, ch 1, 2 dc where last 2 dc were made, ch 5, in next knot make (sc, ch 5) 3 times and sc. Continue thus around, ending with 2 dc in last shell, ch 1, sl st in sp of first shell, 2 dc where last 2 dc were made, ch 4, sc in ch-3 loop, ch 4, sl st in top of starting chain. Break off.

No. 7859 . . . . . Tablecloth

Approximately 68 x 80 inches

Materials: BEST SIX CORD MERCERIZED CROCHET, *Size 30,* **Big Ball:** *39 balls of White, Ecru or Cream . . . Steel Crochet Hook No. 10.*

Each motif measures 2 inches in diameter

FIRST MOTIF . . . Starting at center, ch 12. Join with sl st to form ring. **1st rnd:** Ch 4, 31 tr in ring, sl st to 4th ch of ch-4. **2nd rnd:** Sc in same place as sl st, * ch 5, skip 1 tr, sc in next tr. Repeat from * around, ending with ch 2, dc in first sc. **3rd rnd:** Ch 4, holding back on hook the last loop of each tr make 2 tr in loop just formed, thread over and draw through all loops on hook (cluster), * ch 7; make a 3-tr cluster in next loop. Repeat from * around, joining last ch 7 to tip of first cluster (16 clusters). Break off.

SECOND MOTIF . . . Work as for First Motif until 2nd rnd is completed. **3rd rnd:** Ch 4, make a 2-tr cluster in loop just formed, ch 3, sl st in corresponding loop on First Motif; ch 3, make a 3-tr cluster in next ch-5 loop on Second Motif, ch 3, sl st in corresponding loop on First Motif, ch 3, cluster in next ch-5 loop on Second Motif and complete rnd as for First Motif (no more joinings).

Make 30 rows of 36 motifs, joining motifs as Second Motif was joined to First Motif, leaving 2 loops free between joinings.

FILL-IN LACE . . . Ch 1, tr tr in first free loop of motif (following any joining), tr tr in next free loop, * long tr (6 times over hook) in joining, (tr tr in next free loop) twice. Repeat from * around. Sl st in first tr tr. Break off. Fill in all spaces in the same manner.

PINEAPPLE BORDER—First Corner Pineapple . . . With right side facing, skip 3 free loops on any corner motif following joining, mark next loop. With wrong side facing, attach thread to center of marked loop, ch 7, sc in next loop. Ch 4, turn. **1st row:** 10 tr in ch-7 loop, tr where thread was attached. Ch 5, turn. **2nd row:** Skip first tr, (tr in next tr, ch 1) 10 times; tr in top of ch-4. Ch 6, turn. **3rd row:** Skip first tr, (tr in next tr, ch 2) 10 times; skip 1 ch of turning chain, tr in next ch. Ch 5, turn. **4th row:** Sc in next ch-2 sp, (ch 5, sc in next sp) 10 times. Ch 5, turn. **5th row:** Sc in next loop, (ch 5, sc in next loop) 9 times. Ch 5, turn. **6th row:** Sc in next loop, (ch 5, sc in next loop) 8 times. Ch 5, turn. **7th row:** Sc in next loop, (ch 5, sc in next loop) 7 times. Ch 5, turn. Continue in this manner, having 1 loop less on each row until row ends with sc in next loop, ch 5, sc in next loop. Ch 5, turn. **Next row:** Skip 1 ch of next loop, sc in next ch, ch 5, skip 1 ch, sc in next ch of same loop. Break off.

SECOND CORNER PINEAPPLE . . . With right side facing, skip next loop on same motif, mark next loop. With wrong side facing, attach thread to marked loop, ch 7, sc in next loop, ch 4, sl st in last tr of first row of previous pineapple, turn. **1st row:** 6 tr in ch-7 loop, tr where thread was attached. Ch 5, turn. **2nd row:** Skip first tr, (tr in next tr, ch 1) 6 times; tr in top of turning chain below, sl st in corresponding st of previous pineapple, ch 4, sl st in next loop of previous pineapple, turn. **3rd**

7859

7859

row: Ch 2, skip next tr, (tr in next tr, ch 2) 6 times; skip 1 ch, tr in next ch. Ch 5, turn. **4th row:** Sc in next ch-2 sp, (ch 5, sc in next sp) 6 times; ch 2, sl st in second turning ch-5 loop on previous pineapple. Ch 2, turn. **5th row:** Sc in next loop, (ch 5, sc in next loop) 6 times. Ch 5, turn. **6th row:** Sc in next loop, (ch 5, sc in next loop) 5 times. Ch 5, turn. Continue in this manner, having 1 loop less on each row and completing pineapple exactly as for First Corner Pineapple. Break off.

THIRD CORNER PINEAPPLE . . . With right side facing, skip next loop of same motif, mark next loop. With wrong side facing, attach thread to marked loop, ch 7, sc in next loop, ch 4, sl st in adjacent st of Second Corner Pineapple. Turn. **1st row:** 10 tr in loop, tr where thread was attached. Ch 5, turn. Complete as for First Corner Pineapple, joining to correspond with previous joinings.

FIRST SIDE PINEAPPLE . . . With right side facing, skip 3 free loops on next motif,

249

mark next loop. With wrong side facing, attach thread to marked loop, ch 7, sc in next loop. Ch 4, turn. **1st row:** 10 tr in loop, tr where thread was attached. Ch 5, turn and complete as for First Corner Pineapple, joining 2 turning chain loops of this pineapple to corresponding loops of adjacent pineapple as before.

Make a Side Pineapple on each motif, joining as before. Continue in this manner all around, making 3 corner pineapples on each corner motif and taking care to join last pineapple on both sides.

EDGING . . . 1st rnd: Attach thread to first free loop on First Corner Pineapple, ch 4, holding back on hook the last loop of each tr make 2 tr in same loop, thread over and draw through all loops on hook (cluster made), (ch 7, make a 3-tr cluster in next free loop) twice; (ch 7, in next ch-5 loop make cluster, ch 7 and cluster) twice; (ch 7, cluster in next loop) 3 times; cluster in next free loop of next pineapple, ch 7, cluster in next loop, (ch 7, in next loop make cluster, ch 7 and cluster) twice; (ch 7, cluster in next loop) twice; * cluster in next free loop on next pineapple, (ch 7, cluster in next free loop) twice; (ch 7, in next free loop make cluster, ch 7 and cluster) twice; (ch 7, cluster in next free loop) 3 times. Repeat from * around, working over corner pineapples as before. Join last cluster with sl st to tip of first cluster. **2nd rnd:** Sl st to center of next loop, * ch 7, sc in next loop. Repeat from * around corner, ending with sc in loop preceding last 2 clusters of Third Corner Pineapple, ** ch 3, tr in next 2 loops, ch 3, sc in next loop, (ch 7, sc in next loop) 6 times. Repeat from ** around, working over corner pineapples as before and ending with ch 3, tr in last ch-7 loop, sl st in center of first loop. **3rd rnd:** (Ch 9, sc in next loop) 22 times; * ch 3, tr in next 2 tr, ch 3, sc in next ch-7 loop, (ch 9, sc in next loop) 5 times. Repeat from * around, working over corners as before and ending with ch 3, tr in last tr, sl st in center of first loop. **4th rnd:** Ch 5, sc in next loop, (ch 11, sc in next loop) 6 times; sc in next loop, (ch 11, sc in next loop) 6 times; sc in next loop, (ch 11, sc in next loop) 6 times; * ch 1, tr in next 2 tr, ch 1, sc in next loop, (ch 11, sc in next loop) 4 times. Repeat from * around, working over corners as before

and ending with ch 1, tr in last tr, sl st in 4th st of ch-5. **5th rnd:** Sl st to center of next ch-11 loop, sc in same loop, * (ch 13, sc in next loop) 5 times; sc in next loop. Repeat from * 2 more times; ** (ch 13, sc in next loop) 3 times; sc in next loop. Repeat from ** around, working over corners as before. Join and break off.

Work Fill-in laces between motifs and pineapples as follows: Ch 1, tr tr in free loop of motif following pineapple, tr tr in next loop, long tr in joining, tr tr in next loop on next motif, tr tr in next loop, tr tr at end of first row of pineapple, tr tr at end of next row on same pineapple, long tr in joining, make tr tr at end of 2nd and first rows of next pineapple. Sl st in first tr tr. Break off. Fill in remaining spaces in the same way.

No. 7853 . . . . . . Tray Mat

16 x 23½ inches

Materials: Best Six Cord Mercerized Crochet, *Size 30*, **Small Ball:** *6 balls of White or Ecru, or 7 balls of any color . . . Steel Crochet Hook No. 10.*

Make 4 rows of 7 motifs as for No. 7859—see page 247, joining motifs and making fill-in laces to correspond.

BORDER . . . Complete as for No. 7859.

No. 7854 . . Night Table Doily

16½ inches square

Materials: Best Six Cord Mercerized Crochet, *Size 30*, **Small Ball:** *6 balls of White or Ecru, or 7 balls of any color . . . Steel Crochet Hook No. 10.*

Make 4 rows of 4 motifs as for No. 7859——see page 247, joining motifs and making fill-in laces to correspond.

BORDER . . . Complete as for No. 7859.

7853

No. 7856 . . . . . . Chair Set

Materials: Best Six Cord Mercerized Crochet, *Size 30,* **Small Ball:** *7 balls of White or Ecru, or 9 balls of any color . . . Steel Crochet Hook No. 10.*

Chair Back measures 14½ x 18½ inches; each Arm Piece 10½ x 14½ inches.

CHAIR BACK . . . Make 3 rows of 5 motifs as for No. 7859—see page 247, joining motifs and making fill-in laces to correspond.

BORDER . . . Complete as for No. 7859.

ARM PIECE (Make 2) . . . Make 3 motifs as for No. 7859, joining them to form a single row.

BORDER . . . Make 3 corner pineapples on end motif as for No. 7859. Then repeat the Second and Third Corner pineapples once more (5 pineapples on end motif). Make a Side Pineapple over next motif (as for No. 7859), then work 5 pineapples over other end motif as before and a Side Pineapple over remaining side of center motif, taking care to join both sides of last pineapple.

EDGING . . . 1st rnd: Attach thread to first free loop of Third Pineapple at one end and, following directions for Border No. 7859, work to same position at other end, then complete rnd to correspond with opposite side. Join. Complete edging (as established) to correspond with No. 7859.

251

7854

7856

7857

No. 7857 . . Round Luncheon Set

Materials: BEST SIX CORD MERCERIZED CRO-
CHET, *Size 30,* **Small Ball:** *8 balls of White or
Ecru, or 10 balls of any color . . . Steel Crochet
Hook No. 10.*

**Centerpiece measures 15 inches across
center; each Place Mat 13 inches.**

CENTERPIECE . . . Make 3 rows of 3 motifs
as for No. 7859—see page 247, joining motifs
and making fill-in laces to correspond.

BORDER . . . Complete as for No. 7859—see
page 247.

PLACE MAT (Make 2) . . . Make 2 rows of
2 motifs as for No. 7859, joining motifs and
making fill-in laces to correspond.

BORDER . . . Make 3 corner pineapples on
each motif as for No. 7859, joining First Pineapple of each corner to Third Pineapple of
previous corner in the same way that the Side
Pineapple of No. 7859 was joined to Third
Pineapple of corner.

EDGING . . . Attach thread to first free loop
on corner pineapple, ch 4 and complete a
cluster in same loop, * (ch 7, cluster in next
free loop) twice; (ch 7, in next ch-5 loop make
cluster, ch 7 and cluster) twice; (ch 7, cluster
in next loop) 3 times; cluster in next free loop
of next pineapple, ch 7, cluster in next loop,
(ch 7, in next loop make cluster, ch 7 and
cluster) twice; (ch 7, cluster in next loop)
twice; cluster in next free loop of next pine-

254

apple, (ch 7, cluster in next loop) twice; (ch 7, in next loop make cluster, ch 7 and cluster) twice; (ch 7, cluster in next loop) 3 times; cluster in next loop of next pineapple. Repeat from * around. Join. Complete edging over each group of corner pineapples to correspond with corner groups of No. 7859.

No. 7861 . . . . . Oval Doily

10½ x 14½ inches

Materials: BEST SIX CORD MERCERIZED CRO-CHET, *Size 30, 3 balls* (**Small Balls**) *of White, Ecru or any color . . . Steel Crochet Hook No. 10.*

Work exactly as for Arm Piece of No. 7856 —see page 251.

No. 7858 . . . . . . Buffet Set

Materials: BEST SIX CORD MERCERIZED CRO-CHET, *Size 30,* **Small Ball:** *8 balls of White or Ecru, or 10 balls of any color . . . Steel Crochet Hook No. 10.*

Work exactly as for No. 7857—see page 254.

No. 7868 . . Night Table Doily

Illustrated on page 259

14 inches square

Materials: BEST SIX CORD MERCERIZED CRO-CHET, *Size 30,* **Small Ball:** *6 balls of White or Ecru, or 7 balls of any color . . . Steel Crochet Hook No. 10.*

Make 3 rows of 3 motifs as for No. 7867—see page 257. Make edging as for No. 7869—see page 268.

7861

7858

No. 7867 . . Pineapple Buffet Set

Materials: Best Six Cord Mercerized Crochet, *Size 30*, **Small Ball:** *19 balls of White or Ecru, or 23 balls of any color . . . Steel Crochet Hook No. 10.*

**Oblong Doily measures 11 x 19 inches;
Square Doily 11 inches.
Each motif measures 4 inches square.**

OBLONG DOILY—First Motif . . . Starting at center, ch 10. **1st rnd:** Ch 3, 31 dc in ring. Join with sl st in top of starting chain. **2nd rnd:** Sc in same place as sl st, * ch 10, skip 7 dc, sc in next dc. Repeat from * around, joining last ch-10 with sl st in first sc. **3rd rnd:** Sl st in next ch, sl st in loop, ch 4, 9 tr in same loop, * ch 5, 10 tr in next loop. Repeat from * around, joining last ch-5 with sl st in top of starting chain. **4th rnd:** Ch 5, tr in next tr, (ch 1, tr in next tr) 8 times; * ch 3, sc in next loop, ch 3, tr in next tr, (ch 1, tr in next tr) 9 times. Repeat from * around, joining with sl st in 4th ch of starting chain. **5th rnd:** Sc in

next sp, * (ch 3, sc in next ch-1 sp) 8 times; ch 5, sc in next ch-1 sp. Repeat from * around. Join with sl st in first sc. **6th rnd:** Sl st in first ch, sc in loop, * (ch 3, sc in next loop) 7 times; ch 3, 3 dc in next loop, ch 3, sc in next loop. Repeat from * around. Join as before. **7th rnd:** Sl st in next ch, sc in loop, * (ch 3, sc in next loop) 6 times; ch 3, 3 dc in next sp, ch 7, 3 dc in next sp, ch 3, sc in next loop. Repeat from * around. Join. **8th rnd:** Sl st in next ch, sc in loop, * (ch 3, sc in next loop) 5 times; ch 3, 3 dc in next sp, ch 7, sc in next ch-7 sp, ch 7, 3 dc in next ch-3 sp, ch 3, sc in next loop. Repeat from * around. Join.

9th rnd: Sl st in next ch, sc in loop, * (ch 3, sc in next loop) 4 times; ch 3, 3 dc in next ch-3 sp, (ch 7, sc in next ch-7 loop) twice; ch 7, 3 dc in next ch-3 sp, ch 3, sc in next loop. Repeat from * around. Join. **10th rnd:** Sl st in next ch, sc in loop, * (ch 3, sc in next loop) 3 times; ch 3, 3 dc in next ch-3 sp, ch 7, sc in next loop, ch 5, holding back on hook the last loop of each tr make 3 tr in next ch-7 loop, thread over and draw through all loops on

Motif for
No. 7867

7867

hook (cluster); (ch 5, cluster in same loop) 2 more times; ch 5, sc in next loop, ch 7, 3 dc in next sp, ch 3, sc in next ch-3 loop. Repeat from * around. Join. **11th rnd:** Sl st in next ch, sc in loop, * (ch 3, sc in next loop) twice; ch 3, 3 dc in next sp, (ch 7, sc in next loop) 3 times; ch 11, sc in next loop, (ch 7, sc in next loop) twice; ch 7, 3 dc in next ch-3 sp, ch 3, sc in next loop. Repeat from * around. Join. **12th rnd:** Sl st in next ch, sc in loop, * ch 3, sc in next loop, ch 3, 3 dc in next sp, (ch 7, sc in next loop) 3 times; 2 sc in same loop as last

sc was made, 3 sc in next loop, ch 3, 3 sc in same loop, ch 5, in same loop make 3 sc, ch 3 and 3 sc; 3 sc in next loop, (ch 7, sc in next loop) twice; ch 7, 3 dc in next sp, ch 3, sc in next loop. Repeat from * around, ending with 3 dc, dc in first sc. **13th rnd:** Sc in sp formed by last dc, * ch 5, skip next ch-3 loop, sc in next ch-3 sp, (ch 7, sc in next loop) 3 times; ch 7, sc in next ch-3 loop, ch 7, sc in next ch-5 loop, ch 7, sc in next ch-3 loop, (ch 7, sc in next loop) 3 times; ch 7, sc in next ch-3 sp. Repeat from * around. Join and break off.

SECOND MOTIF . . . Work as for First Motif until the 12th rnd is completed. **13th rnd:** Sc in loop formed by last dc, ch 5, skip next ch-3 loop, sc in next sp, (ch 7, sc in next loop) 3 times; ch 7, sc in next ch-3 loop, ch 7, sc in next ch-5 loop, ch 3, sl st in corresponding loop of First Motif, ch 3, sc in next ch-3 loop of Second Motif, (ch 3, sl st in next loop of First Motif, ch 3, sc in next loop of Second Motif) 4 times; ch 2, sl st in ch-5 loop of First Motif, ch 2, skip next ch-3 loop of Second Motif, sc in next ch-3 sp, and complete Motif as before, joining next 5 loops in the same way.

Make 2 rows of 4 motifs, joining adjacent sides as Second Motif was joined to First Motif.

RUFFLE . . . 1st rnd: Attach thread to first ch-7 loop on side of corner motif, ch 4, tr in same loop, * ch 5, 2 tr in next loop. Repeat from * around, making 2 tr, ch 5 and 2 tr in each corner loop and ending with ch 5, sl st in top of starting chain. **2nd rnd:** Sc in same place as sl st, sc in next tr, * 3 sc in next sp, sc in next 2 tr. Repeat from * around. Join. **3rd rnd:** Sc in same place as sl st, * ch 5, sc in next sc. Repeat from * around, ending with ch 2, dc in first sc. **4th to 10th rnds incl:** * Ch 5, sc in next loop. Repeat from * around, ending with dc in dc. Break off.

SQUARE DOILY (Make 2) . . . Make 2 rows of 2 motifs, joining motifs as before. Complete as for Oblong Doily.

7868

No. 7863 . . . . . . Vanity Set

Materials: BEST SIX CORD MERCERIZED CROCHET, *Size 30,* **Small Ball:** *7 balls of White or Ecru.*

Oval Doily measures 10½ x 15 inches; each Round Doily 9 inches in diameter.

OVAL DOILY—First Motif . . . Starting at center, ch 10. Join with sl st to form ring. **1st rnd:** Ch 3, 23 dc in ring. Sl st in top of ch-3. **2nd rnd:** Ch 4, * dc in next dc, ch 1. Repeat from * around. Join last ch-1 to 3rd st of ch-4. **3rd rnd:** * Sc in next sp, ch 5. Repeat from * around, ending with sl st in first sc. Break off.

SECOND MOTIF . . . Work as for First Motif until 2nd rnd is completed. **3rd rnd:** * Sc in next sp, ch 5. Repeat from * until 6 loops are made, sc in next sp (7 loops), ch 2, sl st in a loop of First Motif, ch 2, sc in next sp on Second Motif, ch 2, sl st in next loop on First Motif, ch 2, sc in next sp on Second Motif, and complete as for First Motif (no more joinings).

Make 3 more motifs same as this, joining 2 loops of each motif to 2 loops of previous motif, having 10 loops free on each side of joining.

Now work all around motifs as follows: **1st rnd:** Attach thread in 5th loop following joining on end motif, ch 4, tr in same loop, ch 5, skip 1 loop, (2 tr in next loop, ch 5) 10 times; skip next loop, 2 tr in next loop, ch 5, skip next loop, d tr in next loop, * d tr in 3rd free loop on next motif, ch 5, skip next loop, (2 tr in next loop, ch 5) twice; skip 1 loop, d tr in next loop. Repeat from * around, working over other end motif as before and joining last ch-5 to 4th ch of ch-4. **2nd rnd:** Sl st in next tr and in next 2 ch, sc in same loop, * ch 7, sc in next loop. Repeat from * around, ending with ch 7, sl st in first sc. **3rd rnd:** Sl st in next 2 ch, sl st in loop, ch 4, holding back on hook the last loop of each tr make 2 tr in same loop, thread over and draw through all loops on hook (cluster); * ch 5, make a 3-tr cluster in next loop. Repeat from * around. Join last ch-5 with sl st to tip of first cluster. **4th rnd:** Sl st in next 2 ch, sc in loop, ch 5, in next loop make 2 dc, ch 2 and 2 dc (shell); * ch 5, shell in next loop. Repeat from * 5 more times; (ch 5, sc in next loop, ch 5, shell in next loop) 8 times; (ch 5, shell in next loop) 6 times; and

complete rnd to correspond, ending with shell in last loop, ch 5. Sl st in first sc. Turn. **5th rnd:** Sl st in next 5 ch, in the next 2 dc and in sp of shell, turn, ch 3, in same sp make dc, ch 2 and 2 dc (shell over shell); * ch 5, in sp of next shell make 2 dc, ch 7 and 2 dc; ch 5, in sp of next shell make 2 dc, ch 2 and 2 dc (another shell over shell). Repeat from * around. Join. **6th rnd:** Sl st in next dc and in sp, * make shell over shell, 14 tr in next ch-7 loop. Repeat from * around. Join. **7th rnd:** * Shell over shell, (tr in next tr, ch 1) 13 times; tr in next tr. Repeat from * around. Join. **8th rnd:** Sl st in next dc and in sp, ch 3, in same sp make dc, (ch 2, 2 dc) twice; * ch 1, sc in next ch-1 sp, (ch 3, sc in next ch-1 sp) 12 times; ch 1, in sp of next shell make 2 dc, (ch 2, 2 dc) twice. Repeat from * around. Join. **9th rnd:** Sl st in next dc and in next sp, ch 3 and complete shell in same sp as before, * shell in next ch-2 sp, ch 2, sc in next ch-3 loop, (ch 3, sc in next loop) 11 times; ch 2, shell in next ch-2 sp. Repeat from * around. Join. **10th rnd:** * Shell over shell, ch 3, shell over shell, ch 4, sc in next ch-3 loop, (ch 3, sc in next loop) 10 times; ch 4. Repeat from * around. Join.

Now work pineapples individually as follows: **1st row:** Sl st to sp of 2nd shell, ch 3 and complete shell in same sp as before, ch 4, sc in next ch-3 loop, (ch 3, sc in next loop) 9 times; ch 4, shell over shell. Ch 5, turn. **2nd row:** Shell over shell, ch 4, sc in next ch-3 loop, (ch 3, sc in next loop) 8 times; ch 4, shell over shell. Ch 5, turn. Continue in this manner, having one ch-3 loop less on each row until one loop remains. **Next row:** Shell over shell, ch 4, sc in next ch-3 loop, ch 4, shell over shell. Ch 5, turn, (shell over shell) twice. Break off.

Attach thread to sp of next free shell on 10th rnd and work next pineapple as before. Work all pineapples in this manner.

ROUND DOILY (Make 2)—Center Motif . . . Starting at center, ch 12. Join with sl st to form ring. **1st rnd:** Ch 3, 27 dc in ring. Join. **2nd and 3rd rnds:** Repeat 2nd and 3rd rnds of Motifs of Oval Doily. **4th rnd:** Sl st in next ch, sl st in loop, ch 4, tr in same loop, * ch 5, skip next loop, 2 tr in next loop. Repeat from * around. Join. **5th rnd:** Repeat 2nd rnd of Oval Doily. **6th rnd:** Repeat 3rd rnd of Oval Doily, making ch 8 (instead of ch-5) between clusters. **7th rnd:** Sl st in next ch and in loop, ch 3, in same loop make dc, ch 2 and 2 dc (shell); * ch 5, shell in next loop. Repeat from * around. Join. **8th rnd:** * Make shell over shell, ch 6, in sp of next shell make 2 dc, ch 7 and 2 dc; ch 6. Repeat from * around. Join. **9th to 13th rnds incl:** Repeat 6th to 10th rnds incl of Oval Doily.

Complete pineapples individually as for Oval Doily.

7863

No. 7770-A . . . . . . **Runner**

Materials: BEST SIX CORD MERCERIZED CRO-
CHET, *Size 30:* **Small Ball:** *6 balls of White or
Ecru, or 7 balls of any color* . . . *Steel Crochet
Hook No. 10.*

Runner measures 12 x 30 inches

**PINEAPPLE MOTIF (Make 8) — Round
Motif** . . . Starting at center, ch 12. Join with
sl st to form ring. **1st rnd:** Ch 3, 23 dc in ring.
Join. **2nd rnd:** Ch 4, * dc in next dc, ch 1.
Repeat from * around. Join last ch-1 to 3rd st
of ch-4 (24 sps). **3rd rnd:** Sc in sp, * ch 5,
sc in next sp. Repeat from * around, ending
with ch 2, dc in first sc (24 loops). **4th and
5th rnds:** * Ch 5, sc in next loop. Repeat
from * around, ending with ch 2, dc in dc.
6th rnd: * Ch 6, sc in next loop. Repeat
from * around, ending with ch 3, dc in dc.
7th rnd: * Ch 7, sc in next loop. Repeat
from * around, ending with ch 3, tr in dc.

First Pineapple . . . **1st row:** Ch 3, in last
loop make dc, ch 2 and 2 dc (shell made);
ch 1, in next loop make 2 dc, ch 5 and 2 dc;
ch 1, in next loop make 2 dc, ch 2 and 2 dc
(another shell made). Ch 5, turn. **2nd row:**
Shell in sp of shell, ch 1, 15 tr in next ch-5 sp,
ch 1, shell over shell. Ch 5, turn. **3rd row:**
Shell over shell, ch 1, (tr in next tr, ch 1)
14 times; tr in next tr, ch 1, shell over shell.
Ch 5, turn. **4th row:** Shell over shell, ch 4, skip
next ch-1 sp, sc in next ch-1 sp, (ch 3, sc in
next sp) 13 times; ch 4, shell over shell. Ch 5,
turn. **5th row:** Shell over shell, ch 4, sc in next
ch-3 loop, (ch 3, sc in next loop) 12 times;
ch 4, shell over shell. Ch 5, turn. Continue in
this manner until 1 loop remains. **Next row:**
Shell over shell, ch 4, sc in ch-3 loop, ch 4, 2 dc
in sp of next shell, ch 1, sl st in sp of last shell
made, ch 1, 2 dc in same place as last 2 dc
were made, ch 5, turn, sl st in joining of shells.
Break off.

Second Pineapple . . . With right side facing,
skip 9 loops on Round Motif, attach thread to
next loop, ch 3, in same loop make dc, ch 2
and 2 dc; ch 1, in next loop make 2 dc, ch 5
and 2 dc; ch 1, shell in next loop. Ch 5, turn.
Complete as for other pineapple. This completes one Pineapple Motif.

Place motifs side by side and sew the center
free loops of the adjacent Round Motifs together.

Work 2 more pineapples on the 2 Round
Motifs at each end, leaving 1 loop free between pineapples.

EDGING . . . **1st rnd:** With right side facing,
attach thread to 3rd loop from base of any
pineapple, * (ch 7, sc in next loop) 11 times;
ch 5, sc in 3rd loop from base of next pineapple. Repeat from * around. Join last ch-5
to base of first ch-7. **2nd rnd:** Sl st to center of
next loop, sc in loop, * (ch 8, sc in next loop)
10 times; ch 2, skip ch-5, sc in next loop. Repeat from * around. Join. **3rd rnd:** Sl st to center of next loop, sc in loop, (ch 9, sc in next
loop) 9 times; * sc in next ch-8 loop, ch 4, sl st
in last ch-9 loop, ch 4, sc in next ch-8 loop,
(ch 9, sc in next loop) 8 times. Repeat from *
around, ending with ch 4, sl st in first ch-9
loop, ch 4, sc in next ch-8 loop of last rnd. Join
and break off. **4th rnd:** Attach thread to next
free ch-9 loop, sc in same loop, * (ch 10, sc in
next loop) twice; ch 10, in next loop make
(cluster, ch 10) twice and cluster—*to make a
cluster, holding back on hook the last loop of
each tr make 3 tr in same loop, thread over
and draw through all loops on hook;* (ch 10,
sc in next loop) 3 times; ch 10, sc in next free
ch-9 loop. Repeat from * around. Join. **5th
rnd:** Sl st to center of next loop, sc in loop,
* (ch 10, sc in next loop) 7 times; ch 3, sc in
next loop, ch 3, sc in next loop. Repeat from *
around, making ch 10 (instead of ch-3) between pineapples at curved ends. Join. **6th
rnd:** Sl st to center of next loop, (ch 10, sc in
next loop) 6 times; ch 5, sc in next ch-10 loop,
ch 10 and continue thus around, making sc,
ch 5 and sc over each joining between pineapples. **7th rnd:** Make ch-10 loops around,
having ch 5 over each ch-5 across long sides
and ch 10 over each ch-5 at curved ends. Join
and break off.

FILL-IN MOTIF . . . Starting at center, ch 10.
Join with sl st to form ring. **1st rnd:** Sc in ring,
(ch 5, sc in ring) 11 times; ch 2, dc in first sc.
2nd rnd: (Ch 5, sc in next loop) 11 times;
ch 2, dc in dc. **3rd rnd:** * Ch 2, sl st in 2nd
free loop on Round Motif, ch 2, sc in next loop
on Fill-in-Motif, ch 2, sc in next loop on Round
Motif, ch 2, sc in next loop on Fill-in-Motif,

7770-A

ch 5, sc in next loop. Repeat from * 3 more times, joining 2 loops to next Round Motif as before and 2 loops to 2nd and 3rd free loops on each pineapple. Join last ch-5 to base of first ch-2. Fill in all other spaces in the same way (14 in all).

No. 7770-B . . . . . Vanity Set

Materials: Best Six Cord Mercerized Crochet, *Size 30:* **Small Ball:** *7 balls of White or Ecru, or 8 balls of any color* . . . Steel Crochet Hook No. 10.

**Oval Doily measures 12 x 17 inches;
Round Doily 12 inches in diameter**

OVAL DOILY . . . Make 3 Pineapple Motifs as for No. 7770-A and join. Work 2 more pineapples on the 2 Round Motifs at each end, leaving 1 loop free between pineapples. Complete as for No. 7770-A.

ROUND DOILY (Make 2) . . . Make 1 Pineapple Motif as for Oval Doily. Work 2 more pineapples on the Round Motif on each side, leaving 1 loop free between pineapples. Complete as for Oval Doily, omitting Fill-in-Motifs and working Edging between pineapples to correspond with curved ends of Oval Doily.

7770-B

No. 7779 . . . . Luncheon Set

Materials: BEST SIX CORD MERCERIZED CROCHET, *Size 30:* **Small Ball:** 8 *balls of White or Ecru, or 9 balls of any color . . . Steel Crochet Hook No. 10.*

Centerpiece measures 16 inches in diameter; Place Doily 12 inches in diameter; Bread-and-Butter Doily 9 inches in diameter; and Glass Doily 6 inches in diameter

CENTERPIECE . . . Starting at center, ch 10. Join with sl st to form ring. **1st rnd:** Ch 3, 23 dc in ring. Sl st in 3rd st of ch-3. **2nd rnd:** Ch 4, * dc in next dc, ch 1. Repeat from * around. Join last ch-1 with sl st to 3rd st of ch-4. **3rd rnd:** Ch 5, * dc in next dc, ch 2. Repeat from * around. Sl st in 3rd st of ch-5. **4th rnd:** Sc in next sp, * ch 5, sc in next sp. Repeat from * around, ending with ch 2, dc in first sc. **5th and 6th rnds:** * Ch 5, sc in next loop. Repeat from * around, ending with ch 2, dc in dc. **7th rnd:** Repeat the 6th rnd, ending with ch 5, sl st in dc. **8th rnd:** Sl st in next loop, ch 3, 4 dc in same loop, 5 dc in each loop around. Join. **9th rnd:** * Ch 5, skip 2 dc, sc in next dc. Repeat from * around, ending with ch 2, dc at base of first ch-5 (40 loops). **10th to 13th rnds incl:** * Ch 5, sc in next loop. Repeat from * around, ending with ch 2, dc in dc. **14th rnd:** * Ch 5, sc in next loop. Repeat from * around. Join. **15th rnd:** Repeat 8th rnd. **16th rnd:** * (Ch 5, skip 2 dc, sc in next dc) 7 times; ch 5, skip 3 dc, sc in next dc. Repeat from * around, ending with ch 2, dc at base of starting ch-5 (64 loops). **17th to 22nd rnds incl:** Repeat 10th rnd. **23rd rnd:** Repeat 14th rnd. **24th rnd:** Repeat 8th rnd. **25th rnd:** Repeat 9th rnd, skipping 3 dc (instead of 2) (80 loops). **26th to 29th rnds incl:** Repeat 10th rnd. **30th to 33rd rnds incl:** Repeat last rnd but make ch-6 loops on 30th and 31st rnds and ch-7 loops on 32nd and 33rd rnds. **34th rnd:** Repeat 14th rnd. **35th rnd:** Sl st in next loop, ch 3, in same loop make dc, ch 2 and 2 dc (shell made); in each loop around make 2 dc, ch 2 and 2 dc (another shell made). Join. **36th rnd:** Sl st in next dc and in next sp, ch 3, in same sp make dc, ch 2 and 2 dc; * ch 1, in sp of next shell make 2 dc, ch 5 and 2 dc; ch 1, shell in sp of next shell (shell made over shell), (ch 3, sc in sp of next shell) twice; ch 3, shell over shell. Repeat

from * around. Join. **37th rnd:** Sl st in next dc and in next sp, ch 3 and complete shell, * 15 tr in next ch-5 sp, shell over shell, ch 3, (sc in next ch-3 sp) 3 times; ch 3, shell over shell. Repeat from * around. Join. **38th rnd:** * Shell over shell, (tr in next tr, ch 1) 14 times; tr in next tr, shell over shell, ch 1. Repeat from * around. Join. **39th rnd:** * Shell over shell, ch 2, sc in next ch-1 sp (between tr's), (ch 3, sc in next ch-1 sp) 13 times; ch 2, shell over shell. Repeat from * around. Join. **40th rnd:** * Shell over shell, ch 4, sc in next ch-3 loop, (ch 3, sc in next loop) 12 times; ch 4, shell over shell. Repeat from * around. Join. **41st rnd:** * Shell over shell, ch 4, sc in next ch-3 loop, (ch 3, sc in next loop) 11 times; ch 4, shell over shell. Repeat from * around. Join.

FIRST PINEAPPLE . . . 1st row: Shell over shell, ch 4, sc in next ch-3 loop, (ch 3, sc in next loop) 10 times; ch 4, shell over shell. Ch 5, turn. **2nd row:** Shell over shell, ch 4, sc in next ch-3 loop, (ch 3, sc in next loop) 9 times; ch 4, shell over shell. Ch 5, turn.

Repeat the 2nd row, having 1 loop less on each row until 1 loop remains. Ch 5, turn. **Next row:** Shell over shell, ch 4, sc in next loop, ch 4, 2 dc in sp of next shell, ch 1, sl st in sp of last shell made, ch 1, 2 dc where last 2 dc were made. Ch 5, turn and sl st in joining of shells. Break off.

SECOND PINEAPPLE . . . Attach thread in sp of next shell, ch 3, in same sp make dc, ch 2 and 2 dc; ch 4, sc in next ch-3 loop, (ch 3, sc in next loop) 10 times; ch 4, shell over shell. Ch 5, turn. Complete as for First Pineapple. Work other pineapples to correspond.

EDGING . . . Attach thread to free loop at point, (ch 10, sc in next ch-5 loop) 5 times; * ch 5, sc between the 2 shells at base of points, ch 5, sc in next free loop, (ch 10, sc in next loop) 10 times. Repeat from * around. Join and break off.

PLACE DOILY (Make 2) . . . Work as for Centerpiece until 14 rnds are completed. **15th rnd:** Repeat 35th rnd of Centerpiece (40 shells). **16th rnd:** Sl st in next dc and in next sp, ch 3, in same sp make dc, ch 2 and 2 dc; * ch 1, in sp of next shell make 2 dc, ch 5 and 2 dc; ch 1, shell in sp of next shell, ch 3, sc in sp of next shell, ch 3, shell over next shell. Re-

7779

peat from * around. Join. **17th rnd:** * Shell over shell, 15 tr in ch-5 sp, shell over shell, ch 2, (sc in next sp) twice; ch 2. Repeat from * around. Join. Complete Doily as for Centerpiece, starting at the 38th rnd.

BREAD-AND-BUTTER DOILY (Make 2) . . . Work as for Centerpiece until 7 rnds are completed. Complete as for Place Doily, starting at the 15th rnd.

GLASS DOILY (Make 2) . . . Starting at center, ch 8. Join. **1st rnd:** Ch 3, 19 dc in ring. Join. **2nd, 3rd and 4th rnds:** Repeat 2nd, 3rd and 4th rnds of Centerpiece. **5th rnd:** Ch 3, in last loop make dc, ch 2 and 2 dc; shell in each loop around (20 shells). Join. **6th rnd:** Repeat 16th rnd of Place Doily. **7th rnd:** Re-

peat 17th rnd of Place Doily, having 10 tr (instead of 15 tr) in each ch-5 sp. **8th rnd:** * Shell over shell, (tr in next tr, ch 1) 9 times; tr in next tr, shell over shell. Repeat from * around. Join. **9th rnd:** * Shell over shell, ch 2, sc in next ch-1 sp between tr's, (ch 3, sc in next ch-1 sp) 8 times; ch 2, shell over shell. Repeat from * around. Join. **10th rnd:** * Shell over shell, ch 4, sc in next ch-3 loop, (ch 3, sc in next loop) 7 times; ch 4, shell over shell. Repeat from * around. Join.

FIRST PINEAPPLE . . . **1st row:** Shell over shell, ch 4, sc in next ch-3 loop, (ch 3, sc in next loop) 6 times; ch 4, shell over shell. Ch 5, turn. Complete as for First Pineapple of Place Doily. Make 5 more pineapples like this. Work Edging as for other doilies.

7869

No. 7869 . . . . Runner
14 x 38 inches

Materials: BEST SIX CORD MERCERIZED CROCHET, *Size 30* . . . **Small Ball:** *12 balls of White or Ecru, or 15 balls of any color . . . Steel Crochet Hook No. 10.*

Make 3 rows of 9 motifs as for No. 7867—see page 257.

EDGING . . . 1st rnd: Attach thread to first ch-7 loop on side of a corner motif, ch 4, tr in same loop, * ch 5, 2 tr in next loop. Repeat from * around, making 2 tr, ch 5 and 2 tr in each corner loop and ending with ch 5, sl st in top of starting chain. **2nd rnd:** Sl st in next loop, ch 4, make 2-tr cluster in same loop, * (ch 5, make a 3-tr cluster in same loop) 2 more times; (ch 5, sc in next loop) twice; ch 5, make 3-tr cluster in next loop. Repeat from * around. Join. **3rd rnd:** Sl st in next 2 ch, sl st in loop, * ch 5, sc in next loop. Repeat from * around. Join and break off.